Technical Workers

Also by Chris Smith

White Collar Workers, Trade Unions and Class
(with Pete Armstrong, Bob Carter and Theo Nichols)

Innovations in Work Organisation: The Cadbury Experience
(with John Child and Michael Rowlinson)

Technical Workers

Class, labour and trade unionism

Chris Smith

MACMILLAN
EDUCATION

© Chris Smith 1987

First published 1987

Published by
MACMILLAN EDUCATION LTD
Houndmills, Basingstoke, Hampshire RG21 2XS
and London
Companies and representatives
throughout the world

Printed in Hong Kong

British Library Cataloguing in Publication Data
Smith, Chris
Technical workers: class, labour and
trade unionists.
1. White collar workers—Great Britain
I. Title
331.7'92'0941   HD8039.M4G7
ISBN 0–333–36320–5 (hardcover)
ISBN 0–333–36321–3 (paperback)

To Joe, Jessica and Sam

Contents

List of Tables and Figures   xi
Acknowledgements   xii
Abbreviations   xiii

Introduction   1

1 Theories of Class and Technical Work   **10**
Explanations for the growth of white-collar workers   10
Patterns of class analysis   13
The new working class thesis   17
   Mallet   18
   Gorz   28
Technology, skill and class   36
   Braverman   36
   Cooley   41
Structural Marxism, the new middle class and
   technical workers   49
   Poulantzas   49
   Carchedi   57
   Wright   60
Technical workers and class   66
Technical workers and some peculiarities of the
   British class structure   69

2 Technical Workers: An Overview   **75**
A profile of technical workers in Britain   75
The origins of technical occupations   80

Differentiation and change within technical
   occupations 85
Job titles, social status and job identity 91
Wages and job identity 96
Technical workers and industrial struggle 100

3 The Local Study: Bristol and Aerospace **106**
The aerospace industry 106
The British industry 114
British Aircraft Corporation: Filton site 117
Bristol: employment structure and labour tradition 119

4 Technical Workers and the Division of **126**
Labour
Introduction 126
Working at the technical–clerical divide 130
   Rate-fixers 130
   Production controllers 136
Established technical occupations 143
   Jig and tool draughtsmen 143
   Tracers 147
   NC part programmers 149
Conclusion 155

5 Design Engineers and the Hierarchy in **158**
Technical Work
Introduction 158
Hierarchy in design: the technical and social elements 159
The design of work 164
Technical change: designers, management and
   corporatism 169
Computer aided design and the position of the
   design engineer 177
Conclusion 186

6 The Craft Tradition under Threat: Technical **192**
Workers' Relations with Manual Workers
Introduction 192
The division of labour in practice 193
Technical workers with no contact with manual

workers 197
Technical workers with some contact with
  manual workers 199
  Jig and tool draughtsman in assembly 199
  Electrical planning engineers and electricians 207
Technical workers in regular contact with
  manual workers around the machine shop 211
  Jig and tool draughtsmen around the machine shop 212
  NC programmers and operators 216
The craft memory: the link between technical
  and manual workers 224

7 **The Work Relations Between Technical** **227**
  Workers and Managers
  Introduction 227
  From company to corporation: BAC to BAe 229
  The job of the technical manager 234
  'Us' and 'them' in the technical area 240
  The unionisation of middle management 246

8 **Technical Workers and Trade Unionism:** **256**
  TASS in the Post-War Period
  Theories of white-collar unionism 256
  Technical workers and TASS 267
  Wages policy and the broad left 271
  Concentration of technical workers and the
    employers' offensive 277
  The amalgamation 280
  Internal changes 287
  TASS policy and the class composition of TASS
    membership 292

Conclusion **298**

Bibliography 304

Index 314

List of Tables and Figures

Tables

1.1 Evolution of the working class: 'changes in the
    organic composition of the working class'   22
2.1 Scientific and technical labour in engineering and
    related industries in 1979: male and female   76
2.2 Educational background of TASS members
    at NEI Parsons: September 1979   79
2.3 The changing complexity of Handley Page bombers   88
2.4 TASS-designated technical occupations at Filton
    by functional location in the production cycle   92
2.5 The relationship between the average pay of
    adult full-time men in higher and lower technical
    bands and skilled manual workers   98
3.1 Employment in the Aircraft Group Weybridge–
    Bristol Division   118
8.1 TASS Conference motions, 1968–80   291

Figure

5.1 The design process   165

Acknowledgements

I am grateful to TASS officials in Bristol for introducing me to members at BAe, and giving me support for the research contained in this book. Particular thanks should go to Dave Yeomans and Tom Lynch – now sadly deceased – for their help. I am also indebted to the management at BAe for allowing me to roam the factory for so long.

Special thanks to Theo Nichols, who supervised, supported and gave much encouragement in the writing of the thesis upon which this book is partially based; to Anna Pollert, who set me straight on many points and gave me constant critical assistance in the final draft of the book; and Steven Kennedy, who continued to believe there was a book in the many draft copies he had to read. Others who have read various drafts and given useful advice are Huw Beynon, Richard Hyman and Paul Smith. Bob Murdock supplied me with much information on TASS at C.A. Parsons and kept up a regular correspondence and interest in this work; Terry Rogers, Harry Blair, Mike Cooley and Ron Whiteley have provided me with many insights into TASS and I thank them for those. Others, who wish to remain nameless, have also given me much information on TASS for which I am grateful.

The Economic and Social Research Council funded my Ph.D. at the Work Organisation Research Centre, and were generous in allowing me time to prepare this book. I am especially indebted to all the technical workers and managers at BAe who agreed to be interviewed by me. Their names have all been changed, but their words are real. Finally, I am appreciative of the typing skills of Ann Lane for preparing part of this book. Needless to say none of the above is responsible for the content of this work.

CHRIS SMITH

Abbreviations

AESD	Association of Engineering and Shipbuilding Draughtsmen
AEF	Amalgamated Engineering and Foundry Workers Union
AEU	Amalgamated Engineering Union
APEX	Association of Professional, Executive, Clerical and Computer Staff
ASSET	Association of Supervisory Staffs, Executives and Technicians
ASTMS	Association of Scientific, Technical and Managerial Staffs
AScW	Association of Scientific Workers
AUEW	Amalgamated Union of Engineering Workers
AUEW-ES	Amalgamated Union of Engineering Workers – Engineering Section
AUEW-TASS	Amalgamated Union of Engineering Workers–Technical, Administrative and Supervisory Section
BAe	British Aerospace
BAC	British Aircraft Corporation
BL	British Leyland
CAD	Computer Aided Design
CAD-CAM	Computer Aided Design–Computer Aided Manufacture
CNC	Computer Numerical Control
CPSA	Civil and Public Services Association
CP	Communist Party

DATA	Draughtsmen and Allied Technicians Association
EOD	Engineering Design Organisation
EITB	Engineering Industry Training Board
EMA	Engineers and Managers' Association
IDS	Incomes Data Services
IWC	Institute for Workers Control
JOC	Joint Office Committee
LPAG	Labour Party Aerospace Group
NALGO	National and Local Government Officers Association
NUBE	National Union of Bank Employees
NUGSAT	National Union of Gold, Silver and Allied Trades
NUSMWCH	National Union of Sheet Metal Workers, Coppersmiths, Heating and Domestic Engineers
NEI	Northern Engineering Industries
NC	Numerical Control
PCF	Parti Communiste Francais
PCU	Production Control Unit
SAIMA	Shipbuilding and Allied Industries Management Association
SIMA	Steel Industry Management Association
TASS	Technical, Administrative and Supervisory Section
UKAPE	United Kingdom Association of Professional Engineers
VDU	Visual Display Unit

Introduction

Technical workers are an unduly neglected and increasingly important stratum of white-collar workers. The archetypal white-collar worker in the literature on social class has been the clerk, and not the engineer, draughtsman or computer programmer. This reflected the numerical dominance of clerical over technical labour, and the fact that clerks were typically concentrated outside manufacturing and therefore more visibly divorced from manual workers. They, in every sense, appeared to be different from the traditional manual worker. The division between clerical and manual work, between 'head' and 'hand', has focused attention on an apparently inherent separation between white-collar and manual workers. It has reinforced common-sense judgements and prejudices. The pen and the machine, the clean and the dirty, the productive and unproductive are dichotomous images with a strong grounding in the material experience of work for the two groups. But with technical workers, the line between themselves and manual workers is not so clear cut, as this book will reveal.

The impact of computer technology, rationalisation and the increasing use of capital equipment in the office, have called into question many of our common-sense assumptions about what constitutes white-collar labour. The boundaries between physical and mental labour are not nearly so clear cut. Within this confusion, the term *technical* is rapidly becoming a catchall prefix to describe former clerical and

1

craft occupations, as well as many of the new computer-based jobs. So what does this term mean? Technical appears to embrace graduates, professionally qualified and specialised manual workers. It includes groups engaged in the development, design and planning of work and commodity production. Equally it involves those engaged in maintenance and post-production functions. Given what seems to be the demise of 'pure' clerical and manual workers, the expansion in the number of those workers labouring under the title of 'technical' looks like continuing. Technical and managerial groups, excluding clerical workers and foremen, made up 29.5 per cent or nearly 7 million employees in Britain in 1984. Within engineering, those in technical and managerial positions constituted over half a million employees in 1980. This represented over a quarter of the workforce in most industrial sectors, but as much as three quarters of employees in some of the new computer goods and electronics areas. It is therefore of considerable importance to examine this stratum, the way it has been perceived, and more importantly, how those in technical occupations understand their place in the class and occupational structures. This book aims to say something fresh about these issues.

Accompanying the historical growth in the number of white-collar workers have been various theories and debates about their significance for society. These debates have addressed fundamental political and social questions about the nature of advanced capitalist societies. Does the decline in the number of manual workers represent the demise of the working class? Conversely the so-called managerial revolution in 20th-century business enterprises has put the owner outside the gates of the firm and delegated control and responsibility to salaried managers and specialists of various kinds. Does this signify the end of the 'capitalist' class, or transformation of capitalism? Are the two major classes in society, labour and capital, now less important and less polarised because of the expansion of those in the middle? Are the new inter-mediate groups closer to capital in their interests and ideas, or are they closer to labour? Alternatively, are they closer in economic and ideological disposition to the small proprietor, shopkeeper or entrepreneur? Questions of this sort have supported at least four basic models of the position of white-collar workers in contemporary society.

Almost as soon as white-collar workers appeared in capitalist society, writers from various shades of the political spectrum considered them a potential buffer between the two major classes of capital and labour. An *embourgeoisement* thesis suggested that white-collar workers represented a privileged, conservative and individualistic force, diffusing middle-class values to manual workers and blocking polarisation and class conflict. Office-based work acted as an upward channel for mobile, ambitious manual workers into positions of high status and reward. Other writers suggested that by delegating duties and tasks to a responsible corps of workers around the boss, capitalism was supposedly transforming itself.

An alternative model, associated with orthodox Marxist writing, argued that as white-collar workers lacked economic ownership, and were formally dependent on wages like manual workers, then they should be seen as members of the working class. Their minor status advantages and more secure employment conditions, would, as their numbers increased, become subject to the same universal pressures of market competition and work control dominating manual workers. The universal consequences of employment concentration, rationalisation and de-skilling of white-collar jobs would, in effect, *proletarianise* these positions. An associated strand of this model appeared in the 1960s, and suggested that technical workers, in particular, were not only increasingly joining the working class, but were becoming a vanguard or leading section within it. French proponents of this idea, especially Mallet (1975) and Gorz (1967), were widely diffused in translated articles, interviews and summaries in the late 1960s. At the centre of this 'new working class' model was the belief that advances in technology – automation and process production – were reconstituting the skills, qualifications and revolutionary potential of the working class and breaking down established divisions between white-collar and blue-collar workers. The emergent unionisation of white-collar workers in France and Italy together with their first experience of independent collective struggle, were thought to offer the prospects of wider demands against capital than the narrow economic claims of traditional trade unionism. As one writer, commenting on the Italian experience, put it: 'the contents of the demands pertain(ed) primarily to the organisation of work rather than to questions of salary alone and aimed at reinforcing solidarity at the expense of individual competitiveness' (Low-Beer, 1978, p. 41). Demands for workers' control over production would be spearheaded by these new groups of workers and this would challenge the hierarchy and authority of capitalist control in the industrial enterprise.

At the other end of the spectrum were those writers who emphasised not an increasing commonality between those engaged in mental and physical labour, but rather, a *class* divide between the two. The identification of white-collar workers as a 'new middle class', is most closely associated with the structural marxism of writers like Poulantzas (1975) and Carchedi (1977). Although there are differences within this school, and I discuss these in chapter 1, what unites them is a view of the working class as becoming a progressively smaller section of society, outnumbered by the growing new middle class. The political implications of this model remain critical for a socialist strategy historically based around the belief of the universal nature of the working class. Theoretically, this school was marked by a shift away from the attention given to the *conditions* of work evident in the new working class writers' focus on technology, work organisation, and industrial sector. For Poulantzas, Carchedi and others, the *place* or functional location occupied by agents of capital and labour, was of a higher theoretical value than either the consciousness or conditions of those within these positions. Class analysis became more abstract, removed and hostile to empirical and historical investigation.

A final model, and one stemming from a critique of the writing of Poulantzas, has been the work of Wright (1977). He argued that white-collar workers did not form a distinct class, but rather occupied 'contradictory locations within class relations' – sort of buffer zones – between the capitalist class, working class and petty bourgeoisie. Twofold or threefold models of class are rejected by Wright who erects a complex 'class map' of structural characteristics and relations between those in the three main classes and the three in-between zones or locations.

This book sets out to assess the merits of these various models in relation to the social position of British technical workers. One of the major absences in the debate about intermediate workers has been any engagement between structural factors and the experience and consciousness of workers themselves. Through detailed interviews with technical workers and managers this book aims to bring their voice into the debate.

The substance of the book is drawn from fieldwork conducted in the late 1970s at a British Aerospace Aircraft Division factory in Bristol. Aerospace was selected because of the large number of technical and manual workers within the sector. These are concentrated in a few large firms, an employment situation shared by the majority of technical workers in Britain today. Viewed through the perspective of product or funding, aerospace appears to have a specificity all of its own. However, state support for the large ship-building and engineering sections of British industry was not as unusual when I conducted the research as it now appears. Moreover, given that total defence activity by British manufacturing industry grew from 8.2 per cent of all manufacturing output in 1979/80, to 13.1 per cent five years later, large defence companies are an increasingly significant part of British industry (Labour Research, July 1986). The geographical and industrial contexts are both in the foreground of the book in order to carefully situate the attitudes of the people I interviewed. They are neither socially nor politically anonymous, but individuals shaped by their experience of a particular sector, place and period. By specifying these contextual features, the lines of generalisation are made clearer than would be the case had I suppressed such details, and simply presented attitudes in a social vacuum. The real names of all those who appear in the book have, of course, been changed in the interests of confidentiality.

Chapter 1 introduces the main theoretical perspectives which have been developed to understand the position of clerical, managerial, and in particular, technical workers. Attention is drawn to the national and historical contexts of the various models, and the distinctiveness of the British class structure. In this regard, I emphasize how the craft tradition of apprenticeship for technical labour has mediated the relations between the technical office and shop floor.

Chapter 2 examines the origins, differentiation and proliferation of technical occupations in Britain. The purpose of uncovering something of the history of British technical jobs is to challenge the idea that the deskilling of the manual craftsman was a rapid affair, and one that constituted a major break in the class structure. The continuity of the craft apprenticeship system of training is seen as a major element mitigating against a major structural rupture between the new technical occupations and existing manual ones. For the current period, different tendencies are identified, some leading towards a growing homogenisation of wages and conditions of both technical and manual workers, others to greater division within technical labour. Employment and market conditions, long held by Weberian writers as a major barrier between white-collar and manual workers, are shown to be equalising. Other concerns, such as authority and status are also examined in this and other chapters and found not to contain the value invested in them by Weberian writers. Occupations like draughting have lost the legitimated power that once marked the draughtsman out from the manual worker.

Following Chapter 3, which explores the local context and specific characteristics of the aerospace industry, Chapter 4 introduces the fieldwork that forms the bulk of the book, with an analysis of the work situations of several different technical occupations. Concrete descriptions of jobs are provided to offset earlier misconceptions and improve upon theoretical statements about the class position of technical workers. More specifically Poulantzas (1975), Carchedi (1977), Wright (1977; 1985) and Johnson (1982), all maintain that technical workers are autonomous in their work situation, perform supervisory functions over manual workers and occupy positions of intellectual labour cut off from manual work. These assumptions are critically examined here and in more detail in Chapter 6. Against the view that technical workers form a single bloc against manual labour, I suggest there are two distinct forms of association between the two groups: the 'qualitative' and the 'quantitative'. Both produce quite independent sets of social relations between technical and manual labour, which in turn influence the types of class alliances open to technical workers. The 'quantitative' form of association refers to how technical workers are forced into a position of monitoring the pace and performance of manual labour, while the 'qualitative' association refers to their identification with the shared product and craft skills rather than manual workers work rate. The craft tradition in Britain has maintained the dominance of this latter form of association. However this situation is not stable, as technology, training and management strategies are altering the relationship between technical and manual occupations.

The history of the classical British technical worker, the draughtsman, reveals that at an early stage employers in the large shipbuilding and engineering industries differentiated their staff into design draughtsmen, detail draughtsmen and copyists or tracers (Reid, 1980). This technical division of labour initially formed the authority structure of the office, which contained, as did the craft shop, a chief, (manager), section leader, (foreman) and ordinary draughtsmen. Unionisation of draughtsmen by the Association of Engineering and Shipbuilding Draughtsmen had the effect of reinforcing the internal divisions within the technical office, as employers conceded recognition to ordinary draughtsmen but resisted the organisation of higher grades. The correspondence between the technical division of labour and the authority structure began to break up in the 1960s as graduate engineers appeared for the first time in large numbers in British technical offices. Chapter 5 examines the hierarchy in technical work and the relationship between graduate engineers, technical workers and management. It shows how the traditionally fluid relationship between draughtsmen and designers, has become more structured and formal as qualifications become increasingly important. The chapter also explores the way new technologies, such as computer aided design, are fragmenting the social cohesion of the drawing and other technical offices.

Chapters 6 and 7 attempt to evaluate, in the light of the

concrete situation, the central issues raised by new class theory in the 1970s, namely, the relationship of intermediate workers to manual workers and management. Building on earlier chapters, I develop the argument that the craft tradition mediates relations between manual and technical workers and acts against any rigid 'collar' divide between the two groups. I argue in both chapters that technical workers, although structurally located within definite social relations, also have to work out their own relationships with manual workers and management in their day-to-day practice. Against the tendency to allocate class position regardless of this subjective component, both chapters allow technical workers at BAe to express their own views on their work relations. Following Mallet, and in a different sense Poulantzas, the role is emphasised of technical workers as productive workers, as distinct from clerical labour and other white-collar groups.

My discussion on management in the technical setting reveals their ambiguous position, since they often assume the status of leading hand rather than an authority figure in the conventional sense. I examine how the autonomy of technical staff interacts with the uncertain authority of departmental managers, who try, not always successfully, to retain both worker and manager functions. The unionisation of management at Filton caused considerable bad feeling amongst many rank-and-file technical workers who resented its confusing further the distinctions between themselves and management. Chapter 7 discusses the contradictory nature of managerial unionism which as a general phenomenon began to grow inside large corporations in Britain during the 1970s.

One of the weaknesses of the new middle class debate in the 1970s has been the tendency to divorce class placement from the issue of collective organisation. This is partially a reaction against the assumption in the 1960s that unionisation automatically signified proletarianisation (Price, 1983). It also reflects the low levels of unionisation among white-collar workers in the countries that spawned the new middle-class debate in the mid-1970s – France, Italy and the USA.

The question of the correspondence between trade unionism and social class concerns the last chapter of the book, which opens with a discussion of Weberian and Marxist theories of white-collar unionism. My discussion of technical trade unionism has a concrete character in that it focuses on the major union for technical workers in British engineering, TASS. This was the only significant technical union on the Filton site and has traditionally been the only union to organise engineering design staff in Britain. The chapter charts the growth of the union and its political character which helped shape its relationship with manual workers. The amalgamation with the AEU, the manual engineering union, in the early 1970s, is examined against the coming together of manual and white-collar workers in the industrial struggles of the period. The demise and break-up of the union in 1986 is explained against the growing heterogeneity of membership within TASS and a decline in the industrial struggles in the 1970s. TASS today is no longer a purely technical union, but contains manual workers as well as managers and clerks. Its growth as a multi-level union is examined in the conclusion, which returns to the central question of the relationship between class and trade unionism amongst new middle-class workers.

1
Theories of Class and Technical Work

This chapter has three basic objectives: to introduce and critically assess theories of white-collar workers' class position; to highlight the importance of historical context for different theories; and to examine the class position of British technical workers. The chapter opens with a discussion of the dominant explanations for the growth of white-collar workers. This is followed by an examination of the relationship between models of the class structure and economic, technological and political change. The aim here is to argue that the insights that can be gained from new working-class and new middle-class theories require an integration that focuses on the historical and subjective components of class. The final part of the chapter examines some of the peculiarities of the British class structure and how these relate to theories of intermediate workers.

Explanations for the Growth of White-collar Workers

The relative and absolute increase in the number of white-collar employees has been the central feature of the class structure of all advanced societies in the twentieth century. In Britain, for example, from representing 3.5 million or 19 per cent of the total occupied population in 1911, non-manual groups have grown to just over 12 million or 52.5 per cent of the economically active population in 1984. Explanations for this growth point to many similar factors, such as the expansion of the state, the development of large-scale enterprises and the growth of the 'service' or tertiary sector of the economy. However, integrated perspectives broadly fall into two categories, the Weberian and Marxist. A Weberian analysis emphasises the growth of bureaucratic modes of organisation and employment sustained by diversification of market relations, and changes in the structure of power from traditional authority to rational–legal calculations under capitalism. As bureaucratic methods of organisation inevitably penetrate all areas of life, employment of white-collar 'experts' and routine support staff accelerates. The expansion of the state into civil society generates the need for more administrators, technocrats, co-ordinators and managers (Mills, 1953). Within enterprises the separation of ownership from control – the emergence of 'managerial capitalism' – promotes the need for managers and their specialised administrative and technical staff. Increases in size, complexity and technological scale of enterprises require the employment of commercial, marketing and distribution functions which are characteristically white-collar in nature. Finally there is the growth of financial and insurance services to support large scale enterprises. While many of these 'factors' are also mentioned by Marxist writers, the core of Weberian explanations lies in changes in power and market relations, which, for Marxists, are more the outcome or effects of changes in the structure and relations of the capitalist production process (Crompton and Gubbay, 1977; Hyman, 1983).

For Marxist writers the expansion of white-collar workers has to be tied into the internal dynamics of the capitalist economy and the state. The accumulation process, the increasing pressures of competition, the growth in the scale of reproduction of labour power and the drive to increase labour productivity have all promoted the growth of white-collar workers. Against the standard assumption that this growth challenges Marx's alleged views on the simplification and polarisation of the class structure between workers and capitalists, it is now more widely accepted that in both his early and mature writings, Marx identified the expansion of non-manual workers as a definite tendency within the system.

Rattansi (1985, p. 653) suggests that Marx located the expansion of 'middle class' groups in the 'growth in the *total* mass of surplus value and profits' which supports an increasing number of unproductive groups in the system. According to this view Marx identified four groups: (i) political and ideological functionaries (civil servants and soldiers), required for purposes of social control; (ii) office workers, 'involved in calculation, administration and sales', and connected with realising, rather than producing surplus value; (iii) managers, created through the 'endemic pressure towards concentration and centralisation of capital' which in turn support large scale enterprises which require coordination and control; and (iv) the growth of domestic servants, an unproductive layer of the working class in a specific work structure (Rattansi, 1985, p. 643).

Marxist writers have focused on different elements within the dynamics of capitalism in exploring the growth in the number of white-collar workers. Braverman (1974), for example, has concentrated on the division of labour and the cheapening of labour power through deskilling, which involves splitting the conceptual and operational elements of work and consequently creating a distinct 'mental' component in the labour force. In addition, he argues that the expansion of supervisory and managerial control functions accompany the decline of craft regulation and rise of mass production and automation. Other writers, Johnson (1982), for example, have attempted to make broader linkages between the accumulation process and the creation of different groups of white-collar workers or as he prefers it, 'new middle class' labour. He has said that 'the process of capital accumulation – while it has an economic appearance in investment decisions, capital movements and paths of historical development – is fundamentally one of formation of classes and transformation of relations between classes' (Johnson, 1982, p. 263). To support his argument he identifies the expansion of wage labour from petty bourgeois positions, the internationalisation of capital, the development of the welfare and military components of the state, and the growth of scientific, technical and organisational innovations as four sources of accumulation which have created different fractions of the 'new middle class'.

These he classifies as administrators, service professionals and semi-autonomous employees. Although Johnson does not introduce enough historical evidence to support his analysis, such attempts to make the connections between accumulation and class structure are an advance on the arbitrary nature of most Weberian expositions.

The central problem with Weber's class analysis lies in the confusion that flows from his view that market capacities or properties, be they capital, specialised knowledge or skills, provide the criteria for drawing the boundary between different classes. Hyman (1983, p. 20) has shown how Marx saw the 'fundamental weakness of any model of class based on purely market criteria, "because of the infinite fragmentation of interest and rank into which the division of social labour splits labourers as well as capitalists and landlords" '. Marx went on to say that 'any attempt to relate class to the identity of revenues and sources of revenues would imply the existence of an infinity of classes'. This was indeed, the problem that confronted Weber who was forced into adopting conventional descriptive rankings of skilled, semi-skilled, etc in his class analysis to impose some order on the class structure. Marx, recognising the limitations of such an approach, used alternative criteria based on ownership and non-ownership of property and the social relations within production, to provide a more coherent and integrated view of the development of classes and nature of class conflict. Given these weaknesses of Weber's analysis of class, this chapter is primarily concerned to explore Marxist accounts of white-collar workers.

Patterns of Class Analysis

Given the fact that capitalism is a dynamic system prone to periodic cyclical and structural crises, it is hardly surprising that the identity of groups in uncertain or ambiguous social positions should fluctuate relative to the influence of economic forces. Class consciousness and action have traditionally been linked to the state of the labour market, and the themes of the moderate and militant worker have a definite recurrence based on the strength or weakness of workers in the labour market (Davis and Cousins 1975). Low-Beer (1978) has argued that theories of the proletarianisation of white-collar workers are associated with stable or worsening economic conditions and rising political class militancy in society. Conversely, theories of their incorporation into the middle class occur in stable or improving economic conditions and a moderate political environment. Low-Beer does not *reduce* theories to economic and political conditions, but merely points out an association. When we are assessing the internal consistency of different theories of intermediate workers' class position, it is important to understand their context. Carter (1985) reviewing the development of the debate on white-collar workers in German social thought has noted how the writing of Lederer, Marschak and Spier shifted between new middle class and proletarian models according to the balance of strength between the dominant classes of capital and labour. Carter (1985, p. 29) indicates how white-collar workers were seen as an 'essentially vacillating social force', this stemming from their close proximity to management and wage labour condition. Given this conception of white-collar workers as *dependent* on the activity or structure of other classes for their *identification*, we can mention at least four contexts in which this dependence can be examined: (i) when the skill composition of the working class undergoes a major change; (ii) in periods of 'acquiescence' for the working class; (iii) in periods of economic and political disunity and fragmentation for the working class; and (iv) in periods of rising militancy amongst the traditional working class.

(i) Changes in skill composition Occupational change is a constant feature of the capitalist mode of production, because the dynamics of accumulation and competition stimulate revolutionary transformation in the forces of production and technical division of labour. However, what Johnson (1982, p. 267) has called 'epoch-making innovations', such as the development of automobiles, aircraft, jet engines, computers, assembly line production and automation, represent novel moments of change. It is during these innovative bursts that occupational structures and skills appear to be *radically* re-

shaped. The reorganisation of British engineering between 1880 and 1914 – based largely on new machine tools – restructured skilled manual work and created the demand for new technical, administrative and supervisory groups; which in turn generated a debate about a new 'class' entering British society (Littler, 1982). The new working class debate in the 1960s was premised on a belief in the radical effect automation would have on the skill structure of the working class, as I will show in this chapter. Child (1985) has argued that the current microelectronic revolution is stimulating a re-organisation of the relationship between producers and consumers and creating a new 'service class' in the economy. This association between radical innovation and class structure is primarily impressionistic, based on the *appearance* of change, not underlying continuities in class relations. It also frequently confuses occupational with class change.

(ii) 'Acquiescent' workers and alternatives In periods when the 'traditional' working class appears to be economically or politically incorporated into the values of capitalist society, the strategic significance of new occupational elements is emphasised. In the 1960s, for example, the image of the 'affluent worker', judged as a new structural feature of capitalism, caused some writers to elevate other groups, such as technicians, students, or marginal groups, as substitutes for the working class (Marcuse, 1964; Anderson, 1965; Birchall, 1980). The perceived incorporation of the working class, the traditional agent of change in capitalist economies, altered the subject of class analysis.

(iii) Fragmentation and alternatives In periods when the political and economic disunity of the working class is acute, as during economic crises, fascism etc, the importance of new groups offering an alternative political programme is frequently posed. For example, in Britain during the 1930s working class institutions, although not destroyed by fascism, did suffer from economic and political disintegration. In such a climate there was considerable interest in the 'new middle class' of managers, professional and technical workers. Cole (1934), for example, proposed an alliance between manual and

'professional' workers to promote workers' control of industry and a peaceful transition to socialism. Conversely, Burnham (1961) saw the emergence of managers representing a new authoritarianism, in which owners and workers would be subordinate to managerial expertise. The number of white-collar workers was increasing during the 1930s, especially in autos, electrical goods, chemicals and aircraft, but their perceived strategic importance was more a reflection of the political and industrial weakness of manual workers, than the numerical significance of intermediate groups. The alleged fragmentation and disunity in the ranks of the working class today has produced a revival of alliance politics and theories of the 'new middle class' as I will later show.

(iv) Periods of rising militancy The perceived significance of intermediate workers is largely dependent on the social action or inaction of the working class. But theories of white-collar workers also reflect the level of activity within the ranks of that stratum. Periods of militancy for white-collar workers typically coincide with a general increase in industrial disputes in the working class as a whole (Carter, 1979). At such times it is difficult to sustain a conservative theory of these groups if they are unionising, striking and forming organisational and political links with manual workers. Certainly British technical workers produced a redefinition of themselves as 'reluctant militants', even amongst non-radical sociologists, due to their increased industrial activity in the 1960s – see Roberts, Loveridge and Gennard's (1972) book of that title. The work of Gorz (1967) and Mallet (1975), as I will later show, is based on a view of the rising self-activity of technical workers. Trade union writing amongst white-collar unions in the 1960s argued that rising unionisation and industrial activity was proletarianising white-collar workers, as I show in Chapter 8. Clearly, this association between industrial conflict and class identity is strong, especially amongst trade union activists who, of necessity, see class in very active terms, as one TASS member from C. A. Parsons said to me:

Are technical staff part of management or are they incorporated as workers? I think you've got to look at specifics. I think in our place they are very definitely workers. They've struggled against redundancies, they struggled on quite a wide political basis against the GEC takeover, we've had overtime bans and sanctions for six months this year on the question of wages . . . In that sense, and I don't see any other sense, other than the commitment to get involved in struggle, they are very much part of the [working] class and playing an active part in it.

These historical dimensions need to be borne in mind when assessing the development of theories of intermediate workers over the past three decades.

The New Working Class Thesis

The theory of the new working class proposed that technological 'advances' in capitalist production, primarily the development of electronics, automation and process production, led to the reconstitution of the working class. Inside advanced production facilities old divisions between productive and unproductive, physical and mental labour would be progressively abolished. White-collar workers, in particular technical labour, far from being increasingly separated from productive labour, were seen as engaged directly and indirectly in the social production process, and part of what Marx referred to as the 'collective labourer' in *Capital* (Marx, 1976). The new working class was, on the one hand, more integrated into capitalism through the material benefits of high wages, job security and specialised skill. On the other hand, it posed a greater threat to the authoritarian structure of work, by demanding self-management and autonomy, stimulated by the technical needs of production for Mallet, and increasing education of labour for Gorz.

The French Debate: 'One Dimensional Man' or 'New Working Class'

Although there was considerable discussion about the impact of automation in Britain (Woodward, 1965) and America

(Blauner, 1964), it was the French context that created a
radical *political* character to the debate. In France, lines were
drawn between Communist and Socialist parties and trade
unions, with the identification of intermediate groups and the
consequences of automation assuming a fundamental political
importance for the future of socialism (Rose, 1979; Ross,
1978). Much of the ferment of ideas around the third industrial revolution (automation) in France occurred around the
journal, *Arguements*, in which industrial sociologists, trade
unionists and political activists established what came to be
called the new working class thesis (Mallet, 1975t, p. 67).

The visible signs of increasing affluence, higher wages,
provision of consumption goods, social welfare etc., created
in the 1960s a strong material basis for the idea of the incorporation of the working class into capitalist society. This, in
turn, produced popular and serious arguments on the right,
for the idea of the embourgeoisment of the working class, its
negation and absorption, through shared consumption habits,
into the middle class. The growing numerical importance of
white-collar workers and consequent decline in traditional
manual workers, appeared to the left as a threat to class-
consciousness, collective values, militancy and any fundamental opposition to capital. Marcuse (1964), who is perhaps
the best known exponent of this belief in the incorporation
of the working class into a technologically organised, one-
dimensional society, lectured in Paris in the early 1960s and
engaged in critical dialogue with the new working class theorists. Mallet shared many of the illusions of permanent economic stability, and the central role science and technology
had played in achieving this situation. However, he projected
a very different intepretation of these conditions than either
the embourgeoisement or one dimensional man thesis.

Mallet

It was Mallet who coined the phrase, new working class
(Howard, 1974, p. 119); his book of that title (*La nouvelle classe
ouvriere*, 1963) actually incorporated models of the 'evolution'
of capitalist production developed by Touraine, Naville and

other French industrial sociologists discussed by Rose (1979) and Gallie (1978). However he developed a political interpretation of these features not shared by Touraine (Rose, 1979, p. 84). Nevertheless his work had much of their concrete character, in contrast to what he regarded as the philosophical view of the working class dominant in the PCF and within orthodox marxism. Mallet conducted case studies of electronic companies and oil refineries in France between 1958 and 1962, in which he argued a marxist case for regarding a qualitative change to have occurred in the structure of the working class under what was called at the time 'organisation capitalism'. This referred to the expansion of planning within the firm and the apparent decline in power of the market in conditions of monopoly production. It also involved the growth of communications and leisure, the expansion of the state and market into all areas of life and the spread of 'rational' calculation into personal relations (Marcuse, 1964).

This concern for the sociological *condition* of the working class, was opposed to what he regarded as the idealisation of the proletariat in orthodox Marxism. Mallet believed it necessary to relate the real possibilities for change to the opportunities and conditions present in advanced forms of production. He was concerned to delineate internal divisions within what he called the working class*es* by *type* of production, rather than exclusively by ownership of property and *relations* of production.

The Class Position of Technicians

Mallet argued against the orthodox Marxist model of the working class as being restricted to productive, manual, waged labour. Within the French Communist Party (PCF) new layers, especially cadres (a complex term embracing 'middle and junior functional managers, routine supervisors and foremen, engineers and commercial travellers' (Rose, 1979, p. 92)) and technicians, were regarded as petty bourgeois because of their connection with management and autonomous, non-manual status. The new working class thesis suggested that, within the new industries, established class barriers were breaking down under the imposition of uniform working conditions and the creation of a collective interest in controlling production. The writers arguing this position:

> Accepted, as important cause for change in the *condition* of the working class the development of factors of integration in the firm, and the increasing importance of the technician and semi-technicians as a distinctive group. This 'technicisation' of the working class could, according to them, lead to a reformulation of working class demands orientated towards a growing awareness of economic problems and the need for the workers to control production at all levels . . . [A] 'technical' way to socialism. (my emphasis)
> (Mallet, 1975s, p. 188)

Mallet is unclear about the boundaries of the new working class, but membership has generally been taken to be 'technicians, researchers and skilled workers in automated firms' (Mallet, 1975t, p. 81). He also claimed that the new working class consisted of 'two different types of wage earners, both born of new technical developments and both involved in this process of 'integration in the firms' (Mallet, 1975s, p. 66). These included those engaged in *production* who are classified into two sub-groups, foremen, loaders, operators, and preparers – workers and supervisory labour; and 'cadres, engineers and white-overalled worker-technicians' – white-collar labour. And those 'exclusively born of automation and numerically greater' who are engaged in *pre-production* research and development, and *post-production*, sales, market research etc. At other times, for example in one of his case studies, Mallet discusses under the heading 'The working classes of Thomson-Houston' four categories of employees: engineers and top managerial staffs; administrative staff; technicians and the workers. The use of the term working class*es* is deliberate and designed to emphasise the heterogeneous nature of the working class on the one hand, and notion of productive 'collective labourer' on the other.

The Theory of the New Working Class

The new working class thesis rested upon several propositions relating to the social impact of automation on the organisation of work, division of labour and political practice of the working class. These can be summarised as follows.

1. Technicism   It was suggested that the 'evolution' of forms of capitalist industry imparts a distinctive character to working class political and trade union practices. Technicism – that is, the attempt to reduce political and ideological structures to production and the structure of labour into the organisation of productive capital – is a key feature of the thesis. It rests upon a linear model of economic development. Mallet said that 'each industrial period, each age of work organisation tends to create a relatively homogeneous structure in the class which operates the means of production. . . It is therefore legitimate to speak, with all the necessary reservation, of the "age of the skilled worker", of the semi-skilled worker and of the technician. Or if one prefers to refer to the organisation of industry rather than that of the worker, to the age of manufactory, of the mechanised factory and of automation' (Mallet, 1975s, p. 23). Table 1.1 demonstrates the character of this model.

Automation – the application of electronics to production; and process production – the integration of diverse tasks into a single process; creates a new structure for the working class. The workers in advanced industries are more integrated into capitalism, have polyvalent or all-round skills, and an identification with the company which is absent from those engaged in mass production and manufacture. Process technology and automation herald a reversal of the tendency towards job fragmentation, deskilling, alienation and the subordination of the worker to routine tasks performed without knowledge of the overall production process. Mallet claimed that automation 'destroys the fragmentation of work and recreates the synthetic vision of a complex task at the level of the team or even whole workforce' (Mallet, 1975s, p. 67). Skills are no longer acquired exclusively through elite educational institutions that perpetuate barriers between technical and

Table 1.1 *Evolution of the working class: 'changes in the organic composition of the working class'*

Type of worker	Character of production	Work situation	Politics and ideology	Trade union form
1. Skilled workers and artisans	*Manufacturing* Occupational or professional Skills. Individualism of small, isolated workshops	Autonomy	Anarcho-syndicalism. Reactionary in the face of advances in capitalist development. Limited production ideology	Craft trade unions
2. Semi-skilled	*Mechanisation* Mechanisation in mass production. Disappearance of occupationally distinctive & individual producer and rise of 'collective labourer'. Emergence of hierarchical and mental/manual division of labour	Loss of autonomy. De-skilling. Decomposition of tasks; interchangable and therefore economic insecurity	Orientation to consumption and revolt economism – revolt against 'work' not capitalism – affluent worker	General unions; industrial unions. Divisions between unions along skill and white-collar/manual lines
3. 'Technicians'	*Automation* Polyvalence & negation of job fragmentation. 'Progressive elimination of the distinction between manual and intellectual labour'	Contradictory integration into the Firm. 'New' autonomy due to specialised skills. Economic security	Re-orientation to production politics. 'Workers' control. Broader vision of production. Self-management	Enterprise-based unionism. Inter-union committees. Joint combines

manual labour. Mallet highlights the importance of on-the-job training in company-specific skills in his case study of the electronics company Thomson-Houston where, in one branch, 40 per cent of the engineers were 'self-made' men (Mallet, 1975s, p. 169). Mallet claimed that in the older industries of coal, construction, textiles, iron and steel, the engineers and cadres were socialised into managerial roles, directly responsible to the employers and cut off through a class barrier from the mass of manual workers. The engineers in the newer, science-based industries are, by contrast, frequently selected by, and responsible to, the work group. This pattern of on-the-job training and mobility between the shop floor and office was new in the French context, but not the British. The consequence of these changes was that social class divisions between engineers and manual workers are under automation, being eliminated or made more contradictory.

2. Agency and change   The new working class thesis argued that the most advanced forms of production created the most advanced forms of class-consciousness. 'The working class in archaic sections of industry cannot formulate a positive alternative to neo-capitalist society. . . It is only the social groups . . . integrated into the most advanced processes of civilisation which are in a position to formulate the manifold forms of alienation and envisage superior forms of development' (Mallet, 1975s, p. 14). For Mallet, the new working class was the new agency of change because the increasing interdependence between production and management in advanced industry conflicts sharply with the continuing private ownership of capital and organisation of managerial power. The integration of workers into the capitalist firm is contradictory.

Modern conditions of production today offer the objective possibilities for the development of generalised self-management of production and of the economy by those who do the work. But these possibilities clash with the capitalist structures of production relations and their profit criteria based on short-term returns to the owners, and also with the companies' techno-bureaucratic structure which appears more and more as a brake on the harmonious development of their productive possibilities.

(Mallet, 1975t, p. 82)

Mallet, unlike Gorz, believed in the neutrality of technology and science. He did not see it necessary to abolish the capi- talist values invested in technology, but merely reorganise that technology. He argued that the 'transformation of the economic, social and political structures cannot be had at the price of the destruction of the existing means of production, or even its serious weakening – "the machine is too valuable to smash" ' (Mallet, 1975s, p. 28). This reformism was based on the assumption of continuing economic stability, and the possibility of gradually extending control over production without revolutionary upheaval. It is also based on the belief in the neutrality of the instruments of production (tech- nology), rather than its infusion with capitalist values of hier- archy and control. 'The more the modern worker reconquers on the collective level the professional autonomy he had lost during the period of mechanisation of work, the more will demands for control develop' (1975s, p. 28).

The focus of new working-class writers was on action, consciousness and social condition. While arguing that different forms of production influenced social action, they also stressed its contradictory nature. Activity could change consciousness and class position. So for example the engineers at Thomson-Houston through refusing to form an exclusive, separate union and affiliating to a workers' confederation were demonstrating 'their feeling not of belonging to a "new middle class" as it has been said of them, but rather ident- ifying socially and economically with the working class which is itself the scene of internal mutations that facilitate the fusion between the two social categories' (Mallet, 1975s, p. 166).

Some Problems with Mallet

Criticisms of Mallet's work focus on his 'technicism', techno- logical determinism and utopian interpretation of the up- skilling effects of automation. I examine these in more detail below. Critics all too often reduce or ignore his views on the contradictory nature of automation and technicians' and engineers' roles within the working class. Because of the absence of an explicit theory of the class structure, a hazy methodology for his case studies, and a tendency towards popular or journalistic style of writing, it has been easy for writers to selectively simplify Mallet's work. His concern to integrate sociological insights on the structure of the working class into a utopian political practice often meant that he simplified the complex relationship between structure and class consciousness. His work is littered with deterministic phrases which reduce the role of human activity to a reflex of capital or technology. Equally, his case studies constantly qualify and complicate the relationship between production relations and trade union and political action. This dilemma was never satisfactorily resolved and may have reflected, as Poulantzas has argued, a model of class that started with condition rather than place.

His attention to conditions of work organisation and the division of labour in advanced industrial sectors did, however, reveal insights which have been buried under the mountain of criticism which has followed his work. For example, his three main case studies of electrical companies and oil refineries remain insightful for their discussion of inter-union rivalries, the contradictory pressures towards corporatism and workers control in the consciousness of engineers, and his distinction between 'climatic' and 'strategic' industrial struggles (Mallet, 1975s, p. 178). The latter point is discussed in the next chapter. These are details and insights supported in other empirically grounded books which focus on the relationship between class situation and condition amongst technical workers, e.g. Low-Beer (1978), Greenbaum (1979). The different forces operating upon the consciousness of engineers and technicians, and the important role of trade union leadership and policy within this process, is certainly something emphasised in this study and my other work on engineers (Smith, 1986). Mallet, in contrast to the structuralist Marxism of the 1970s, did utilise empirical evidence to support theoretical propositions, and retained a concrete concern for *class relations of production* which had been ignored

in later Marxist work. These points are not an apology for
the errors of his analysis, but rather comprise an exhortation
to re-read the rich quality French writing on social integration, class, skill and the firm in this period.

Major Criticisms of Mallet

Moving on to the substantive faults with Mallet, we can
say that the tendency to discuss the abstract or technical
possibilities of machinery outside definite social relations has
strong parallels in French social thought. Mallet comes close
to paraphrasing Proudhon who, in an earlier debate with
Marx on the nature of manufacture, imposed positive social
characteristics on technology. Mallet called automation, 'the
real dialectical negation of job fragmentation' while Proudhon
considered machinery, 'the antithesis of the division of labour
in the factory' (Rose, 1979, p. 66). Writing against what could
be called this 'romance of automation', Mandel (1978)
conceded that, in principle, automation if it displaces the
'conveyor belt and parcellized labour', makes possible 'an
intelligent comprehension and control of the overall
production process by the producers'. But in practice, 'the
increased level of skill of the collective labourer takes the form
under capitalism of only a slight increase in the average skill
of each worker, combined with a substantial increase in the
skill of a small minority of highly qualified producers (polyvalent technicians and repair workers)' (Mandel, 1978,
pp. 269–70). Poulantzas has made the same criticism, when
he observed that Touraine's model of the 'three phases' of
the capitalist labour process, shown in Table 1.1, 'failed to
take into account a dual process, one of qualification *and*
disqualification of labour under monopoly capitalism, and
assumed an inherent and self-sufficient "technological
process" independent of capitalist relations of production'
(Poulantzas, 1975, p. 243). Empirical evidence from Gallie's
studies of English and French oil refineries suggests that in
the French case, 'frequent experience of work in different
units was confined to a fairly small number of people who
were officially polyvalent' (Gallie, 1978, p. 81).
    Studies of plants that have moved from traditional to

process technology have found a general downgrading of skill, (Salaman 1981). My own work on the introduction of automated and semi-automated plants at the Cadbury factory in Bournville indicates the continuity of routine job design and a highly fragmented division of labour (Smith, Child and Rowlinson 1987). Nichols and Beynon's (1977, pp. 18–23) study of a chemical plant, revealed not only the continuity of repetitive, heavy manual labour – so called 'donkey work' – but also its dominance within a supposedly sophisticated modern factory. Moreover those workers connected with the 'scientific work' in the control rooms also spoke of the noise, isolation and stressful nature of their work. A vision of the overall production system was not evident. The shift systems operated in most factories engaged in continuous process production are a major disruption to the lives of the workers, but appeared to have been completely overlooked by Mallet and other new working class theorists. In addition, workers continued to have the same regard for issues to do with wages and conditions as workers in non-process production plants. Halle (1984) has made similar observations about work in an American chemical plant, stressing in particular the educational barrier between blue-collar and white-collar jobs.

The two central weaknesses of the new working class thesis were its technological determinism and its overemphasis on the discontinuity of work relations in the new science-based industries. This latter position is, as I have indicated, understandable given the fact that on-the-job training challenged the established pattern of training for technical workers in France. But in the British context, sectors like aerospace, although employing equally large numbers of scientific and technical workers as their French counterpart, trained them through a pattern of apprenticeship and practical experience that was standard across the engineering industry as a whole.

For Mallet, the earlier system of craft production in diverse workshops created the conditions for workers to have a high degree of autonomy and control over their working environment. The weakness of the craft system was that it produced a view of politics limited by the narrowness of the isolated craftsman and a vision of socialism dominated by an individualism that was ultimately reactionary in the face of the expansion of unskilled labour in large scale industry (Ridley 1970). In automated industries the individualism of the workshop was crushed, but the vision of production was broadened and therefore the potential for workers' control over work increased. Mallet romanticised the idea of comprehensive knowledge of production residing in polyvalent workers, and underestimated the extent of technical specialisation and fragmentation of knowledge.

Gorz, associated with the new working class thesis in the 1960s, rejected much of the determinism of this model in his later writing. This reflected not only the criticisms raised above, but also changes in the political and economic environment. Moreover, his position within the new working class debate was different, in many respects, from that of Mallet, as I will now indicate.

Gorz

André Gorz, a French latter-day marxist, has been a commentator on changes in the class structure of advanced capitalist countries for three decades. Unlike Mallet, Gorz is primarily theoretical, or one should say conjectural, his writing being characterised by crystal-gazing about political trends in advanced capitalist economies. He has rarely conducted primary fieldwork, unlike Mallet, and is eclectic in selecting illustrations for his ideas. Despite some dramatic political changes in his perspective, he has a constant concern with consciousness and ideology, focusing upon the question of agency and the prospects for a transformation of capitalist society. His writing is generally within the humanist Marxist tradition, counterposing a critique of capitalist society with an abstract commitment to human freedom, creativity and potential. My purpose here is to briefly examine his discussion of the class structure and the position of technical labour over the last three decades.

An Overview

Gorz in the 1960s was strongly influenced by the new working class analysis of the class structure. He argued that the progressive proletarianisation of educated and qualified labour was the central feature of advanced economies and focused on the contradictions posed by this development. By the early 1970s, with the emergence of the new middle-class thesis, itself a reaction to the 'utopianism' of the new working class ideas of the 1960s, Gorz changed his analysis of qualified labour. Unlike Poulantzas and Carchedi who focused upon the emergence of a *new class*, Gorz persisted with a two-class model of society with qualified labour *ideologically*, not structurally, wedded to capitalist relations of production. Gorz argued, in Maoist fashion, that the formal working class position of qualified labour had to be brought to bear on its ideological position by a 'cultural revolution' in the division of labour that separates technical and manual workers (Gorz, 1976). By this he meant a questioning of hierarchical values and monopoly of technical knowledge exercised by qualified labour over manual workers. (Cooley, who was also influenced by the cultural revolution and Maoism, has argued a similar line in Britain.)

Gorz has changed his position again in the 1980s. Now he argues that the workplace is losing its meaning and role as the main site of the struggle to transform capitalism. Unemployment, the re-structuring of the working day and jobs, is increasing the number of temporary and part-time workers and weakening class ties with work identified by writers in the 1960s. Within the organised sectors, trade unions are increasingly demanding a shorter working week and greater individual and collective control over working time. This new flexible pattern of work in the organised sectors, combined with a growing under-class, or non-class at Gorz calls it, of marginal, subcontract workers, means that an orientation of socialist politics towards work and production – self-management, workers control, etc. – is anachronistic. The 'new politics' is enhancing individual choice over working time, leisure time and life style. Collective or class wide transformations are, according to this prognostication, no longer structurally possible. This is partially because of the growing fragmentation of labour under the impact of global crisis. But more importantly, because labour *cannot* overcome the structural divisions imposed upon it by capital and by the growing diversity and internationalisation of capitalist production. This pessimism, which discounts the option of a working-class-led transformation, is in stark contrast to his earlier work, when the agency of change was always the working class.

My purpose here, having introduced Gorz, is to focus on that part of his work most relevant to the class position of technical labour.

Gorz in the 1960s

In his early writing, the identity of qualified labour was primarily defined by its wage labour status and consequent experience of proletarian conditions of work:

> Technicians, engineers, students [and] researchers discover that they are wage earners like the others, paid for a piece of work which is 'good' only to the degree that it is profitable in the short run'.
>
> (Gorz, 1967, p. 106)

More than traditional manual workers, this new working class was drawn into a series of *distinct* contradictions with the capitalist relations of production. Firstly, the arbitrary nature of the market was in contradiction with the growth of planning and increasingly 'rational' organisation of work. Gorz suggested that competition, changes in the product market, movement of capital to sites of cheaper labour, redundancies due to corporate takeovers and rationalisations, all offend the rationality of qualified labour. Relatedly, engineers' and technicians' expectations, shaped by long-term planning of products and production, conflicted with the short-term orientation to profitability of capitalist industry, where 'there (may be) less risk and more profit in manufacturing saucepans' (Gorz, 1967, p. 104). The qualified working class 'discover that long-range research problems, creative work on original problems, and the love of workmanship are incompatible with the criteria of capitalist profitability'.

The second major contradiction was the increasingly routine nature of work performed by qualified workers, something not stressed sufficiently by Mallet. Not only are abilities progressively under-utilised, but the quantum leap in skills initially flowing from automation, was considered a short-term, not a permanent feature of industrial development:

> The contemporary transition from mechanisation to automation will bring about a crisis in the organisation of work and the technique of domination founded upon it . . . Manual and intellectual work will tend to go together and cause a rebirth of humanism of work which had been destroyed by Taylorism. *But this humanism of work is itself only a transitional form*: automation will cause it in turn to disappear. (my emphasis)
>
> (Gorz, 1967, p. 126)

This contradiction has an abstract or universal dimension, based on the distinction between capitalist and human needs, and a concrete dimension based on the institutional organisation of the training and preparation of technical labour. The first level of contradiction lies in the clash of 'values' between the capitalist goal of efficiency, profitability, short-term gain and hierarchy, against the 'human values' based on the freedom of man and the 'irreducible autonomy . . . located in the worker himself and considered as sovereign praxis' (Gorz 1976, p. 165). The second, or concrete level, is the contradiction between a training in independence and creativity, and its stifling by the limitations of market rationality.

> The industry of the second half of the twentieth century increasingly tends to take men from the universities and colleges, men who have been able to acquire the ability to do creative work, who have curiosity, the ability to synthesise, to analyse, to invent, and to assimilate, an ability which spins in a vacuum and runs the risk of perishing for lack of opportunity to be usefully put to work.
>
> (Gorz, 1967, pp. 105–6)

Thus the central contradictions are not between ownership and non-ownership, productive and finance capital, indigenous versus international capital, although all these are considered. They are the contradictions between 'creative abilities' and the organisation of production for the market:

A fundamental contradiction is that between the requirement and criteria of profitability set by monopoly capital and the big banks on the one hand, and on the other the inherent requirement of an autonomous, creative activity which is an end in itself.

(Gorz, 1967, p. 103)

The capital/labour relationship is central, but this is not primarily an economic – wages and profits – contradiction, but one of the stifling of human creativity, a clash between socialised forces of production and capitalist relations of production. Gorz, like Mallet, accepted the economic boom conditions of the 1960s as relatively 'permanent'. His belief in the radical potential of qualified labour arose from the belief that their education, and the high expectation of creative work that it fostered, was bound to come into conflict with the narrowing of autonomous opportunities in the workplace. This would lead to political demands for 'self-management'.

Gorz in the 1970s

Gorz's writing in the 1970s continued to show concern for the new elements in the class structure. He also remained preoccupied with the question of agency, ideology (educational and cultural change), rather than economic issues. But the optimism of the 1960s, with progressive proletarianisation of qualified labour, and the issue of encroaching control spearheaded by technical labour, disappeared. In Gorz (1976) the *ambiguity* in the position of technical labour is central. At the beginning of an article variously titled, 'Technical Intelligence and the Capitalist Division of Labour (1971) or Technology, Technicians and Class Struggle (1976) Gorz identifies technical workers as inextricably part of the capitalist division of labour, monopolising technical knowledge and enmeshed in the hierarchy of control over manual workers. This is because: 'In performing their technical functions, [they] are also . . . reproducing the conditions and the forms of domination of labour by capital' (Gorz, 1976, p. 162). Gorz asks the question whether this is inevitable – a technical or neutral requirement of production – or whether it is fulfilling strictly capitalist functions. This leads him into a discussion on the status of science under capitalism and, more importantly for Gorz, the nature of products produced by capitalism. He suggests that the drive for research and development is 'to counteract the tendency for the rate of profit to fall and to create new opportunities for profitable investment' (Gorz, 1976, p. 164). Much R & D is directed towards what he sees as waste production – the substitution of relatively simple goods for more elaborate and costly commodities. He suggests, that many such services and products are superfluous 'from a socialist point of view'. Consequently much of the knowledge, skills and techniques needed to produce these commodities is also superfluous because they are tightly geared towards 'monopoly capital's needs' and would be unnecessary in a 'communist society'. Therefore, large numbers of technical and professional workers are currently in conservative and defensive positions in relation to socialism:

> If scientific and technical workers are to be politically radicalized we must call into question and contest the content and orientation of the professional activities and skills, and thus contest the capitalist ideology with which science and technology are thoroughly infected.
>
> (Gorz, 1976, p. 165)

Gorz also stresses the exclusivity of technical knowledge, the idea of a technical 'sub-culture' where language, techniques and jargon are partially technical but primarily a method of preserving existing power relations and separating technical workers from manual, production workers. Moreover, Gorz suggests that the technical knowledge accumulated by technicians during their training in college is not necessarily utilisable. In the 1960s, he argued that this inability to use the available technical skill was a *loss* to the technician and a condition of the capitalist emphasis of production 'efficiency'. In this article he says 'useless knowledge', like an awareness of algebra, serves to perpetuate the subjugation of manual workers to intellectual labour. Gorz cites an example of a technician who maintained his distance from shop floor workers through a repeated emphasis on his knowledge of calculus, despite his not using calculus in his work. For Gorz this is 'proof' that it is the knowledge that is not gained through experience that is the key to the mental/manual division of labour. At this level, there appears no way of resolving the division, short of exposing all workers to abstract knowledge.

But there is a way out. Gorz focuses on the product – use value of commodities – and the knowledge necessary to produce them, as the key element. This is the *material* prop of capitalist values, the embodiment in physical commodities and the organisation of production of capitalist values. Radicalisation of technical workers must be done from the 'outside' and through a questioning of the utility of products. Hence, what is necessary is an *ideological* or cultural challenge to the products, technology and organisation of technical and scientific education.

In spite of his concern with the oppressive and elitist role of technical workers, Gorz returns to his earlier theme of proletarianisation of technical labour, rather pinning his hopes on *young* technicians:

> As technical or further education and the technicisation (or intellectualisation) of work becomes more and more widespread, the distinction between the 'old' and 'new' working class is becoming obsolete, at least as far as younger workers are concerned. They know or sense that the technical worker is the proletarian of the 'technological society'.
>
> (Gorz, 1976, p. 182)

Proletarian condition stems from their wage labour, regimented schools, the repressive and hierarchical organisation of work, and the rapid obsolescence of skills. Because of this condition there is, Gorz insists, an 'objective basis, in their common attack on the capitalist division of labour, for the political and ideological unification of technical and manual workers' (Gorz, 1976, p. 183). But this can lead two ways. Either a 'cultural revolution' is required, a 'destruction of inequalities, of hierarchy, of the separation of intellectual and manual work and between conception and execution; the liberation of the creative capacities of all workers' (Gorz, 1976, p. 184), by struggle 'in the factories and the education system'. Or, the alternative scenario, the 'non-revolutionary attitude', is to aspire to 'responsibility, respectability and initiative' within the structure of capitalist hierarchies. That is, the rebellion against alienation can also work against proletarianisation; not for a working-class practice, but for securing privileges bestowed by education.

Problems with Gorz's Work

Criticism of Gorz's work should begin with his lack of attention to historical context. His treatment of qualified labour in the 1960s and 1970s ignores the specifically French context of his analysis. His use of Marx similarly shares an abstract, ahistorical character (Gorz 1976; 1982). Secondly, his lack of attention to the economic character of class leads him to place too much emphasis on the apparently *voluntary* nature of class identification. His focus on technical knowledge and capitalist 'products' is confusing. Why, if the utility/non-utility of products defines the distinctively capitalist form of production, are workers in armaments factories still regarded as members of the working class? Gorz wrongly identifies the *product* of production, rather than the *relations* of production, as conferring class position and an objective interest in an alternative economic system. Moreover, how is Gorz able to say in advance of any collective evaluation, what is to be the nature of products under socialist production? His writing frequently has a one-dimensional and deterministic character and is consequently subject to dramatic reverses in logic, e.g. the under-utilisation of knowledge is a source of opposition for technical labour in the 1960s, but a source of elitism over manual labour in the 1970s. There is a strong element of technological determinism in all his writing, especially his recent work, where he suggests that capital has deskilled all industrial work (Gorz, 1982, p. 72).

Against these criticisms, Gorz remains insightful, with an eye on the totality of capitalist development and class identity within broad political trends. His attention to class struggle is also refreshing, given the barrenness of much structuralist writing on class. However, the tendency to locate class primarily at an ideological level means that there are also dramatic shifts in analysis which are never adequately theorised, reflecting as they do peaks and troughs in class conflict. His work in this respect, is similar to early German writing on the new middle class (Carter, 1985). There is no question that Gorz has been an inspiration to the radical science and alternative planning movement – most strongly developed in Britain by Cooley. These qualities do not outweigh the fallacies of Gorz's work, but they nevertheless make him a writer with some interesting insights on intermediate workers.

Technology, Skill and Class

Braverman

Gorz's attention to the capitalist division of labour was developed more fully by the American Marxist, Harry Braverman (1974) in his influential, *Labor and Monopoly Capital*. For Braverman, craft control over production was the high watermark of workers' control under capitalism, the deskilling of the craftsman representing the universal degradation of work in the twentieth century. Automation, far from signalling a reversal of this trend, accelerated the subordination of labour to capital by objectifying relations of domination and control in the forces of production. The technicians created through the application of science to capitalist production and the destruction of the manual craftsman, are not representatives of a working class vanguard, but very much the agents of management and capital. Braverman puts the elements of technology, skill and class together in quite a different dynamic from the automation romantics of the 1960s.

If Mallet idealised technology to the advantage of labour, Braverman, by contrast, has been most criticised for a one-sided materialism, investing in capital an omnipotent power to mould labour according to the needs of accumulation and managerial control (Thompson 1983; Burawoy 1985). According to Braverman, capital in its pursuit of control over the labour process has systematically raided the craft skills that supported an autonomy and counter-authority absent from mass production. The application of science to production and the emergence of scientific management are identified by Braverman as removing on a massive scale the conceptual dimensions from manual work, and transferring these to the office, which, under conditions of monopoly capital, is dominated by management and its agents. Technical workers – engineers, designers, planners – are considered the creation of monopoly capitalism – products of the deskilling of the manual craftsman, (something that is open to doubt as I indicate in Chapter 2).

While Mallet saw the proletarianisation of technical workers coming through changes in the work situation, Braverman, in an almost Weberian fashion, suggests that their position in the labour market is a key determinant of their class location. Through the market situation, rather than their position in production relations which remains contradictory, draughtsmen and some engineers are forced towards a working class location. Braverman begins his analysis of intermediate employees by stating that as dependent wage labourers, they are 'formally' part of the working class:

That is, like the working class, it possesses no economic or occupational independence, is employed by capital and its offshoots, possesses no access to the labour process or the means of production outside that employment, and must renew its labours for capital incessantly in order to subsist.
(Braverman, 1974, p. 403)

Braverman, following the work of Lockwood (1958) suggests that within their work situation white-collar employees' authority relations mark them off from manual or blue-collar workers:

Since the authority and expertise of the middle ranks in the capitalist corporation represent an unavoidable delegation of responsibility, the position of such functionaries may best be judged by their relation to the power and wealth that commands them from above, and to the mass of labour beneath them which they in turn help to control, command and organise.

(Braverman, 1974, p. 405)

Sitting between manual workers and management white-collar workers exhibit 'the characteristics of the worker on one the side (and) manager on the other in varying degrees' (Braverman 1975, p. 405). Within what he sees as a continuum between the two polar positions, draughtsmen and technicians are located towards the working class, while engineering heads are given a definite bourgeois 'polarisation'. Foremen, petty managers and certain technical specialists are, somewhat confusingly, seen as occupying the 'middle ground'. This continuum is not static, as it serves as a 'status ladder', a hierarchy of command, authority and privilege instituted and perpetuated by senior management as a mechanism of 'divide and rule' amongst employees:

Among the intermediate groupings are parcelled out bits of specialised knowledge and delegated authority without which the machinery of production, distribution and administration would cease to function. Each of the groupings serves as the recruiting ground for those above, up to and including top management. Their conditions of employment are affected by the need of top management to have within its orbit buffer layers, responsive and loyal subordinates, transmission agents for the exercise of control and the collection of information, so that management does not confront unaided a hostile and indifferent mass.

(Braverman, 1974, p. 406)

Here Braverman is describing the managerial or political side of the continuum. There are also economic pressures, from the demands of the capitalist accumulation process, operating on the labour market position of these intermediate positions. Undercutting his above portrait of a fluid and mobile pool of middle-class labour around top management, is the growth of a mass labour market for groups like draughtsmen and some engineers. With this development the privileges offered such occupations due to their scarcity value are undermined. This has been the hallmark of the difference between white-collar workers under conditions of private and monopoly capitalism. Discussing this process Braverman has said:

> Not only does it receive its petty share of prerogatives and rewards of capital, but it also bears the mark of the proletarian condition. For these employees the social form taken by their work, their true place in the relations of production, their fundamental condition of subordination as so much hired labour, increasingly makes itself felt, *especially in the mass occupations* that are part of this stratum. (my emphasis)
>
> (Braverman, 1974, p. 407)

Mass labour markets have developed for such intermediate occupations as technicians, draughtsmen, teachers, accountants, supervisors, junior management and clerks. These occupations are subject to economic pressures, unemployment, deskilling and loss of control in the labour process and it is because of these changes, which stem from the market, that:

> the proletarian form begins to assert itself and impress itself upon the consciousness of these employees. Feeling the insecurity of the role as sellers of labour power and the frustrations of a controlled and mechanically organised workplace, they begin, despite their remaining privileges, to know those symptoms of dissociation which are popularly called 'alienation' and which the working class has lived with for so long that they have become part of its second nature.
>
> (Braverman, 1974, p. 408)

Braverman's analysis in Chapter 17 of *Labor and Monopoly Capital* maintains that market situation determines the work situation and class position of intermediate groups. However his central thesis in the book, that of the degradation of work through the divorce of conceptual and operational elements in the capitalist labour process, intersects the above analysis. It also confuses his position on the class position of intermediate workers and this is apparent at the end of the book when he returns to the central issue of deskilling and the potential for a resolution to degradation that favours labour. Here Braverman claims that technical workers are unambiguously incorporated into management through their role in deskilling craft work and monopolising the 'technical knowledge of production'. He says:

> the extreme concentration of this knowledge (scientific, technical and engineering) in the hands of management and its closely associated staff organisations have closed this avenue to the working population.
> (Braverman, 1974, p. 443)

For 'working population' read 'manual workers', because it is they who are excluded from sharing in or entering this store of technical knowledge, sealed in via the capitalist division of labour. Technical workers here are definitely part of the bourgeoisie as agents of capital in the production process. The idea of technical workers acting as gatekeepers to a store of technical knowledge is strongly challenged by the evidence of this study. Indeed the concept of a single source of knowledge or technical information, does not hold up under empirical investigation, where the informal division of labour and regular association between technical and manual workers increases the sources of ideas. Braverman's world allows for no such interaction as the flow of knowledge is always *downwards* to manual workers, and their participation in conceptualisation is virtually non-existent. All of which is, as I will later show, open to strong theoretical and empirical questioning.

What lies behind the above criticism is an absence at the heart of Braverman's work, of the question of human agency. This applies as much to his portrait of capital as it does to his failure to discuss the reaction and challenge from labour to changes in the conditions of exploitation generated by the capitalist production process. Technical workers and engineers are never really active in the process of deskilling, they are rather controlled through the capitalist division of labour and senior management to act in the interests of capital, which are always assumed to be readily known. A view of technical workers which has, at one level, strong similarities to Braverman's, comes from the writings of an Irish engineer, Mike Cooley. But what distinguishes Cooley from Braverman is the stress the former places on the ability of technical workers to choose, within economic limits, the way work is designed under capitalism. As one of the few writers in Britain to discuss technical workers in this way, he deserves some attention here.

Cooley

Engineers and Scientific Management

Braverman identified Taylorism as a universal and irresistible managerial ideology and practice. All other managerial approaches to labour were subordinate to the premises of Taylorism, those of the fragmentation of work and managerial control over the conceptual aspects of production. Technical labour as we have seen was the product of monopoly capitalism and ultimately subordinate to management and the forces of capital accumulation. Noble (1977), in a pioneering work on the structuring of technical and scientific education in the monopoly phase of American capitalism, identified in the person of the engineer, rather than the ideology of Taylorism, prescriptions of scientific rationality and capitalist efficiency. He has said:

> The distrust of human beings by engineers is a manifestation of capital's distrust of labour. The elimination of human error and uncertainty is the engineering expression of capital's attempt to minimize its dependence on labour by increasing its control over production. The ideology of

engineering, in short, mirrors the antagonistic social relations of capitalist production.

(Noble, 1977, p. 30)

Noble gives subjectivity to technology through the person of the engineer. However, he also strives to show how this figure has been incorporated into capital and his design choices shaped by the exigencies of profit maximisation or managerial control of labour for its own sake. Cooley represents a position close to that of Noble, but one arrived at via a different route and within a different political and industrial context. Cooley is more optimistic about the possibility of radicalising engineers than Noble, who, within an American context where they largely represent a non-unionised, professional elite, has few grounds for anticipating close bonds emerging between this group and manual workers. This is not the case in Britain.

Cooley: The Engineer and Trade Unionist

Cooley, like Braverman to some extent, has not been raised within a university or academic environment but within industry and trade unionism. Up until 1981, Cooley worked at Lucas Aerospace as a designer and leading member of the Lucas Aerospace Combine Shop Stewards Committee. His writings about science, technology, skill, workers' control and workers' alternative plans, have largely been produced within a trade union context and for an audience of trade unionists, managers, technical workers and socialists within British industry. Partly as a consequence of this context and the practical political nature of much of his writing, Cooley has not developed his ideas into a single coherent text. Many of his articles repeat familiar illustrations and examples of the contradiction in capitalism's ability to create powerful technical forces while not solving basic social questions of poverty, bad housing and unemployment. Many of these examples compare the tensions between the forces and relations of production within capitalism, something standard to an orthodox Marxian view of science and technology. However Cooley is also very critical of what he regards as the Stalinist or orthodox Marxist conception of science as an essentially neutral or independent force only distorted by capitalist relations of production. He argues instead, that science itself is full of bourgeois values and requires re-thinking rather than applying in a neutral way. A major sign of this interpretation of science and technology is his concern to challenge the way designers and other technical workers design the technology and work organisations of other workers. Hierarchy, elitism and the Taylorian conception of work are seen as part of an engineering ideology or what Rosenbrock (1981) has called an 'engineering paradigm' and have all been targets of attack.

Cooley has consistently tried to expose the theoretical and political inadequacies of a conception of engineering practice that rests on a divorce between mental and manual labour and the subordination of the latter to the former. The tradition of a long practical and theoretical training for engineers, which is peculiarly British and a legacy of craftism, is defended, for the *technical* reason of being more efficient, and the *political* reason of strengthening the cooperation between technical and manual workers. Rising out of this critique has been the support for ways of designing jobs to enhance the skills of manual workers and maintain the craft association between conceptual and operational elements in the broad engineering labour process.

One of his primary concerns has been the impact of new computer technologies on white-collar workers, in particular those groups like designers who are technically highly qualified (Cooley, 1972, 1976, 1980). The threatened impact of computer aided design on the engineer has been interpreted by Cooley as evidence of Taylorism entering design, with the implication that the long-term job prospects for engineers will become similar to skilled manual workers who have suffered deskilling and routinisation. What separates his analysis of the deskilling of technical workers from that of Braverman is that Cooley is concerned to halt the process and re-direct technology away from deskilling towards skill enhancement. For Braverman, such a possibility is not actively present in his analysis.

The Lucas Plan

Cooley as an active trade unionist in TASS has attempted
to challenge what he regards as the deskilling intentions of
computer aided design by trying to influence TASS policy at
a national and local level (Cooley 1972). But perhaps his
greatest contribution, and one which has drawn a wider audience to his work, has been his involvement in formulating a
workers' alternative plan at Lucas Aerospace in the mid-
1970s. In response to rationalisations and redundancies inside
Lucas Aerospace, shop stewards developed an alternative
plan to job loss that called on the company to support investment in a list of products drawn up by the workforce through
the shop stewards' combine. The plan challenged managements' right to determine product range and mix, and centred
around moving the company out of the defence sector into
civilian or what the plan described as 'socially useful
production'. The plan was strongly influenced by many of
Cooley's ideas and views of technology, skill and technical
labour. It contained a critique of deskilling, for example,
which was probably penned by Cooley himself: 'it is clearly
evident from some of the Lucas Aerospace plants that
attempts to replace human intelligence has had quite disas-
trous results. It is intended to campaign for quite radical job-
redesign which protect our members from this' (LACSSC,
1976).

The origins and philosophy of the LACSSC Corporate Plan
has been carefully analysed by Wainwright and Elliott (1982),
and I am not detracting from the complex and collective
forces that shaped its development, by suggesting that Cooley
exercised a key intellectual influence within the shop stewards
committee. Latent within the alternative plan's movement
was a revival, within a British context, of the idea of technical
workers being some kind of vanguard for the working class.
Technical workers within the combine, through a technical
sub-committee, exercised the major role in drawing up the
alternative product designs at the centre of the workers'
corporate plan. It is also evident that attempts to generalise
the experience of Lucas into other companies, were only
'successful' where technical workers existed as an organic

resource integrated into the trade union structure at plant level through a combine committee, as at C. A. Parsons (Smith, 1979).

The Lucas plan, as Rustin (1980) has usefully argued, represented an attack on attempts to change the division of labour between technical and manual workers. In a climate when the Finniston inquiry into the status of engineering was promoting the professionalisation of British engineers, the corporate plan argued strongly for engineers and other technical workers' integration into the trade union and labour movement. The shop stewards' combine brought together 'the analytical power of the technologist and the class understanding of those on the shop floor' (LACSSC, 1978). It aimed at creating a new vision of production control and pro-active trade unionism stemming from the unity between these two elements of the collective worker.

With a firm commitment to trade unionism and workers' self activity through such syndicalist-type practices as worker plans, it is clear that Cooley regards technical workers as a vital part of the British working class. From joining TASS in 1959 he has helped build up the broad left in the union which, as I later indicate, was responsible for bringing technical workers into industrial action on a significant scale in the 1960s.

Cooley and Computer Aided Design

As a trade unionist his conception of class as *class struggle* is apparent, but what of his writing on class, technology and engineers? How has he integrated his political practice into his analysis of these areas?

As mentioned earlier, the impact of CAD on engineers has occupied Cooley for over a decade. Between his pioneering book on the social implications of CAD published as a TASS pamphlet in 1972, and an article on the same theme written for a conference on CAD in the early 1980s, little has changed in his argument. The 1972 book suggested that CAD would deskill and proletarianise designers. It argued that CAD represented the emergence of Taylorism in the technical department. These themes continue to occupy Cooley as I

will now indicate through a brief analysis of the 1981 paper
(Cooley, 1981).

Cooley begins the article with a discussion of Taylorism
and the capitalist division of labour. Like the earlier book he
considers 'techniques such as computer aided design as a
trojan horse with which to introduce Taylorism into the field
of design' (Cooley, 1981, p. 98). He explains that technical
labour initially benefited from Taylorism and the 'clear cut
and novel division of mental and manual labour'. Indeed the
deskilling of the craftsman stimulated the growth of technical
labour: 'throughout the [twentieth century] most industrial
laboratories, design offices and administrative centres were
the sanctuary of the conceptual, planning and administrative
aspects of work' (Cooley, 1981, pp. 98–9). The existence of
centres of conceptualisation outside the workshop is taken as
evidence of Taylorism in practice. The integration of science
into production has the consequence of rationalising the work
of those in the offices and laboratories and preparing the way
for Taylorism and the separation of whole processes into
quantitative (routine) and qualitative (creative) elements.
The application of computers to the design area enhances
these developments: 'CAD tends to deskill [and] subordinate
the designer to the machine and [produce] . . . industrial
alienation' (Cooley, 1981, p. 103).

For Braverman the logic behind attempts to deskill manual
workers through mechanisation and automation was
primarily economic, whereas for both Noble and Cooley its
political determination is emphasised. This is chiefly the
outcome of their attention to the military-industrial complex
where 'economical production is not necessarily the prime
motivation behind automation (or even the chief means of
profit maximisation' (Noble, 1984, p. 340). The nature of the
defence industry is discussed in Chapter 3. Cooley argues that
the failure of corporations to concentrate funding on skill-
enhancing techniques, equipment and research is not because
machinery and skill are somehow inherently oppositional,
but rather that increasing workers' skill strengthens their
independence from capital and threatens managerial prerogatives. The opposition to the corporate plan by Lucas management was interpreted, with some justification, as evidence of

the unwillingness of management to abdicate from certain strategic decision-making areas. It was strongly believed by Cooley and other stewards, that exposing managements' reluctance to cooperate in key areas of corporate power would have a radicalising effect on those groups of workers, such as engineers, who have some belief in the reasonableness of management. The work of Professor Rosenbrock on interactive computing and skill enhancement demonstrates, according to Cooley, the *technical* possibility of designing for human beings rather than capital accumulation and profit. Indeed, such work indicates the greater degree of efficiency obtained by utilising human creativity and resourcefulness, rather than working to destroy these factors by making workers machine minders. Again Noble supports these arguments with plenty of illustrations on the inefficiency of automation in the machine tool industry.

One of the consequences of this political interpretation of deskilling is to see the extension of skill as a challenge to capitalism. New alternatives to skill destruction will not be adopted 'since they challenge power structures in society' and 'those who have power in society, epitomised by the vast multinational corporations, are concerned with extending their power and gaining control over human beings rather than with liberating them' (Cooley, 1981, p. 110). Summing up the consequences of this analysis of deskilling, Cooley says:

> The reality is that as we design technological systems, we are designing sets of social relationships, and as we question those social relationships and attempt to design systems differently, we are then *beginning to challenge in a political way power structures in society.* (my emphasis)
>
> (Cooley, 1981, pp. 110–11)

Some Problems with Cooley's Work

This article, like much of Cooley's writing, contains a strong element of technological determinism. In this respect there are certain similarities to be made between him, Gorz and Mallet. In addition, his conception of Taylorism as an all powerful engineering and capitalist ideology that pervades engineering practice is expressed in strongly deterministic language. Can the introduction of computers actually change the class structure? Do engineers using CAD begin to experience so-called 'industrial alienation'? Such statements perceive engineers solely through their technical function, not their social place in the hierarchy of command and division of labour. Engineers as *managers* may support CAD precisely because it does all the things Cooley accuses it of. Engineers in non-supervisory positions may still welcome the independence CAD can give from other technicians. Both these views were expressed to me by engineers at BAe, as Chapter 5 indicates.

Were Cooley to be judged purely on these confused aspects of his writing, he could be dismissed as a crass determinist. However, this is only one side of his work. He needs to be seen as an engineer, and a trade union and political activist. His writing, aimed at the engineering community through articles in institute journals and at conferences, is directed at theoretically challenging the dominant engineering paradigm and defending the position of engineers as a status group. In this arena, he is appealing to engineers purely as technical experts, not as individuals within a social context. As to the efficacy of such an appeal, it is also evident that he does not rely on the goodwill of the engineering profession or management to see the sense of his or others' critique of Taylorism and CAD, and voluntarily change their approach to design. He recognises the vested interests within the engineering community, in particular the power of capital to maintain domination over labour by removing the independence and economic strength skilled labour can possess. As a trade union activist, and one of the main figures in the workers' alternative planning movement, he is attempting to bring the critique of Taylorism and capitalist technology into the heartlands of working class industrial power to change the orientation of trade union practice. This concern with a new agenda for trade unionism, places him above any crude determinism which assumes that either technology will shape political practice or engineers will voluntarily identify with the trade union movement. All these things have to be consciously struggled for. This active element in his political practice stands in contrast, and to some extent contradiction, to the determinism of his writing. Any assessment of his contribution to the debate on the nature of skill, technology and the class situation of technical staff must look at both the man and his writing for a fair portrait of his work.

While I have been critical of Mallet and Cooley, their strength lies in their concern to relate the question of class in the workplace to industrial and political action in the workplace. What stands out in the debate on class within marxism from the mid-1970s is the universal abandonment of this concern. This idea of a growing working class which is more educated, qualified and confident, is replaced by the opposite view, where the proletariat is a shrinking, minority force, composed of unqualified manual workers, alienated from technical knowledge by an expanding 'new middle class'. The concern with the idea of a single agency of change or a vanguard capable of spearheading independent working class activity is replaced by a stress on the *limits* of autonomous action and the need for class alliances between a dwindling working class and ever-increasing new middle class. This concern with alliance politics was accompanied by a much more rigid, and supposedly scientific, distribution of the population into definite class positions with prescribed patterns of behaviour. By way of an assessment of this so-called structural or functionalist marxism, I will now examine the work of three of the most influential writers of this school, Poulantzas Carchedi, and Wright.

Structural Marxism, the New Middle Class and Technical Workers

Poulantzas

Nicos Poulantzas was probably the most influential marxist theorist of class structure in the 1970s. His approach to the subject was primarily abstract and came from a political concern with the nature of the state in capitalist society. This is in contrast to the orientation of new working class writing, with its focus on technology, the workplace, trade unions and consciousness. Poulantzas, although a Greek marxist, developed his ideas inside French social thought, indeed some argue that it is not possible to explain his views without looking at this French context (Ross, 1978). His main theoretical perspective is structuralism, or functional Marxism. This is in contrast to humanist Marxism which was developed against a critique of Stalinism and orthodox Marxism by French writers like Lefebvre and Goldmann, both key influences on Mallet (Howard, 1974). For humanist Marxism, the focus is on the contradiction between existing and potential class consciousness, the relationship of the individual to the group or collective, and *crucially*, the importance of action to class analysis. For the structuralists, by contrast, empirical individuals or groups are not the focus; attention is rather on the external, material relations that operate independently of social agents, and shape class struggles. Individuals as conscious *subjects* are irrelevant to this focus, indeed they only exist as 'bearers' of social relations. Classes are abstract 'places', not empirical and historical conditions. The language of humanism speaks of consciousness, action and struggle, in contrast to Poulantzas who emphasises objective structures, formal relations and abstract places.

At the beginning of his book, *Classes in Contemporary Capitalism*, Poulantzas (1975) asks the question: what are classes in Marxist theory? This he answers with a formal listing of features of class analysis, not culled from Marx, but from within structuralism. They include the following:

1. Classes are social agents defined primarily, but not exclusively, by economic relations of production. Ideological and political relations are also important.
2. Classes are only defined through mutual opposition, they do not firstly exist as independent entities and then come into conflict. Conflict is endemic to an understanding of class.
3. Classes exist independently of the will of social agents.
4. There is a difference between the determination of social agents by economic, political and ideological class relations, and the actual class position social agents may operate within. In other words, social agents do not always correspond to their class determination, they may share

political and ideological positions of other classes, or enter alliance strategies which are not immediately reducible to their class interests.

5. Social class 'places' are distinct from the people who make up these positions, that is persons are different from places. Moreover social origins – educational and family background – are not relevant to class placement. 'Social classes are not empirical groups of individuals . . . [and] social class membership depends on the class place that they occupy' (Poulantzas, 1975, p. 17).

Poulantzas's object in this book is to divorce class theory from an historical, sociological and empirical understanding of class. It is to drive a wedge between what we could call an historical class formation, involving real individuals, groups and class struggle, and a kind of supra-structuralism, separate and above historical reality. Although many of the elements mentioned are in keeping with a Marxist understanding of class, the polarisation between structure and action/consciousness does not accord with Marx. Before examining his analysis in detail, it should be noted that the contents of the book consists of sections on the state, the bourgeoisie and the petty bourgeoisie, but nothing on the working class. This, for a Marxist text on the class structure is astonishing, and indicative, as I will argue, of an attempt to eliminate a conception of socialism as the result of the self-activity of the working class.

Nichols (1979) suggests that Poulantzas builds his analysis of social class on three foundations: (i) the labour theory of value; (ii) an emphasis on 'place' in the social division of labour which precedes considerations of 'condition'; (iii) the view that class structure precedes class struggle, for instance the adoption of working class methods of struggle, unionisation, strikes, etc., by the new petty bourgeoisie does not alter their class position.

From these conceptions Poulantzas constructs a theory of the structural determination of social classes along three axes; the economic, the political and the ideological. The 'economic' determines all the other levels within the social formation but not in a linear or causal way. In practice, the political and 'ideological' levels are given the same weight as the 'economic base'. The relationship between dominance of any level or levels and determination is also crucial. Because the economic level is not seen to influence all other levels of a group's class position, ideological and political levels can take pride of place in certain classes. Technicians, for example, are part of the working class at the economic level, i.e. they are productive workers, however, ideologically and politically they are part of the new petty bourgeoisie.

What does Poulantzas mean by ideological, political and economic levels? The economic is reduced to considerations of productive and unproductive labour. Political is likened to supervision within the productive enterprise, i.e. political with a small 'p'. Ideological refers to the division in social relations between 'mental' and 'manual' labour. Examining these three 'levels' in more detail it is possible to show that Poulantzas's theory rests on a revision of Marxism, through the creation of 'class divisions' out of structures not given that status in Marx's work.

At the economic level technical workers are part of the collective labourer and therefore produce surplus value for capital. The entry ticket into the ranks of the collective labourer is the ability to produce 'material' commodities. Marx has several definitions of 'productive labour' and Poulantzas is wrong to attempt to restrict Marx to this one, Marx argued that it was not the 'product' that defined whether a worker was productive or unproductive, but rather the social and economic organisation involved in the production of that product.

Marx in criticism of Adam Smith in *Theories of Surplus Value* (1969 p. 171) argued against what he saw to be an empiricist or 'Scottish' definition of productive labour. Namely, that it required a material manifestation of labour power in the commodity before productive labour could be said to have been performed. This 'mystification arises from the fact that a social relation appears in the form of a thing' (Marx 1969, p. 172). Marx argued that teachers, writers and prostitutes could be productive if they were organised by capital to produce exchange value from their surplus labour. Poulantzas however, says:

We shall say productive labour in the capitalist mode of production is labour that produces surplus value while directly reproducing the material elements that serve as the substratum of the relation of exploitation: labour that is directly involved in material wealth.

(Poulantzas, 1975, p. 216)

With this revised definition of productive labour Poulantzas concludes that technicians are part of 'capitalist productive labour' and therefore potentially members of the working class. However economic criteria *alone* is not sufficient evidence of class identification or sufficient to delimit the boundaries of the working class and certain fringe sections of the new petty bourgeoisie.

Moving to the political level in class determination, it is important to note that Poulantzas uses the term 'political' in two senses. Firstly, political in the state apparatus outside of production, and secondly political at the economic level, within production. It is in this second sense that Poulantzas is most controversial, building on the work of Gorz (1976) and systematising an account of supervision and its role within production. For Poulantzas supervision and management are political, and therefore technicians in co-ordinating the labour process of other workers are acting in the interests of capital:

The work of management and supervision, under capitalism, is the direct reproduction within the process of production itself, of the political relations between the capitalist and the working class.

(Poulantzas, 1975, pp. 227–8)

This is an important point for many critics of Poulantzas, especially orthodox Marxist critics, who say that he over-politicises the work of co-ordination which is essentially 'technical' and not social in nature.

I support Poulantzas in regarding management as a function that produces and reproduces capitalist relations of exploitation and not, as some orthodox marxists claim, neutral or collective labour functions. But whether technicians

perform managerial functions is an empirical not theoretical
question, something Poulantzas's theory of class denies.

For Poulantzas technicians are excluded from membership
of the working class because of their role as agents of capital
in 'politically' supervising the labour process. He says that
their involvement in supervision is of a twofold type. Firstly,
they are themselves responsible for the work of management
and supervision, thereby controlling the 'efficiency of the
workers and the achievement of output norms' (Poulantzas,
1975, pp. 239–40). And secondly, technicians are indirectly
part of the process of separating workers from the conditions
of work and subordinating them to an ideological class knowledge. This second function is important, because whether
technicians are aware or critical of their role in production
does not negate their objective 'complicity' as agents of
capital. That is, the *consciousness* and *content* of their work is
irrelevant to the *form* in which the work takes place, namely
within mental labour. It is here that Poulantzas begins to
differentiate himself from Gorz and Cooley, who would argue
that a new consciousness amongst engineers would also
represent a change in their class position. For Poulantzas the
separation between mental and manual labour presents an
irresistible class barrier, it is the form of the 'capitalist subordination of the working class to the hierarchy of bourgeois
factory despotism'. The separation between mental and
manual labour represents the interlocking of the political and
ideological levels:

> Their [i.e. technicians and engineers] mental labour separ-
> ated from manual, represents the exercise of political
> relations in the despotism of the factory, legitimized by
> and articulated through the monopolisation and secrecy of
> knowledge, i.e. the 'reproduction of the ideological relations
> of domination and subordination'.
>
> (Poulantzas, 1975, p. 240)

Poulantzas incorporates the work of Gorz (1976) on the
class nature of science, and the oppressive role of technicians
within mental labour He argues that mental labour performs
a dominating and controlling function *vis-à-vis* manual labour

because it operates within a monopoly of knowledge and hierarchy of secrecy which rests on a specialisation and mystique of formal qualifications. All these elements are considered the material base of ideological practice, i.e. they are the material constituents of ideology and ideological control rather than ideas in the sociological sense of attitudes in people's heads. He defines mental labour in this structural way:

> We could say that every form of work that takes the form of knowledge from which the direct producers are excluded, falls on the mental labour side of the capitalist production process, irrespective of its empirical/natural content, and this is so whether the direct producers actually know how to perform this work but do not do so (again not by chance), or whether in fact they do not know how to perform it (since they are systematically kept away from it)!
> (Poulantzas, 1975, p. 238)

So, by the criteria of productive labour technicians would be members of Poulantzas's working class, but because of the dominance of the politico–ideological levels in their class determination they are excluded entrance and form a fraction of the new petty bourgeoisie. Poulantzas's definition of technicians insists on supervision as an essential element in their work, but even where they are non-supervisory because they remain a part of mental labour, they are denied a working class identification.

Poulantzas delineates three fractions of the new petty bourgeoisie: (i) non-productive groups in the commercial, retailing and service sector of the economy, such as shop assistants, cafe workers; (ii) office workers in lower-level positions within the public and private bureaucracies; (iii) technicians and what he calls 'subaltern engineers', that is lower level or subordinate engineers. All three fractions are given a 'proletarian polarisation', this means, for technicians, they have:

> objective preconditions for grasping the essential mechanism of capitalist exploitation, [but] still remain marked

by their place in the politico-ideological relations of the
enterprise as an apparatus.

(Poulantzas, 1975, p. 326)

The idea of proletarian and bourgeois polarisations has
obvious similarities with Braverman's continuum, along
which professional engineers represent one pole around the
capitalist class, and draughtsmen the opposite pole, around
working class.

Reactions to Poulantzas were quick to develop in Britain
and structuralism did not fit into the political and trade union
movement with any ease. Criticism of Poulantzas should start
with his revision of marxism. It was not part of Marx's
analysis of social classes to isolate three separate structural
features of society and from these features build a 'class structure'. Clarke (1977) has said:

The social classes of Poulantzas's theory are not constituted
by the relations of production, in the Marxist sense, but
are rather distributive classes defined by reference to the
technical functions of their members in production as well
as by political and ideological, 'social', factors.

(Clarke, 1977, p. 14)

Clarke points out that Poulantzas's triple formula is more
closely modelled on Weber's approach than on Marx: *class*
becomes economic, *status*, ideology, and *party*, political. The
absence of class struggle and therefore history from his work
is also in sharp contrast to Marx's work. Another feature is
the absolute differentiation between 'place' and 'condition',
again something alien to classical Marxism, where the contradiction between these two levels is all important. Another
criticism is his 'politicisation of supervision' which has been
attacked by Hunt (1977), and Hyman and Price (1983).

When examined empirically, it is obvious that Poulantzas
is too crude in not differentiating the levels of the command
structure and seeing the ambiguity in the role of groups like
foremen or line managers. They are in a particularly contradictory position where they are unionised and share collective
structures with manual workers as in Britain. However,

against the allocation of working class identity by non-ownership and status as wage labour, Poulantzas's discussion of the political function of supervision is a considerable advance.

Poulantzas's construction is an ideal type that is ahistorical and resistant to empirical testing. When we introduce the material background to his theory we note that technicians in France, his implicit model, are more likely to be supervisory and college-educated than technicians in Britain. Here, the division between mental and manual labour, so tightly imposed on the class structure by Poulantzas, when examined empirically is seen to be much more complex. Craft consciousness, rather than educational superiority, while continuing to place an important wedge between the different sections of the collective labourer, also acts as an important bond between technical (mental) workers and manual workers. Poulantzas disembodies class structure from class practice. Class consciousness is turned into a subliminal structure (ideology) with external categories which are abstracted from conventional class conflict. Politics is relegated to an organisational appendage of the division of labour, again in the form of a reified structure. When *structure* does not incorporate struggle but replaces it at all levels of social class formation, then Marxism is transformed into a form of behaviourism, whereby human actions are mechanically plotted along a predictable path laid down by a structural map that is established and maintained in the head of the theorist without any human intervention on the part of the subject of investigation.

Carchedi

Carchedi like Poulantzas bases his theory of the 'economic identification of social classes' on the Marxist theory of value. The production of surplus value requires certain functions which the socialisation of capital and labour within monopoly capitalism makes global not individual in form (Marx, 1976, pp. 643–9). The two basic functions are:

1. Global functions of capital – surveillance and control of the labour process in the interest of exploitation and profit.

2. Global function of the collective worker – unity and co-ordination in the production of surplus value.

Carchedi builds on Marx's analysis of modern industry where the 'collective labourer' or 'aggregate labourer' progressively increases and enriches the co-operation and complexity of the capitalist labour process (Marx, 1976, pp. 643 and 1040). But whereas for Marx the 'aggregate' worker is not a social class, and neither did Marx examine social classes when discussing the changing nature of productive labour, for Carchedi the technical division of labour is the central *site* of the origins of social classes. The new middle class is created out of the two functions mentioned above. Carter (1985) has summarised Carchedi's analysis of the new middle class by saying that it has no legal or real ownership of the means of production and performs both the global function of capital and function of collective worker. This dual function is the contradiction at the heart of its class position. Carter believes such an analysis of the new middle class is consistent with 'a coherent Marxist approach' to class founded on the labour theory of value. It has the advantage, he claims, of getting beyond the simple dichotomous class structure based on ownership and non-ownership of the means of production – an orthodox Marxist position which he claims ends up within a Weberian perspective. That is, when Marxists introduce factors like status, market differences and links to authority, in order to explain why, in practice, white-collar workers remain oppositional to the working class, despite sharing the same objective class position as manual workers. Other critics, especially Hyman, find the apparent coherence of Carchedi's dual analysis difficult to reconcile with craft differentiation. This criticism of Carchedi is not at all surprising given my argument that 'craft' rather than 'class' has been the hallmark of internal differentiation within the collective labourer in Britain. Hyman is articulating this legacy when he says:

> Hierarchy commonly exists within the collective labourer especially where clear craft demarcations exist. A bricklayer or a maintenance fitter traditionally exerts control (at times overtly and coercively) over his labourer, does that mean

that he is an 'agent' of the global function of capital? Ultimately the boundary between these two functions is both empirically and conceptually more imprecise than Carchedi can admit.

(Hyman, 1983)

Carchedi quotes approvingly from the work of Fairbrother in the introduction to *On the Economic Identification of Social Classes*. Fairbrother (1978) bases his class analysis firmly on job analysis, and this, according to Carchedi is the way into 'class identification':

A 'job account' then, i.e. technical description of a function, if sufficiently specified should always provide us with enough information to judge about not only that function's technical content but also that function's social nature.

(Carchedi, 1977, p. 6)

Carchedi quotes from job descriptions given in Fairbrother's work and then translates these job descriptions (chemical supervisor, production assistant and metallurgy technician) into functional categories and hence to class identifications. There are three logical steps in Carchedi's analysis: (1) technical job description; leading to (2) imputed social relations; leading to (3) class identification of the 'agents' performing the functional tasks in capitalist production relations. Classes are intellectually created from the empirical make-up of jobs. But this is purely 'analytical class' not 'historical class', i.e. individuals are conceptually posited as embodying or personifying different functions in the process of production. Their real empirical relations are not considered. Carchedi does not really create *classes* through this juggling with job contents, he merely describes in different terms those job contents. We start and finish with 'job description'. Historical class is divorced from these rationalistic sequences, and his method fits exactly with what Thompson (1978) has described as placing class *before* class struggle and class-consciousness.

There are strengths within this analysis, which I draw on in the following chapters to understand the class situation of technical workers, but there are also great dangers of ascribing behaviour to occupational categories in an ahistorical and abstract way. It is important to understand the separate functions of labour and capital and to evaluate social work roles against these criteria for purposes of understanding basic class relations. However, a job description for a draughtsman in Britain and another for one in America may entail similar ingredients, but the arrangement of these features, their evaluation by the general culture, the background and training required to obtain these qualities could be very different. More importantly, the pattern or form of association between the occupation, capital and labour, challenge any straightforward utilisation of occupation for class location. These are not simply contextual or conditional characteristics that only modify in a small way basic relationships. They are as much a part of class understanding as structural criteria.

Wright

Both new working class and new middle class models of intermediate workers draw heavily on Marxist writing for their inspiration. Weberian writing, as mentioned earlier, has historically differentiated the working class from non-manual workers by criteria of market capacities or skills. There have always been writers who have borrowed from Marx and Weber to theorise intermediate workers, Lockwood (1958) and Parkin (1974), with a definite Weberian appropriation of Marx, and Allen (1971), with an implicit Marxian utilisation of Weber. Those writers arguing for a marriage between the two classical protaganists of the class structure increased in the 1980s, with their models becoming more sophisticated. This partly reflects the economic and political context social theorists faced in the late 1970s, a weakening and fragmentation of working class consciousness under the impact of recession. But just as important was the failure of structural Marxism to develop an adequate conceptual apparatus into the empirical reality of class and an identifiable political practice. Evidence of the emergence of a synthesis between

Weberian and Marxist perspectives on class is clearly demonstrated by the self-conscious eclecticism of writers like Abercrombie and Urry (1983). But perhaps the most dramatic shift in position comes from the American Marxist, Eric Olin Wright.

Wright in the mid-1970s advanced a model of the class structure in a critique of Poulantzas's structural analysis of class, particularly his failure to accord the 'economic' decisive influence over the distribution of classes. Wright (1977) attempted to put the 'economic' back in centre stage by posing the distinction between ownership (legal entitlement) and possession (real control). Class relations in capitalist societies were structured by three underlying social relations of production: (i) control over labour power; (ii) control of the physical means of production; and (iii) control of investments and resources. Possession represents (i) and (ii), while (iii) is essentially economic ownership. None of this was new to Marxist theory, as Nichols (1986, p. 8) has rightly argued. What was new was the way Wright used this classification. Wright said that the central forces in capitalist society were the capitalist class and the working class. In relation to the three forms of control, the capitalist class has possession and ownership, while the working class has neither possession nor ownership. This polarisation marks capitalist society. The petty bourgeoisie is defined as having control over the means of production and investment and resource allocation, but not control over labour. Between these classes are what Wright calls 'objectively contradictory locations within class relations', or contradictory locations for short. Wright acknowledges the contradictory nature of all class positions – there is never a straightforward division between classes. The term contradictory locations refers to situations in which the three types of control do not perfectly correspond to the basic class forces within the capitalist mode of production or to the petty bourgeoisie in simple commodity production.

Expressly concerned with the issue of how to define the 'boundaries' between classes, and against a new middle-class model of intermediate workers, Wright put forward a three-class model of capitalism – capitalists, workers and the petty bourgeoisie – with three 'contradictory locations', not classes

or fractions, between the major classes. Managers and supervisors between the capitalist class and working class; small
employers between the petty bourgeoisie and capitalist class;
and semi-autonomous employees between the working class
and the petty bourgeoisie. In pure form capitalism is characterised by the basic polarisation between capitalists and the
working class. However, in every historical formation there
are both vestiges of other modes of production, petty
commodity production, and locations that do not coincide
with the basic classes.

This typology, or what Wright calls a 'class map', places
technicians and engineers in two positions. Firstly, between
the capitalist class and the working class lie middle managers
and what Wright terms 'technocrats', that is technicians and
professionals of various sorts within the corporate hierarchy
who maintain limited autonomy over their work (control of
the physical means of production) and a limited control over
subordinates, but who are not in command positions over the
productive apparatus, and lack economic ownership.
However, Wright also places technicians between the petty
bourgeoisie and the working class as semi-autonomous
employees. This is both confusing and inaccurate. Most technical labour is waged labour located in large industrial enterprises of capitalism, not 'petty commodity production'. The
ideological and political conflicts within technical labour are
between corporate/managerial and working class orientations,
not a working class/petty bourgeois conflict.

Wright does not concentrate solely on economic relations,
but introduces political and ideological relations into class
placement. Political struggle by class organisations can
counteract or heighten the contradictory quality of locations
not completely determined by the economic level. In other
words, those in contradictory locations can be more influenced by economic and political relations. Technical workers
may be within mental labour ideologically, but a strong trade
union movement can, according to Wright, constitute a
political influence to counter the ideological factor, or push
them closer to the working class. Wright concludes where he
should have started, by saying:

in the end, class struggle will determine the extent to which people in these contradictory locations join forces with the working class in a socialist movement . . . Class struggle shapes the very contours of the class structure itself, which in turn shapes class struggle.

(Wright, 1977, p. 41)

Wright, in using the term 'contradictory class location', was developing a purely analytical understanding of social class; a concern for the distribution and classification of the population rather than a more dynamic understanding of capitalist society. Effectively, 'class locations' are non-classes, abstract categories in the head of the theorist. However, by retaining a three-class model of capitalism, with two dominant places, Wright keeps an element of movement in his work. His latest book, *Classes* (1985), throws out his previous limited dichotomy for a fragmented and static 'class map'. Developed in the classical structuralist mould of an auto-critique, Wright identifies four conceptual problems with his earlier work:

The contradictoriness of contradictory locations, the status of autonomy (as boundary criteria), the absence of an analysis of post-capitalist societies and the displacement of exploitation by domination in the concept of class. [Of these four faults] the fourth seems to me to be the most fundamental. In one way or another, each of the other issues is tied up with marginalisation of exploitation.

(Wright, 1985, p. 57)

Under the influence of Roemer's (1982) *A General Theory of Exploitation and Class*, Wright recasts his conceptualisation of class, especially the place of the 'middle class'. He moves closer to a Weberian definition of class by seeing 'effective control over resources as the material basis for class relations' (Wright, 1985, p. 106). These resources are not restricted to ownership/possession and non-ownership/non-possession of property rights, but are extended to include the control of organisational assets and skills or credential assets. Introducing terminology like 'assets' is indicative of Wright's drift

out of a marxian political economy. Indeed, he gives exchange, rather than production, a central place in his theory
of exploitation: 'In all capitalist exploitation the mediating
mechanism is market exchanges . . . [The] surplus is appropriated through market exchange' (Wright, 1985, p. 106).
For Marx the appropriation of surplus occurred within the
production process, it is only in the early works that the
market is central – see Rattansi (1985) for a discussion of this
transition in Marx's work.

'Skill-asset exploitation' is based on the restriction in supply
of specialised knowledge; the transfer of information into
credentials. Organisation-asset exploitation is based on access
to 'organisation', that is 'the conditions of coordinated cooperation among producers in a complex division of labour'
(Wright, 1985, p. 79). Managers, who do not formally own
the 'resources' they utilise, but have command over the
division of labour, are said to benefit from 'organisational
assets'. By introducing 'organisational assets' and 'skills
assets' as mechanisms of exploitation, Wright is arguing that
those who possess such 'resources' receive an additional wage,
which is extracted from those who do not possess such assets.
Wright speaks of additional income, rather than surplus value
and there is no discussion of the labour theory of value in the
book, which is again indicative of a non-marxian political
economy.

The model of the class structure to emerge from Wright's
new 'class map' fits exactly the fragmentory picture of an
infinite sub-division of classes that Marx said flows from a
theory of class based on the market. Wright severs any sense
of the dynamic within the class structure, and produces a
distributive classification with 9 groups of wage labourers
defined by the degree of possession of organisational and skill/
credential assets. These are not classes, but 'locations', places
as defined by structuralists. Proletarians are placed in 'box
12', semi-credentialled workers in 'box 9', semi-credentialled
supervisors in 'box 8' experts and non-managers in 'box 6',
etc. Nine 'class locations' for non-owners and 3 locations for
owners – the bourgeoisie, small employers and petty bourgeoisie. The distinction between the latter two 'class locations'

is between those who employ others but also have to work, and those who are simply self-employed.

Many of my criticisms of structuralist Marxism apply equally to Wright. My discussion of the weaknesses of Weberian class analysis is also pertinent. We learn nothing of the *relationship* between social classes from his model; nor of the relationship of middle groups to the class struggle. What does emerge is the fact that the working class is no longer the only agency of change, 'other class forces . . . have the potential to pose an alternative to capitalism' (Wright, 1985, p. 89). Wright asserts, with no theoretical or historical justification, that managers, with no stake in capital ownership, have an interest in establishing state ownership, which is supposedly closer to socialism than is private capitalism. The ideological and political affinities between managers and the capitalist class, their performance of capitalist functions, as discussed by Carchedi, are not seen as evidence of their inherent interest in capitalism. Other problems result from his use of skills as a basis for exploitation. There is no reason why those with skills receive an additional wage because of 'exploitation transfer' from those without skills. Payment for skills can equally come out of profits, and bargaining by trade unions around the value of labour power can be a mechanism to reduce, rather than increase exploitation, that is, increase labour's share of the surplus from capital not from other workers. Indeed, trade unions, far from being a potential challenge to capital, are logically, according to Wright's analysis, a mechanism for securing skill-asset exploitation. This ignores the role of trade unions as political and ideological centres for working class struggle against capital, by a narrow focus on their impact on income differentials.

Wright misunderstands the asymmetrical relationship between labour power and capital. Skills cannot be stored, as can capital, or transferred from one form to another. They are possessed by the individual and commodified by capital. There is an inherent unequalness between capital and human labour power regardless of whether this is skilled or average labour. It is the experience of commodity status that places skilled and unskilled workers within the working class, rather than two separate class positions as Wright suggests. Technical workers, for example, have more in common with manual workers due to their exploitation by capital, than differences based on specialised skills. Moreover Wright does not examine the social construction of skill, the dynamics, in the case of technical workers, between manual craftsmen and technicians, around the question of cooperation, solidarity and trade union organisation discussed in later chapters.

The debate on class at this ahistorical level looks like continuing. It is not the primary aim of this book to review all the theories and variations on theories that have appeared in the past decade, but I have covered the basic positions. In emphasising, as I do, the centrality of historical context and empirical reality, I do not mean to abandon the role of theorising class at an abstract level. Structure has a place in historical analysis, to ignore it is to sink into idealism or voluntarism. But stuctural*ism*, without reference to concrete history and empirical reality, degenerates into endless taxonomies and a 'search for magical formulations that will reconcile as yet irreconcilable contradictions' within the class structure (Carter, 1985, p. 83).

Technical Workers and Class

This review of the literature on the class situation of intermediate workers reveals two sets of problems. Firstly definitional or semantic questions over what constitutes technical labour, and secondly theoretical judgements about the class position of technical workers.

There is considerable confusion over the term 'technical worker' in the literature. Within different institutional and national contexts divergent functions are embraced by the term 'technical' – specialist skills, expertise, conceptual knowledge, supervision and authority. It is therefore important to uncover the *particular* meaning of the term in different contexts. There is also the related question of the social status of technical and engineering activities across countries; on the Continent engineering technique is elevated as an abstract process, whereas in Britain engineering has a practical and implicitly manual meaning. Finally there is the question of technical workers' location by type of production (mass, automation, one-off, batch, etc); and place in the production cycle. The relative size of the technical component within a particular sector or company is also relevant to any assessment of the relationship technical workers are likely to enter into with other workers and with capital. In consumer goods sectors technical workers tend to form an elite, close to managers, since by function, skill and usually gender division, they will be strongly differentiated from directly productive manual labour. Within capital goods sectors, skill ratios may be more equal and the barriers between a technician and craftmen less tightly constructed.

One way of tackling these problems is to stress the national and industrial context whenever using the term technical worker. Similarly, the authority position of technical labour requires emphasis, as does the location of technical workers within the cycle of production and product type. The generic term 'technical' carries little generalisability without these qualifications. And these details are very much part of my approach within this book.

The second problem level is theoretical. How do we characterise intermediate workers in the class structure? In my view, a humanist Marxist perspective which approaches class through social relations in production and encompasses ideological and political relations has greater analytical depth than a one-dimensional focus on structure. It is also wider than a narrow attention to particular conditions – like types of technology or production systems. An awareness of different levels of experience of production relations becomes increasingly important with the growing imprecision of terms like 'manual' and 'mental' labour and greater internal diversity within waged labour in advanced capitalism. While there are problems in the class identification of groups which are economically oppressed but dependent upon *revenue* generated by other workers, most British technical workers are not in that position. They are productive non-supervisory wage labourers, working within social and institutional practices that foster a working class identity. They are concentrated within collective work situations alongside manual workers and have historically borrowed trade union practices from skilled manual workers. However, this picture is complicated by two sets of experiences: office life and relations with manual workers. Technical workers work in departments and contexts which contain a mixture of class positions which are not so clearly differentiated as on the shop floor. Technical managers and supervisors, because of their surveillance and control functions, 'command during the labour process in the name of capital' (Marx, 1976, p. 450). Where 'the work of supervision becomes their established and exclusive function' they are a 'special kind of wage labourer' distinguished by a class division from those in non-supervisory positions. The office also contains many who have been downwardly mobile, ex-owners or managers, as well as aspirant managers with ideological attachments to capital functions. Consequently there exists a material support for a mixture of ideological practices, reflecting different class interests of the groups in the office. Moreover working class technicians share certain common conditions – autonomy, responsibility, absence of rigid job controls – with managerial or new middle class labour, which structures their everyday experience and generally reduces their awareness of a rigid class division between themselves and managers.

All technical workers experience their relations with manual workers through three primary contradictions: their position as part of 'office' or 'mental' labour; their indirectly productive position; and the relative autonomy fostered by their working conditions. Although not evidence of a *class division* between technical and manual workers, these conditions structure everyday relations and experiences and support common sense distinctions which can *in practice* assume the position of a class barrier. Moreover capitalism elevates 'mental' over 'physical' labour, therefore technical workers' position within conceptualisation means they share with all 'mental' labour a common status over manual labour. Where technical workers are unlike other non-manual groups is their engagement with production and the stress placed on practical as well as abstract knowledge. Added to this, manual workers have had relatively open access to technical jobs, something maintained in Britain by a craft apprenticeship training. Where this access is closed, then we see a greater emphasis on the superiority of 'mental' labour, authority based on technical competence and the isolation and subordination of manual workers to these positions. Qualified engineers are in such a position over manual and other technical workers. As such they tend to be closer to management, or the new middle class, and removed from working class technicians.

If we exclude from the new middle class white-collar workers who lack a control and surveillance function over manual workers, and those groups, like the majority of technical workers, who are productive of surplus value, then we are left with those within managerial and supervisory positions and those who possess qualifications or credentials inaccessible to the majority of the working class. By this criterion, the working class is more numerically dominant in British capitalism, and most other capitalist societies, than structural Marxist models suggest.

But class analysis is not just about analytical placement, 'counting' the size of social classes in different countries. We also need to consider the wider cyclical and historical conditions discussed earlier, and integrate these into an analysis of class based on the social relations of production. This means looking at specific national contexts of class formation. The dominance of craftism as the main avenue of training across the 'collar' divide, made it inevitable that most British technical staff should share with skilled manual workers a sense of being the aristocracy of *labour* rather than the poor relations of *capital*. Given the centrality of the craft tradition in the British context, it is important to conclude this chapter with a brief analysis of its origins and function.

Technical Workers and Some Peculiarities of the British Class Structure

Carter (1985, p. 36) in a review of the literature on white-collar workers has noted: 'Judged by the attention paid to the history, growth and function of middle class labour in Britain social theorists have regarded this social group as a force of little significance.'

This he puts down to the 'lack of social conflict on the scale that took place in Germany' and the fact that 'middle class labour formed a much lower percentage of the employed population'. The historical peculiarities of British capitalism are too great to enter here, but it is worth noting some of the features that relate to the class structure, especially with regard to technical workers.

In Britain the manual working class achieved numerical superiority over other productive classes, notably the peasantry and petty commodity producers, at an earlier stage relative to other countries. The dominance of capitalism over other modes of production and early industrialisation ensured the expansion of wage labour in industry and agriculture, and depleted the economic and political importance of dependent social classes peripheral to capitalism. One consequence of this was the theoretical focus on the traditional manual working class and a concern with intra-working class differentiation. The earlier appearance, and persistence in different forms, of the embourgeoisement and labour aristocracy theses both reflect the size and importance of wage labour within the British class structure (Davis and Cousins, 1975).

White-collar workers were slower to gain prominence in Britain relative to Germany and other European countries. This is not surprising given early industrialisation and the prevailing strength of basic industries (cotton, textiles, iron, steel, coal and shipbuilding) where traditional methods of craft control ensured the dominance of manual workers. Crossick (1977) has also noted that other countries entered the world economy:

> not just at a higher technological level, but also at a higher commercial and bureaucratic level. Thus the expansion of white collar occupations would come far sooner after initial industrialisation in the rest of Europe than it had done in Britain.
>
> (Crossick, 1977, p. 21)

More (1980) argues that the craft apprenticeship system, omnipotent in the basic industries, spread into newer industries, especially light engineering, to ensure the continuity of craft control and therefore hold up the expansion of supervisory and technical white collar labour. Those sectors that did not expand on a craft basis, food, drink, tobacco, chemicals, etc. were generally in the process and/or consumption goods areas (Littler, 1982, p. 115). When technical workers began to appear in large numbers, they themselves came through the apprenticeship system, thus ensuring a *craft* not an autonomous professional or university base to British engineering (Ahlström, 1982, p. 16; Whalley, 1984). The premium craft apprenticeship system for technical workers, also prevented education being utilised as a way of dividing manual and white-collar labour, as it did in Germany (Kocka, 1980). Craftism aided trade union organisation amongst foremen and technical staff, which originated in the established working class industrial sectors, especially shipbuilding, and the predominantly working class towns of Glasgow, Newcastle and Sheffield (Melling, 1983; Mortimer, 1960). Reid (1980) notes that in contrast to the hostility of Edwardian clerks to trade unionism and the labour movement noted by Crossick (1977) draughtsmen established strong links with manual workers. Their common training and family background cemented work bonds, while their experience of changes in employment conditions and craft control promoted the need for collective organisation. The importance of the craft tradition is a theme that pervades my understanding of the class position and relations between British technical and manual workers in this book.

Given the concentration on polarisations between capital and labour and intra-working class skill differentiations, the strategic importance of declining classes, or a socially and politically coherent 'new middle class' has not been a strong theme within British social thought. The strength of the labour aristocracy and the incorporation of trade union officials into the state, were encouraged by certain brands of social thought, especially Fabianism, and strongly rejected by others, notably Marxism. The professions were regarded by the Webbs, Shaw and left Fabians, such as Cole, Laski and Tawney, as a moral and ideological counter to business values (Callaghan, 1987). Cole, from his early writings on workers' control, also regarded scientists, engineers and technical

workers as 'professional labour', capable of uniting with the
manual working class to lead a peaceful expropriation of
capital by removing the capitalist from the process of
production (Cole, 1934; Smith, 1982). This early 'new
working class' thesis was, nevertheless, not very strong in
Britain. The establishment of the Federation of Professional
Workers in 1920, under the direction of G. D. H. Cole, was
aimed at encouraging infant white-collar industrial unions
into the ranks of the TUC and not a professional middle
ground.

Attempts to find a theoretical link between 'all' intermediate groups have existed; MacDonald, (1923) attempted
to locate a common ingredient in the work of journalists,
designers, architects, draughtsmen, management experts and
engineers, around the notion of 'intellectual' or mental labour
as against routine clerical or manual labour:

> While the product of intellectual labour may take the
> physical form of a drawing, a manuscript or an improved
> tool or machine, it quite as often takes the intangible form
> of a chemical process, a method of organisation or an
> instruction. What the capitalist pays for in wages or salary
> is not what is commonly classed as goods or material pro-
> ducts, things that can be measured or numbered, but
> thought, education and intellectual ability and it is from
> these that he derives his profit.
>   (MacDonald, 1923, pp. 10–11)

Such an attempt to define a distinct 'product' for new
middle class labour, intellectual skill, ignored the different
social relations and economic situations of intermediate
groups, and also underestimated 'status' fragmentation within
similar occupational bands, such as between different types of
engineer (Watson, 1975). For British engineers and technical
workers within engineering at least, craft training prevented
the elevation of abstract knowledge, cut off from 'manual
skills' in MacDonald's sense. MacDonald's approach is
unusual in the British context which has, in general, produced
unsystematic and confused theories around the vague category of 'middle class'. These have concerned differences

between professional and manual workers, status differences, pay and conditions, rather than more fundamental statements around the issues of mental and manual labour and the political role of supervision discussed earlier by new middle-class writers. Carter (1985, p. 37) puts this down to the weakness of Marxism in Britain, the strength of post-war Weberian writing in sociology and the traditions of labourism in politics and trade unionism. But also significant is the weakness of a politically organised 'middle-class' voice, supporting a programme which claims independence from capital and labour. The 'middle-class' movements of the 1970s, described by Hutber (1977), and King and Nugent (1979), have concentrated on appealing to the traditional petty bourgeoisie on conventional small business issues such as tax relief for the self-employed, rates, inflation and state support for the little man. This, as I suggested above, reflects the origins, size and traditions within the British working class more than the significance of the 'new middle class'.

These observations about the peculiarities of the British class structure, while a useful corrective to ahistorical and global theorising, should not be interpreted as implying too close a correspondence between social theories of class and national class formations. Theoretical statements of classical revisionists such as Bernstein (1961), drew heavily on Webbsian Fabianism which came out of British not German class history (see Davis and Cousins, 1975 pp. 177–9). Attention to the relationship between national occupational structure and class theory gives us a starting point, but why distinct theories are dominant in distinct periods in several countries e.g. the 'new middle class' debate during the mid-1970s, is perhaps more associated with political and economic conjunctional factors. The traditions of particular countries and the historical class formation, offer only theoretical predispositions but the history of class analysis is also related to occupational change, the business 'cycle' and the political conjuncture of social classes at societal levels.

The main purpose of this book is to locate the structure of social relations both within technical work and between technical labour, manual labour and management. These issues have previously been explored from an abstract perspective, which has not enabled technical workers' experience and consciousness to enter the complex matrix of theoretical categories that form the 'class structure'. My research has been informed and was initially provoked by new class theory, but I do not subordinate my data or analysis to a single author because of the weaknesses discussed above. Carchedi and Poulantzas especially implicate *all* technical workers, at a certain level of analysis, as the oppressors of manual labour and therefore the working class. Gorz is close to this position, as is Braverman in the final analysis. I want to argue that the majority of British technical workers are not excluded from the working class. They are productive, overwhelmingly non-supervisory and work through the possession of 'knowledge' not cut off, via credentialism or monopoly, from those they instruct. This book seeks to give technical workers some say in the debate, while locating social class in the context of the workplace.

2

Technical Workers: An Overview

A Profile of Technical Workers in Britain

Government reports and industrial training board studies have placed technical workers below professional engineers and technologists and above skilled manual and clerical occupations. Such studies separate 'draughtsmen' from 'other technicians', and training programmes separate 'other technicians' into 'technician engineer' and 'technician'. All these efforts are directed at trying to improve the status of technical work in general. In practice however, this separation is difficult to sustain, and the status of the British technician remains comparatively low. The majority of technical workers I interviewed had little confidence in the broad labels which are used by others to conveniently summarise their place within the division of labour. Most preferred to be called by a specific title, e.g. draughtsman, or 'jig and tool draughtsman' or estimator, or 'tool designer'. General titles such as technician engineer, technician or technologist, were considered vacuous.

Outside the category of draughtsman, which is the best known technical occupation, technical workers were acutely aware of society's confusion about who they were and what they did. The proliferation of technical job titles in the 1970s, was seen as compounding the confusion and, within the engineering industry itself, a draughtsman or estimator frequently had little idea what a 'Loadcell Technician' or 'Machinability Services Investigator' actually did (AUEW-TASS, 1974).

75

Technical workers are concentrated within manufacturing industry. A survey in 1972 revealed that eighty-five per cent of all scientific and technical staff in British industry were located in just five industrial sectors; chemicals, metals, engineering, electrical goods and vehicles (Roberts, Loveridge and Gennard, 1972, p. 122). An Engineering Industry Training Board report on technicians in 1970 discovered that one in seven workers in aerospace were technical and one in thirteen in mechanical engineering and engineering as a whole. In metal manufacture, motor vehicles, and other metal goods manufacture, technical workers represent fewer than one in twenty of total employees (EITB, 1970, p. 7). Engineering and related industries absorb the vast majority of Britain's technical and scientific labour. In 1979 there were just under one million or 30.8 per cent managerial, administrative technical and clerical workers within an engineering sector of just over three million. Technical and scientific labour accounted for 262 230 or 27.7 per cent of that one million. Examining the statistics more closely, Table 2.1 indicates the broad occupational categories that account for engineering's technical and scientific labour.

Table 2.1 *Scientific and technical labour in engineering and related industries in 1979: male and female*

Category	Number	% of total white-collar employees
Professional engineers	79 530	8.4
Scientists, metallurgists, and other technologists	16 750	1.8
Draughtsmen	61 430	6.5
Other technicians	104 520	11.0
Total	262 230	27.7

SOURCE: *Department of Employment Gazette, 1979* (1980).

The proportion and rates of growth within the four major categories have undergone considerable change in the post-war period, especially from the mid-1960s. Draughtsmen have declined, while professional engineers, technologists and other technicians have all expanded. Routh (1980, p. 17) has shown that between 1931 and 1951 draughtsmen numbers increased by 4.2 per cent per year, while between 1951 and 1971 they increased by only 0.8 per cent per year. These changes have challenged, but not destroyed the craft-based mobility tradition in British engineering which allowed craftsmen to move into the technical area without significant additional qualifications. It has been suggested that the decline in the numbers of draughtsmen and the rise in the category of specially trained other technicians, may have blocked the craftsman's access into the technical area. My own findings indicate that craftsmen still provide the main reservoir of recruits into the new technical occupations. In the British engineering industry, technical workers have traditionally served a craft apprenticeship or at least spent some of their technical apprenticeship on the shop floor. Prior to the expansion of technician and technician engineer courses, a craftsman frequently went to night school in order to enter the office. Moving into the drawing or planning department was often an experiment and the worker held dual membership of DATA or the old AESD, and the AEU, in case the experiment did not work. The official historian of the AESD, Jim Mortimer, has noted the close relationship between craftsmen and draughtsmen:

> Many draughtsmen remain fairly closely associated with the workshops throughout their career . . . Draughtsmen usually have a strong sense of craftsmanship. In this repsect they tend to differentiate themselves from other sections of the staff. They are very conscious that they possess technical skill and that unlike most of the weekly or monthly paid staff in other departments, they are *engineers* . . . It is not uncommon for draughtsmen to feel a closer sense of kinship with the most skilled workers in the shops, including tool makers, panel beaters, pattern makers and foremen, than with clerical staff workers.
>
> (Mortimer, 1960, p. 416)

Although the craft avenue into technical work has declined, I found this sense of craftsmanship and animosity to clerical

workers a universal feature amongst middle level technical
workers. Much of this reflects a common attachment to
production and the gender division between the two sides.

The main area of blocked mobility has been within the
categories of draughtsmen and other technicians, as the rise
of degree-holding (qualified) engineers has created a graduate
ceiling that those without degrees cannot break through. The
continuum that used to exist from craftsmen to professional
engineer, is today more fractured and hierarchical, as
draughtsmen and technicians are polarised towards skilled
manual workers and graduate engineers towards management. But management as a group are no longer as homogeneous in function, identity or ideology; and managerial
status, as I indicate in Chapter 7, is no longer a major source
of division, particularly in industrial sectors where management duties are technical and co-ordinative, rather than
supervisory and controlling. I was unable to obtain a comprehensive educational breakdown of technical workers at the
Filton site, but Table 2.2 indicates the educational background of technical staff organised by TASS for a company
of comparable size located within the power engineering
industry. The data reveals the significance of higher education
qualifications, and the overall importance of qualifications for
technical staff.

Alongside these emerging sources of differentiation within
technical work, there persists an established division between
men and women. Women workers are almost totally excluded
from the technical and skilled areas of engineering employment. As I will later show, in only one technical occupation
outside of the traditional female occupation of tracing, did I
encounter a single woman technical worker. Technical work
is male-dominated and although TASS and ASTMS, the
major technical unions, have promoted equality of opportunity in recent years, their success has been negligible. In
1979 in all engineering and related industries, women
represented 1020 of the 79 530 professional engineers (1.3 per
cent); 400 of the 16 750 scientists, metallurgists and other
technologists (2.4 per cent); 1150 of the 61 430 draughtsmen
(1.9 per cent); and 2610 of the 104 520 other technicians
(2.5 per cent). The supervisory and skilled manual categories

Table 2.2 *Educational background of TASS members at NEI Parsons: September 1979*

Qualification	Number	% of Sample
Ph.D	23	3
M.Sc.	22	3
Degree	136	17
C.Eng.	41	5
H.N.D.	17	2
H.N.C.	132	17
O.N.D.	3	–
O.N.C.	148	19
Full C. and GT5, T6	55	7
Full C. and GT4	51	6
(No qualification or not included above, e.g. Board of Trade)	161	20
Total in sample	789	100

Abbreviations

C. and G.   = City and Guilds.
T6, T5, T4 = Technician 6, 5, 4.
C. Eng.   = Certification Engineering (Professional Qualification).

NOTE: Where a return includes both a C.Eng. and a degree, only the degree is entered above.

SOURCE: C. A. Parsons, TASS, ACAS Submission (1979, p. 9).

display equally stark gender divisions (*Department of Employment Gazette*, 1980, p. 636). The male dominance in both skilled manual and technical areas of engineering has undoubtedly contributed to the craft affinity between the two areas. Relations would have been structured in very different ways had technical jobs, like those of clerical staff, been predominantly female in nature.

Women occupied technical positions during World War II, the typical pattern being tracers – traditionally allied to the drawing office to enhance drawings – moving into the plan-

ning office or becoming draughtswomen. But tracing is today
virtually a dead occupation, and women have not entered
either the established or newer technical occupations. Where
women appear within the membership of technical unions, it
is overwhelmingly from administrative and clerical occupations. TASS appointed a women's organiser in 1976
specifically to break into these non-technical areas as part of
the union's increasingly general recruitment policy. Black
workers too are under-represented in technical occupations
(Lee and Wrench, 1981, 1983). At the Filton site of British
Aerospace, I did not interview, encounter or observe a single
black technician in the course of my eighteen months of
fieldwork.

These, then, are some of the social features of technical
workers. They are a predominantly white, male and increasingly qualified group with those at the higher end of the
spectrum more likely than before the 1950s to have been
through higher education. But what of the origin of technical
work, and particularly the distinctive craft tradition in Britain
which has allowed apprenticeship entry into the technical
field and a fluid, rather than immutable social relationship
between technical staff and craftsmen.

The Origins of Technical Jobs

Technical occupations expanded with the increasing application of science to the capitalist production process. Between
the 1880s and 1918 a massive reorganisation took place in
British engineering industry. Significant developments in this
period were the ending of internal contracting and the appearance and growth of a new grade of worker, the semi-skilled
labourer. The generation of this new stratum was
accompanied by an expansion of indirect, office based labour.
Some technical occupations were generated by the deskilling
of the manual craftsman and expansion of semi-skilled labourers (Jeffreys, 1945). Rate fixing, progress chasing, inspection
and planning engineering all appeared as discernible separate
occupations at this time. Other duties were hived off from
the foreman's function and parcelled into clerical-technical

occupations (More, 1980). Estimators, calculators, and time control clerks, can all trace the origin of their jobs in work previously carried out by the foreman.

Differentiation of occupations was largely confined to large companies. Estimating for example, is generally only a separate occupation in the larger engineering firms, in smaller firms it is combined with planning, rate-fixing and commercial functions. Estimating books written during the 1920s and 1930s were written for an audience of 'engineering students, draughtsmen, cost clerks, foremen and works managers'. Estimators as a discernible, separate grouping were not mentioned. By the 1940s, especially during the war, the occupation developed in its own right. A book written in the late 1930s on estimating was aimed at all technical and managerial staff in production engineering including 'mechanics, draughtsmen, estimators, rate fixers, planning engineers, cost accountants, foremen and others who now control or who will one day control production'.

Planning engineering today is well established, although the precise origins of the occupation are unclear. It has largely been assumed that planning engineers grew up in the late nineteenth century in association with new machine tools and the premium bonus payment system (Jeffereys, 1945). Reid (1980) does not mention planners in his history of the division of labour in shipbuilding, 1880–1920. It is the drawing office and not the planning office that developed as the centre of design activity, and foremen, shipwrights and pattern makers who controlled the sequencing of work and mediated the flow of information from office to shop floor. Melling (1983) also sees the drawing office as the outward manifestation of rising technical standards of machine design, especially in the larger factories in the marine and electrical engineering sector. Others have suggested that the major development of the occupation occurred in the 1910s and 1920s. Maclean (1978), in a brief overview of industrial engineering theories of 1919, implies that planners developed in opposition to PBS schemes and rate fixers, an occupation that owed its existence to new machines and payment systems introduced from the 1880s. Paraphrasing an article from *The Engineering Industrial Management*, entitled 'Eliminating the

82   *Technical Workers*

Stop Watch from Industry', he says: 'Better than the stop-watch is proper organisation, reliable records production, properly controlled and good working conditions' (Maclean, 1978, p. 198). His description of the operation of the planning department at Weirs, Glasgow, is an accurate reflection of the function of the office described in Chapter 4. This was not the all-embracing Taylorian planning department (confirming Littler's (1982, p. 54) and Melling's (1983) claim that it never existed in Britain), but a more discrete technical office.

Draughtsmen have a much longer history of independence from foremen and craftsmen, going back in engineering to at least the 1850s (Booker, 1963; Mortimer, 1960). Reid (1980) has shown that in shipbuilding the name draughtsman is derived from the practice of making a 'draught plan' from the wooden models of ships hulls used for tendering the contracts and in the actual construction of vessels. The draughtsman originally prepared the wooden models and the draught plan. In the course of the last century the function of draughting became more standardised, and divided between 'design' and 'detail' operations. This may have first occurred in railway workshops and shipyards and then spread throughout other engineering sectors. Reid has carefully documented the development and changes within the shipyard drawing offices of the Clyde, describing their expansion together with an internal functional differentiation into design draughtsmen, detail draughtsmen and copyists or tracers. The economic rationale for expanding indirect labour followed the increasing capitalisation of industry and the need to get a greater return on fixed capital. This entailed a tighter control of manual workers through incentive schemes, new machinery and more timed work combined with a reduction in preparation time by transferring certain planning, processing and progressing operations off the shop floor and into the office. In the technical field this logic helped expand the number of draughtsmen and has remained a central dynamic behind the growth of other technical occupations.

Reid bases most of his analysis of shipbuilding draughtsmen on the firm of William Denny. Archibald Denny wrote an article entitled, 'The Drawing Office' in which he described and championed the economic benefits of expanding a separate design office. The following quote from that paper illustrates management's economic rationale in expanding technical work:

> In 1868 the foremen got more general plans and were allowed to scheme out their work as best they might. Nowadays all that has gone and I believe for the better, as a whole: plans are very detailed, carefully thought out and much increased in number. This is necessary partly because of the more complex nature of modern vessels, but really induced by the desire to see the end from the beginning, to avoid mistakes and changes and also with a view to more rapid and cheaper production. This is really the key-note – cheapness of production; and while the drawing office expenses are enormously increased, I believe that every pound spent judiciously in the drawing office saves two or three in the yard.
>
> (Reid, 1980, p. 82)

More (1980) and Melling (1983) have noted that it was cheaper to retain skilled workers in most functions unless the scale of production was expanded sufficiently to justify the introduction of the new automatic machines operated by semi-skilled workers. It was therefore the larger firms who pioneered these changes which led to the formal movement of engineering knowledge away from the shop floor and into the drawing, and later the planning office. Those writers who see in these changes the subordination of manual labour under the domination of mental labour, ignore the continued interaction between craftsmen, draughtsmen and the newer technical occupations. Reid noted that the shipwright performed operations that were a 'crucial check on the accuracy of [draughtsmen's] plans' (Reid, 1980, p. 83). My own work highlights this continued co-operation.

The notion of a static pool or store of knowledge monopolised by one group, does not square with the actuality of production where there are many sources of knowledge, although access to formal sources is heavily weighted in favour of technical stuff.

Along a similar axis writers have also interpreted these developments as representing the political subordination of craftsmen to office workers. However, power and control within the office was centralised in the office manager, checker, or section leader, not the non-supervisory draughtsman or planner. And even within the hierarchy of the office, control and power over manual workers is not apparent. It is part of the analysis of Poulantzas (1975), Gorz (1976) and ultimately Braverman (1974), as already mentioned, that technical staff control the labour process of manual workers. The technical workers I interviewed and observed were bound up with the servicing, checking, preparing, designing and programming of work for manual workers to execute, they did not directly control the production process or product of manual workers.

There is a translation stage at each moment in that information flow, and innovation is possible in the transformation of a set of instructions, plans or drawings, into a physical commodity. Technical workers create drawings or instructions or data which is controlled by management who act as agents of capital in the process of production. The emergence of technical departments, especially the Drawing Office, also provided a new space from which to begin a career in management.

The history of the creation of the new technical occupations is far from clear. What is apparent, however, is that the process of generating new technical and clerical jobs was not rapid, but occurred over a twenty or thirty year period. There was not a dramatic deskilling of individual craftsmen or a sudden recruitment of foreign technicians. Functions were changed in an almost imperceptible way. Craftsmen did not wake up, with their skills and initiative removed, suddenly confronted by a new army of technical workers. Individual craftsmen were promoted into the new technical fields, feeding the growing demand for draughtsmen. Technical education began to grow from the mid 1880s, and the development of new science-based industires increasingly meant that on the job training could no longer provide the knowledge needed for production in those industries. More has said that:

occupations in electrical and gas supply, and increasingly in engineering, demanded considerable theoretical knowledge. Because of this theoretical trade training and even techno- logical education provided a more general theoretical back- ground, [and] was increasingly relevant not just for aspiring supervisory and technical staff, but also to ordi- nary manual workers in the above mentioned occupations.

(More, 1980, p. 203)

But technical education did not outstrip apprenticeships or other methods of training in either the newer or established industries. Technical staff were the main recipients of tech- nical education, but only a minority of employers insisted on technical staff attending colleges and only a minority of technical employees sat technical examinations (More, 1980, p. 200).

The First World War acted as a tremendous stimulus to the new technological-based industries, (vehicles, aircraft, radio, chemicals and electricity) and therefore to technical occu- pations. The membership of the AESD was under 1000 in 1914, and over 10 000 in 1918. This dramatic increase reflected the growth in demand for technical staff, which, without a rapid expansion of technical education (which did not take place), could only be satisfied by encouraging skilled manual workers into the technical field. Dilution on the manual side, with the introduction of women workers, had a knock-on effect of dilution in the technical field, with the large-scale recruitment of manual workers into technical jobs (Marwick, 1978, pp. 226–38).

Differentiation and Change within Technical Occupations

Part of the problem of Braverman's thesis on the centrality of the manual craftsmen to industrial occupations, is that it does not sufficiently explain the differentiation within occu- pational bands historically removed from the craftsman. Technical occupations are subject to a process of specialis- ation that generates new functions and fragments existing

ones. A major differentiation occurred with the break up of the
design draughtsmen's function during the 1930s and 1940s.
Cooley (1972) described these changes in the following
terms:

> The function of the design draughtsman is . . . becoming
> more and more fragmented and specialised. The
> draughtsman in the '30s was the centre of the design
> activity. He would design the component, draw it, stress
> it, select the materials for it, write the test specifications
> for it, liaise with the workshop floor for production.
> Towards the end of the '30s and certainly during the war,
> all these functions were broken down into discernible
> separate jobs. The calculations were carried out by the
> stressmen, the materials selected by metallurgists, the form
> of lubrication determined by the tribologist. The
> draughtsman did the drawing, production engineering was
> carried out by methods and planning engineering, and
> customer liaison by specialist customer liaison engineers.
>
> (Cooley, 1972, pp. 77–8)

In an interview Cooley told me he based this description on
three sources: an examination of design files at de Havillands
during the 1930s; his own experience as a mechanical designer
and the evolution of grades and salary scales of the AESD,
the forerunner of TASS.

Cooley is describing the break up of the design draughtsman's function, as detail draughtsmen were around in large
numbers before the Second World War. The relationships
between technical workers and manual workers, and within
technical staff as a whole, was disturbed by the war. It was
not simply the division of labour but a spatial separation
created by the special conditions of war production that accelerated the differentiation between designers, draughtsmen
and production engineers. John Stevens, an old production
engineer, remembered how the co-operation and interplay in
the labour process amongst technical workers was broken off
by the war:

The influx of people blew that all apart and work had to then spread out, because physically you separated people, . . . because we didn't want everyone under the same roof. The factory became a target for enemy action and you're liable to lose people and jigs and tools. And one thing you mustn't lose is the drawings, the designs and the designers, because otherwise you could never start again. And so the design offices were taken away, put in big houses in the country . . . and we lost contact with them, because you can't walk into a country house, twenty miles away, especially during the war you couldn't, and talk to old Bob Jones that you knew well. And suddenly at the end of the war there was a new breed of people there, because they had grown also, many, many times in number and so suddenly you didn't know all these guys . . . that were drawing drawings and designing aeroplanes.

The First World War had accelerated the creation of technical and clerical occupations out of functions formerly performed by foremen and skilled manual workers. The Second World War acted as a catalyst on technical jobs, polarising, in particular, the work of technicians in design and those in production engineering. In the production of aeroplanes, techniques, materials and skills changed dramatically during the war. Airframes were originally made of wood therefore wood-based skills and crafts were needed. The changeover to metal airframes changed the skill base of the industry and increased the flow of scientific and technically qualified staff into the industry. The development of the jet engine had a similar effect.

Aero engine and airframe design, in its infancy in 1914–18, made considerable technological strides during the inter-war period even without the massive financial stimulus created by the demand for aircraft following rearmament in 1934–5. Table 2.3 indicates the changing design inputs and requirements for Handley Page Ltd, the main supplier of British bombers. The twenty technical staff employed in 1918 still represented a minute fraction of the 1120 workforce: by 1935 the proportion of technical staff had grown to 42, still a tiny fraction of the 1160 workforce. These figures indicate a rising

technical input, but the proportions suggest that the industry
was labour-intensive, and that technical workers were still
heavily dependent on the skills of operatives to build aircraft.
The aircraft industry employed 10 per cent more white-collar
employees compared with total manufacturing (Fearon, 1978,
p. 81). The term 'technical staff' in Table 2.3 may only indicate drawing office staff.

Table 2.3   *The changing complexity of Handley Page bombers*

Type	AUW lbs	Design begun	Prototype flew	Av. no. of tech. staff	Design weeks	No. of drawings
0/100	14 000	Jan. 1915	Dec. 1915	6	300	295
V/150	30 000	Oct. 1917	Apr. 1918	20	600	2 025
Hampden	20 000	May. 1934	Jun. 1936	21	2 364	8 000
Harrow	23 500	Sep. 1935	Oct. 1936	42	2 500	7 000
Halifax	65 000	Aug. 1937	Oct. 1939	71	8 320	13 000

SOURCE: Fearon (1978, p. 80).

These very major changes in production were accompanied
by smaller changes, e.g. designers originally designed large
sections of the aircraft, while today designers, draughtsmen
and planning engineers are locked into a small sub-section of
airframe design, e.g. mechanical, avionics, or electrical
design. Moreover the possession of a specialised knowledge
within a specialist area of design was increasingly common,
e.g. circuitry within electrical design. John Pill had been
designing aeroplanes since 1945, and described to me the
moves towards specialisation he had personally witnessed:

> in the older days where you had a designer, a design
> draughtsman as we would call him, he not only designed
> the circuit, he also designed all the hardware, and the
> places in the panels where all the switches were going. But
> as aeroplanes got bigger and more complex this just wasn't
> practical so a split came. Then they had a Circuit Design
> section, and they had an Electro-Mechanical Installation

section, and so now you have divorced one from the other. But that was alright in the '50s when aeroplanes weren't too big, you come to the '60s and '70s, and aeroplanes have now become so complex that no one man can master everything on the electrics side. So now you have technicians and electrical designers like myself who specialise in certain subjects. Now my subject happens to be all the warning systems: master warning, audio-warning, smoke detection and various other things. You have another chap who is responsible for engine circuitry, another who is responsible for the hydraulic system, another for fuel and so on.

This specialisation existed within the Design Engineering Organisation. This large building housed over 300 designers and draughtsmen and was situated close to the Assembly area, one mile away from the manufacturing area and machine shop. This specialisation obviously limited the technical knowledge of the designer and draughtsmen. John Pill again:

If the hydraulic design section leader had four men, all they did was hydraulic circuits and their knowledge of any other system was fairly limited.

The reason given for this fragmentation of technical knowledge is that 'aircraft got bigger' or 'aircraft got more complicated'. Why they *had* to get bigger and more complicated is not really considered. It was just 'the way things were going'.

Designers or design engineers had originally been called design draughtsmen to distinguish them from detail or routine draughtsmen. The difference was in scope and breadth of knowledge; the design draughtsmen being the source of the original *idea*, the detail draughtsmen graphically enlarging and elaborating on instructions given to them by the design draughtsmen.

The design draughtsman frequently exercised a supervisory function as a Section Leader or Manager in the office. One designer I interviewed said that the general variety of functions attributed to the design draughtsmen in the 1930s by

Cooley were carried out by Filton designers at the end of the
1950s.

> Cooley's time scale is wrong. We had that happy situation
> at the beginning of Concorde which was 1958–1960. There
> you had a senior Design Engineer who was responsible for
> the original conception of a system and his responsibility
> took him all the way through. I mean, he had a draughting
> group which could draw pretty pictures for him, but he
> made the rough sketches and the original scheme layout . . .
> And he then chose the material, saw the vendors and got
> the pieces in. And he had the test rigs liaise with him to
> try the equipment out. And that was up until 1962.

During the Concorde programme compartmentalisation of
designer functions accelerated. The designer, Paul Coggan,
again:

> Technicians do a bit of investigation for suppliers, tech-
> nicians do your calculations, someone else does a few draw-
> ings for you and somebody else does your ordering. Diversi-
> fication hasn't added to the interest of the job.

To some extent Cooley and Coggan are dealing with different
realities. Coggan is describing the design engineers' loss of
'managerial' control over work, with the growth of mediating
occupations and specialisms between the designer and 'his
system'. Cooley is concerned with the actual sloughing off of
design-based functions for the generation of new technical
occupations. The authority over 'the system' is a separate
issue which Coggan deals with because, as a manager, it is
more pertinent to his work. For Cooley it is not the loss of
control, or authority or responsibility that is at stake, but the
apparent loss of skill, and the routinisation of skill.

   It is not only at the higher end of the technical spectrum
that   specialisation   and   differentiation   occurred.
Draughtsmen, and 'other technicians' are now operating in a
rapidly changing environment that is threatening old technical occupations (e.g. tracing, planning, estimating and
draughting) and generating new specialisms primarily based

on computing technology. I will now examine some of these changes and the reactions of technical workers at Filton to their development.

Job Titles, Social Status and Job Identity

In 1963 TASS discussed at their annual conference, the changing nature of technical occupations and the need to change the rules governing eligibility of membership. At that time technical workers consisted of draughtsmen, designers, tracers, calculators, estimators, planning engineers and 'other technicians however designated, whose function related [them] to design' (AESD, 1963, p. 50). A decade later TASS issued a list of the 'typical posts' held by the membership in the higher and middle range. The total number of jobs mentioned was 468 as opposed to seven in 1963. The 1963 designations were broader and if they had been described in more detail perhaps fifty titles could have been catalogued. Nevertheless the expansion of titles from fifty to 468 in a decade is a phenomenal growth in titles, if not occupations. Of the 468 titles, over 400 were of a technical nature, the rest being clerical, administrative and supervisory. The complexity of the division of labour and the separation of worker from worker is reflected in the profusion of job titles and the gap between job function and job title.

At Filton there were around 100 technical job titles on the company's personnel files, but TASS, the main technical union on site, had reduced these into just twenty-six occupational categories. Table 2.4 lists these titles and their functional location in the company's production cycle.

Occupations like draughtsmen occurred with a variety of prefixes, but were identified by TASS under a generic title and the major specialism, 'jig and tool draughting'. My research was concerned with occupations in the design and production engineering areas. I showed John Stevens, who had worked as a production engineer since 1935, TASS's list of occupations:

Table 2.4   *TASS-designated technical occupations at Filton by functional location in the production cycle*

Design Engineering
This incorporates the initial design and development of the product

Design Engineers	Wind Tunnel Technicians
Project Engineers	Draughtsmen
Electrical Engineers	Loftsmen
Systems Engineers	Stressmen

Production Engineering
This includes the preparation and organisation of the product for production

Planning Engineers	Jig and Tool Draughtsmen
N.C. Programmers	Production Engineers
Estimators	Cost Control Engineers
Work Study Engineers	

Product Support
This is chiefly a post-manufacture stage in production

Technical authors	Service Engineers
Technical Illustrators	Spares Engineers

Maintenance
This includes technical workers who are attached to one or more of the other stages

Plant Engineers	Technicians
Works Engineers	Draughtsmen
Sanitary Engineers	

Flight Testing
As the name implies – the flight testing of the completed aircraft.
Flight Test Engineers

If you go back pre-war all we had were draughtsmen, we had a few estimators, we had tracers of course, we had technical illustrators, although we called them a different name. We didn't have spares engineers, standards engineers, stress men, weights engineers, we had a very few jig and tool draughtsmen and we had no loftsmen and no planners.

There is an increasing lack of fit between the title and content of a job. When I began my research I had a naïve idea that engineering technicians were somehow a readily identifiable group. I quickly found that the enormous number of titles that come under the general title 'technician' or 'engineer' created confusion within engineering and prevented those outside the industry having any real understanding of a person's work. Job identity, in the traditional sense – of a miner, nurse, doctor or mechanic – possessing a definite status through a readily identifiable image conveyed to the public by the job title, was largely absent except for the category of draughtsman. But even within occupations that supposedly confer a clear social identification such as draughting, there still exists a sense of 'lost' identity, bound up with a feeling of declining status. Graham Ell, was a second generation draughtsman in his late twenties. He reflected on the changes in the position of draughtsmen between his father's generation and his own.

> My father was a draughtsman in the early days and when I was at school I always got the impression that a draughtsman [did] a good job, and the older people, you ask the older people and they will tell you that a draughtsman was a cut above the rest and he would come with his briefcase and his tie. That's all gone, a draughtsman is just anybody [now]. That's how I feel, I'm just like a shop floor worker. I'm equal to them, that's how I put it.

Another draughtsman in his thirties who had entered the drawing office after working on the shop floor echoed this position. He had maintained, as had Graham Ell, close contacts with old mates on the shop floor, and considered himself the same as a skilled manual worker:

> To my way of looking at it, a skilled miller, a skilled turner, isn't any less or any more skilled from a bloke on the drawing board, you know. I don't see how they're professional people as such, they are just another skilled man as far as I can see.

Both draughtsmen could not separate identity from status, wages and their attitude towards manual workers. The decline in the position of the draughtsmen from being 'a cut above the rest' to 'just like a shop floor worker' could not be halted by changed job titles. Both were jig and tool draughtsmen, although the new title for the job was 'Tool Design Engineer'. For some in the jig and tool/tool design department, such a change was cosmetic. Titles had proliferated, but beneath the titles the quality of the work and more importantly, the social relations between draughtsmen and manual workers, had significantly altered. Their status, authority and wages had declined and consequently for some the general consciousness of being 'just like a shop floor worker' had developed. This loss of authority was bemoaned by several draughtsmen in their fifties, Eric Ham for example:

Well in my lifetime the role of the draughtsman has changed dramatically. Certainly the status of a draughtsman has changed . . . I can remember when the draughtsman went into the shops. I mean his word was absolutely law and the men on the shop floor used to say 'Oh, there's a Draughtsman coming down'. You know, it was quite an event. But now it's not like that at all, it's not, it's changed a lot.

How then did the majority of technical staff see themselves? If new job titles were seen as cosmetic by some, others thought they did 'improve the image' of the technical worker, and compensate for some of their lost status. As I indicated earlier, most thought generic titles like 'technician' or 'technologist' very vague. But despite confusion, a lot found the title 'engineer', with different descriptive prefixes, 'weights', 'design', 'stress', etc. useful. For the higher technical staff the search for *authority* in titles was considered very important. Reference was continually made to the status of engineers on the continent or in the United States. Many had worked in France during the *Concorde* project which was a joint Anglo-French development, and enjoyed the higher status and better wages and conditions of design engineers there. Similarly with the United States. The Finniston Report (1980) on the status of the engineering profession was also attracting a lot of attention when I was doing my interviews. One senior draughtsman who was not a professional engineer, i.e. not a graduate or member of a professional engineering association, said to me:

> I should like to think it was a profession, but it's not really recognised as such. You know, there's a great deal of discussion about this lately, you know, with a lot of people going to France. An engineer over there is really something, they are treated like the cream but it doesn't really apply here.

With the internationalisation of the aerospace industry, an international labour market for skilled labour was created. Professional engineers had been part of this world market for several years, and the engineer, who was manager of a small design team, and had worked in France and the United States, told me:

> Well in this country if you say to someone you're an engineer, they think you work in a grease pit, somewhere under a car. In the States and on the continent an engineer is in fact regarded with the same sort of status as a G.P. or a lawyer or someone of that nature . . . This is unique to this country and you just have to live with it.

Eric Ham, who as I have already indicated, was very troubled at the loss of respect for the draughtsmen, looked to the situation in Europe as a possible remedy. He certainly wanted the status of the word 'engineer' to be improved, i.e. professionalised:

> On the continent an engineer is classified as a professional. Well I think the whole thing ought to be raised to engineer, I'm classified here in the office as a 'Tool Engineer' but I think whether it would serve any useful purpose to regrade or re-title the occupation, I don't know. Certainly it would have to be done throughout the whole country to up the status of these people.

By and large this view was in a minority at Filton. It was

voiced by some older technical workers or those who had experienced managerial and supervisory status. Ham was in a supervisory position; Hill was a senior tool designer, and Coggan a managerial designer. The younger technical workers and those who had recent experience of the shop floor, considered themselves to be 'technical craftsmen', certainly not professionals. For them the term professional was reserved for those who were university educated, or chartered engineers. However one young chartered engineer I interviewed in NC programming, did not consider the term 'professional' meant anything. It certainly did not provide additional status, or identity. Moreover it did not guarantee additional wages, and it was money more than identity, that most technical staff were interested in.

Wages and Job Identity

Technical workers, like all wage labourers, evaluated themselves by the wages they received relative to the wages of other workers. Job identity was connected with their level of remuneration, and increasingly staff status, privileges and special conditions were subordinated to the issue of the level of pay they received at the end of the month. The harmonisation of conditions of work (holidays, hours, sick pay, etc.) between manual and non-manual workers has been increasing during the 1960s and 1970s, especially in the thoroughly unionised sectors of engineering (Incomes Data Services 1982a). At Filton there were few real differences in conditions of employment between technical and manual workers. Their hours were the same following the reduction of the working week to thirty-nine hours after the 1979–80 AUEW national strike. Manual workers started work at 7.30 a.m. and finished at 4.30 p.m. Technical staff started at 8.00 a.m. and finished at 5.00 p.m. Manual workers overtime premiums were better than those of technical staff, i.e. they were paid double time for Sunday working while technical staff only received time and a half. Technical staff had twenty-one days holiday and manual workers twenty days, and they had better sick pay, although this was being equalised. The implication of these changes, and Filton was part of a general trend, was that 'staff status' was increasingly an anachronism, a category that contained few additional benefits to the worker who transferred from the shop floor to the technical department. Formal conditions of employment were moving towards a common norm, although on the issues of autonomy at work and job control, there were major differences between technical and manual workers. This was reflected by the larger number of formal agreements between shop management and unions. The shop floor was a highly controlled, supervised and regulated environment relative to the drawing office or planning department, and there was more bargaining by manual shop stewards over changes in jobs and a greater chance for sectional wage drift.

It is against this background that one should examine the issue of wages and wage differentials in the technical area. For although concern about wages is as old as technical trade unionism, the decline in significance of non-wage formal conditions of employment has left technical workers at all levels interested in wage rates more than ever before. Many of the older technical workers I interviewed spoke of this new wage consciousness in the technical departments.

Routh (1980) in his study of pay in Britain between 1906 and 1979, has shown that technical staff have mainly been trailing skilled manual workers. He divides the period into nine categories and in most of them the wage differential was increasing in favour of manual workers (Routh, 1980, p. 178). During the inter-war period there was basic parity between draughtsmen and skilled manual workers. However, from the mid 1930s the differential increased dramatically in favour of manual workers. Routh examined draughtsmen's earnings as a percentage of manual earnings and produced the following ratios: in 1940, a draughtsman's wage was worth 83 per cent of an average manual workers; in 1942: 74; 1944: 73; 1946: 70; 1948: 73; and 1950: 70 per cent (Routh, 1980, p. 155). This trend was halted during the late 1950s and 1960s, and from the 1970s there has been a general parity between technicians and craftsmen. The militant wages policy of TASS during the 1960s accounted for much of the increase in draughtsmen's pay, as I will later demonstrate.

Quoting average pay does not always present the true extent of the differential as manual workers had greater access to bonus work, shift work and overtime working at higher rates. One draughtsman I interviewed recalled the differential between himself and the skilled craftsmen:

Thirty odd years ago, just after the last war, the position was that the young fellow in the office would probably be, in earning terms, getting as little as fifty per cent of the wages of someone on the factory floor. The young fitter or turner would be earning twice as much as someone in the drawing office, in terms of bonuses, etc. So it's been a long, long haul to get some sort of relationship between the young draughtsman or technician (and his equivalent) on the shop floor.

Table 2.5 highlights the average pay relativities between higher and lower technical workers and skilled manual workers during the 1970s.

Table 2.5 *The relationship between the average pay of adult full-time men in higher and lower technical bands and skilled manual workers*

	1970	1971	1972	1973	1974	1975	1976	1977	1978
Engineers, scientists technologists	£39.6	44.1	49.5	53.9	59.9	77.2	93.9	102.0	114.5
Technicians	£31.0	34.5	37.9	41.4	46.7	59.0	71.9	78.5	90.8
Skilled manual[a]	£28.6	31.3	34.8	45.4	50.1	60.5	70.5	77.5	89.8

[a] From 1973 skilled manual workers equals toolmakers and tool fitters.

SOURCE: Routh (1980 pp. 175–6).

Again the average in favour of technical workers may actually disguise the reverse, when bonus payments, shift allowances and higher overtime premiums are considered. At Filton in June 1981 the manual workers minimum rate was £120 per week at twenty, while for technical workers the minimum was only £115.76p per week at twenty-six years of age. The average in the technical offices, which was a more realistic figure than the minimum, was between £123 and £125 per week. Whether the differential favours manual or technical workers, it is only a question of one or two percentage points and nowhere near the gap that existed in the immediate post-war period.

Most technical workers I interviewed wanted improved differentials and saw new job titles as a way of getting more money. During my period at Filton, Government pay policy was squeezing pay differentials. Just as the two world wars had caused technical staff wages to be held back, because they could not so readily supplement their basic pay with bonuses as could manual workers, so government pay restrictions affected technical staff more than manual workers. In the nationalised sector government policy was rigorously enforced.

From the late 1960s grading schemes have been introduced in technical areas. These have been associated with productivity schemes in some instances. TASS policy was to resist all productivity and job evaluation schemes in the late 1960s and early 1970s. This changed in the mid-1970s as job evaluation became recognised as an 'inevitable' feature of the working environment. At Filton there was a growing demand for a grading scheme amongst some technical workers. But the senior TASS negotiator at Filton considered that a grading scheme would give management an instrument of 'divide and rule', introduce competition and fragment the unity of staff workers. He also thought that a lot of TASS members would be in for a shock if their jobs were graded by job evaluation experts. The lack of fit which I have described between job title and job content would inevitably result in a downgrading. In the planning area he said everyone was basically a planner – although some were called production engineers. He believed that job evaluation would classify a lot of the planners as 'technical clerks' and production engineers as planners. TASS would not accept any 'lowering' of the status of existing jobs, but because the average age is so high, in a decade there would be a retirement bulge, and younger staff would then be brought in on a lower grade and a lower salary.

The 'rational ordering' of career patterns and the bureaucratic desire to 'know where you are and where you are going' was especially common among the higher grades of technical workers. The confusion with job titles was thought to be surmountable if they were graded and workers moved through grades over time. John Mulvey was the office representative for TASS in the avionics design section of the Engineering Design Organisation and he wanted a grading scheme:

> I was very confused moving from a sort of civil service background where jobs are defined rather accurately, coming to an organisation where they are much looser, to the point where you tend to lose your bearings. Until you come to your own definition rather than what's written down by the company.

This desire for structure and hierarchy frequently substituted for the need to improve wages of all technical staff across the whole plant. TASS had been resisting a grading scheme for these reasons, although in other plants, C. A. Parsons for example, a grading scheme and general wages militancy did coexist.

These uneven developments have a reason: technological changes are introducing new jobs and changing the content of established occupations. Technical workers, consequently, inhabit an uncertain, dynamic work environment, in which the demand for a grading scheme can be seen as one attempt to find certainty and identity. The demand for new titles for old jobs, is another way of enhancing wages, and perhaps addressing disquiet about lost status and position. However, technological change has also provided technical workers with more potential industrial power than ever before. It is this new consciousness that I will now examine.

Technical Workers and Industrial Struggle

Technical staff have traditionally had a low level of industrial activity, partially because their distance from production makes their withdrawal of labour a long and expensive affair. This is proven by the existence of long disputes amongst draughtsmen, even when the labour market conditions are favourable. In the 1950s and early 1960s, when disputes by manual workers were measured in days and hours, TASS members continued to have month long disputes. During the 1960s TASS effectively developed work to rule, over-time bans and most importantly, especially in the large firms, sub-contract bans. These methods were used on their own as 'guerilla type campaigns' or in preparation for strike action. Anderson (1965, p. 268) praised TASS's industrial activity as being 'more imaginative and aggressive' than the traditional strike of manual workers. What he was referring to was the strategic use of sanctions and guerilla-style action of TASS. Given technical workers slowness to stop or significantly disrupt the wheels of industry, they needed gradually to build up to a strike, with overtime bans, work to rule and sub-contract bans. This strategic, sanctional form of action, summed up in the phrase, 'working without enthusiasm', was pioneered in the stronger, more self confident sections of TASS (Parkin, B., 1974, p. 17). It is wrong to romanticise this form of action without seeing it as an accommodation to the weakness of technical workers' strike power. Anderson is expressing many of the illusions about technical workers which began in France with Mallet and Gorz. In fact the most important weapon TASS developed during this period was the industrial support of other unions who were instrumental in blacking drawings, plans and instructions to slow down production at a much faster rate. This takes us back to the craft tradition and the importance of co-operative, social relations between British technical and manual workers in engineering.

What characterised industrial struggle amongst technical staff in a large establishment like Filton was central control and the lack of isolated sectionalism at the level of the department. I asked a leading militant at Filton to describe the steps involved in a wages dispute in the early 1980s. Firstly there would be some consultation with other unions on the site to ensure that blacking was solid. Secondly there would be an overtime ban and a sub-contract ban, imposed in the early stages of a dispute. It may take as long as six months for these actions to bite in a slack period, but obviously they

are more effective when a contract or programme is seriously
threatened with delay. Thirdly, the departments closer to
production or the shop floor take sporadic action. In the
case of Filton, this involved liaison planners, staff in goods
outwards (to hold up the completed product) and staff in
goods inwards (to hold up supplies to the shop floor). As
overheads and costs are far greater in the capital-intensive
areas of the shop floor, the more they can disrupt production,
without causing loss of pay to manual workers, the better.
Everything is planned to slow down production with the
minimum amount of wage loss. It was calculated that the
members of TASS at Filton could strike for a day and a
quarter – however that amount of time is aggregated – before
they suffered financially, as the tax relief balances with wages
lost. The fact that such details are worked out gives an insight
into the approach to industrial action adopted by TASS. Alan
Mann, the TASS convenor, told me: 'It's a war of attrition,
clean and surgical. We don't want any SAS merchants in
here'. Sectional action that does not accord with the central
thrust of the Joint Office Committee (JOC) strategy, was
looked down on. The loss of initiative from the JOC or Industrial Committee to a section was seen as weakening the overall
effect of the action. I found the same emphasis on central
control in other large factories – Rolls-Royce, Bristol and
Coventry, NEI, Parsons and Lucas Aerospace.

Along with overtime bans and sub-contract bans, there
were also work to rules, i.e. members only performing one
job at a time, refusing to fill out forms, stopping travel
between the different BAe. sites. The involvement of the office
representative (shop stewards) in the campaign was
considered essential as they were needed to identify the 'really
important people' in their section so that if they withdrew
their labour it would have the maximum effect on production.
It was common practice to pull out key sections or just individuals and pay their wages out of a common dispute fund.
Alan said that in each office there was always one or two
really central individuals. Finally, when the dispute was near
to be settled, Alan said 'you pull out your main weapons'
(e.g. computer staff), 'just to make management move further
and a bit faster'. This planned pattern is typical of technical

workers' industrial action, although the legacy of a successful lockout of TASS members of BAe meant there was great difficulty in getting a mass strike, which must have conditioned aspects of the picture described here. This is discussed in Chapter 3.

Mallet (1975s, p. 178) suggested that disputes by workers integrated into the firm are more co-ordinated, planned and disciplined. He called these 'technical' or 'strategic' disputes, in contrast to the traditional 'climatic' dispute of manual workers, which is based on the strength of individual sections who autonomously initiate and spread a dispute by means of agitation and example. This characterisation has definite parallels with the pattern described above by Alan Mann.

Cooley (1972, p. 87) in an early analysis of the industrial impact of computer-aided design and draughting, suggested that technical workers' control of such high capital equipment would 'increase their strike power'. When I interviewed TASS activists at Filton, two examples of the power new technology offered were mentioned to me. One involved engineers in the electricity supply industry in Dublin who had to be released from prison because, having been put there for striking and breaking essential services law, their expertise was such that Dublin was blacked out without them. The other involved a lone computer operator who wrecked a computer programme by inputting incorrect codes. This act of sabotage was by an individual angry about not getting a £1 per week merit review. He allegedly wiped out £10 000 for the sake of £50. I tried to find an account of the Dublin strike without success, and am inclined to believe both examples to be more mythical than real. But their symbolic value does reflect a change in attitude amongst technical workers about their ability to halt or disrupt production. The standard evaluation of their absence of industrial muscle was nicely described to me by Alan Law, an estimator:

Chris: What would happen if you withdrew your labour?
Alan: Nothing . . . we couldn't stop them from carrying on doing work as such . . . I think it would take a long time if this department stopped before the company folded up. Probably ten years. [laughter]

This view remains prevalent, but a new sense of power was mentioned by some workers, especially those who were active in TASS. Neville Green, a draughtsman and office representative, who had only ever experienced the negligible 'power' of putting down an H4 pencil, waxed lyrical about the future prospects of technical workers' industrial strength:

> if we had a future dispute we could use the computer staff without touching another member of our membership, all they would do is cough up £1 or £2 every week to keep twenty people out. Take them [computer people] out and you completely stop the company . . . My attitude to computers is that they are very vulnerable.

Ken Gill, TASS General Secretary, speaking at the 1978 annual Conference on the need to broaden the membership base, used the new-found power of white-collar workers in general, as an argument for recruiting them:

> Technological change meant the elimination of old skills and the creation of new ones. The shift of power moved at the same rapid pace as technological change, the telephonist, the wage clerk and the computer programmer becoming, in turn, the most effective industrial lever against obstinate employers. The ability to stop production was the real measure of industrial strength.
>
> (AUEW-TASS, 1978)

One needs to separate the rhetoric of such claims from the reality of work experience and the balance of forces between labour and capital within specific circumstances. At one level the capitalisation of technical functions and the integration of design and production through CAD-CAM, and other computer systems, does increase the speed with which technical workers' industrial action affects production. Batstone, Boraston and Frenkel (1978, p. 28) identify four sources of industrial power: scarcity of skills, strategic position in production, the immediacy with which a group can disrupt production and finally the ability of workers to generate uncertainty in the production process. Technical staff handling computer equipment may be more likely to generate uncertainty and quickly influence production, but their skills may also be increasingly substitutable and easier for individual managers to handle, in the event of a dispute.

In other words increasing the overheads in technical areas has both negative and positive features in terms of the workers' industrial power. Moreover, as I discuss in Chapter 8, employers may be more willing to lock out all technical staff in response to the strategic action of one group. The withdrawal of key groups is more likely to fit into the coordinated pattern of industrial action described earlier, rather than as a magical fix by one group. TASS computer staff at Westland Helicopters were on strike for several months in 1981 with non-union contract workers doing their work. This indicated the isolation of this section within the larger body of technical workers, (something noted at BAe), but also the general decline in worker solidarity in the recession. Mechanical equations about the computer allowing small groups to dramatically halt production and quickly bring the employers to the negotiating table need to be tempered by the above comments and illustrations.

Industrial action is a major way in which workers establish their independence from the views and interests of their employer. I have suggested that the pattern of industrial activity amongst technical workers is shaped by their place in production which has traditionally meant fewer strikes and a slower preparatory build-up to industrial action. The industrial strength associated with having an immediate impact on production has not shaped their experience of wage labour, although as design and production becomes more integrated and synchronised, and the magical 'point of production' becomes harder to define, their industrial power and confidence will also change.

3

The Local Study: Bristol and Aerospace

The Aerospace Industry

There are two related reasons for choosing to examine technical workers within an aircraft company. Firstly, technical workers, together with clerical and managerial staff, are more heavily concentrated in aerospace than in most other major engineering sectors. Secondly, where technical and manual workers are employed in roughly equal concentrations, one is better able to assess the moves toward trade union unity across the manual/white-collar divide. In such situations the importance, if not necessity, of unity between the various sectors of labour is raised, especially in relation to company-wide issues like redundancies, productivity deals, and government pay policies.

One can differentiate between industries where technical workers are a tiny fraction of the total workforce, and where they are a significant section. Invariably where the product is of a highly technical nature, produced in one-offs or batch-size units, technical workers will represent a significant section of the total workforce. In this situation it is harder for management to 'buy them off' with higher wages and status privileges, because of the sheer volume of their employment. In situations of heavy concentration it becomes necessary for management to hold down wages and reduce privileges and

106

important for technical staff to defend themselves against management. In a sector where technical staff are in a minority, courting their support by manual workers is not perceived as necessary – let alone desirable. At Filton, three waves of redundancies in the 1970s brought technical and manual trade unions together in important but brief periods of solidarity (Dey, 1979).

Aerospace has a high proportion of the predominantly male total technical workforce of the British engineering industry. The statistics on the broad occupational employment pattern in the aerospace industry did not begin until 1962. In that year, of the 260 040 male and female employees 39.5 per cent were in the managerial, administrative, technical and clerical category. This proportion increased to 44.6 per cent by 1970, out of a total workforce of 225 830. This remained the same during the 1970s although the total number of employees in the industry in 1979 was only 193 440, a loss of nearly 70 000 in just under two decades. Technical workers enlarged their numbers against manual workers both absolutely and relatively during this twenty-year period. Comparing the situation to other industrial sectors, however, reveals a remarkable stability in the skill composition of the total workforce. In motor vehicle manufacture, craftsmen declined from 29.1 per cent of the total workforce to 23.4 per cent, and in radio and electronic components from 17.3 per cent to 10.5 per cent in the equivalent period. But in aerospace the decline was only from 36.5 per cent to 32.2 per cent.

The aerospace industry has other fairly unique features apart from the skilled labour force. Throughout the history of the British aircraft industry the State has acted as the chief investor and purchaser. There has been no 'golden age' of *laissez faire* independence, as from its inception it has used State money to develop and exist. It was, for example, the impetus of the First World War that stimulated an infant group of aircraft companies into a large industry. In 1914 the British air services had 272 machines, and by October 1918 the RAF possessed 22 000 machines.

While in Britain, and most other European countries, it has been the State's need for military aircraft that has sustained civilian products, the geography and size of corporations in

America have sustained a large market for civil aircraft. The civilian aircraft industry has been dominated by three American companies – Boeing, McDonnell Douglas and Lockheed – although their share of the market has declined in the 1970s. It would be wrong to conclude, however, that the US Defense Department has not figured significantly in the American aerospace industry as a whole. Harris (1983) has written of the enormous contribution made by the State to the US industry:

> Of the 1980 Pentagon contracts (valued at 48 billion dollars) 16.4 billion dollars worth were awarded to six companies – General Dynamics, McDonnell Douglas, United Technologies, Boeing, General Electric and Lockheed. Ninety per cent of the contracts issued, it is said, were awarded without competitive bidding and in conditions of secrecy.
>
> (Harris, 1983, p. 224)

The funding of aerospace industry as a whole is permeated by a pattern of cost maximisation and subsidy maximisation, known as cost-plus funding. The normal capitalist pressures of minimising the cost of a commodity to compete in the market place do not always apply to the aerospace industry. Aerospace companies are frequently funded on the 'total costs' of a project or contract and there is an inbuilt incentive to maximise costs because profit margins (especially when fixed by governments) depend on this. Aerospace companies on fixed cost-plus contracts are:

> Insulated by the flexible attitude of the Ministry of Defence towards delivery dates . . . In theory, of course, there are strict controls on the profits to be earned on such contracts . . . [but] despite a ruling by the House of Commons Committee on Public Accounts that non-competitive military contracts should yield profits equal to the average rate of return on capital for the whole of manufacturing industry, the M. of D. admit that they earn at least 3% above that rate.
>
> (CIS, 1982, pp. 11–14)

The British civil aircraft manufacturers are heavily subsidised by the State. The Plowden Report (1965) noted:

Since the Second World War it has been Government policy to encourage the development of civil aircraft in this country. Promising aircraft and aero engines have been aided by Government finance when the manufacturers could not find all the money themselves or considered the risks too great to bear on their own. Whenever possible the Armed Forces have ordered a derivative of civil types to meet their needs for military transports.

(Plowden, 1965, p. 18)

Civil aircraft like the *BAC 1–11* or the *HS 125* or *Concorde* are examples of civil aircraft with large State fundings. The research and development costs of the new *BAe 146* have all been met by the State. *Concorde* smashed through government budget estimates on several occasions. The special relationship between aerospace companies and the State means that profits are guaranteed to private companies on Ministry of Defence contracts in a way that they are not in the commercial field.

Seymore Melman, who has written extensively on the economic disadvantages for private capital of high defence spending, has commented on the peculiarities of the arms economy:

It is difficult to conceive of a civilian [industry] that might operate in that fashion for an extended period – since those conditions of operation would force a progressively lower level of productivity if applied on an economy-wide basis.

(Personal correspondence)

This is not the place for a discussion on the function of the arms economy or the aerospace industry as it relates to the world economy. The drain on raw materials, scarce labour power and capital equipment into an industry that creates products which neither the consumption or capital goods sectors utilise has led some commentators to use the term 'waste' to describe the industry as a whole (Kidron, 1968,

Melman, 1978). I recorded the unease in the minds of those
I interviewed about the military and civilian sides of the
industry. This tension has long produced a demand by the
labour movement for an extension of civilian aircraft
production. My fieldwork was within the civilian or commercial aircraft side of British Aerospace, however most of those
interviewed had spent a large portion of their working lives
on *Concorde* and some felt this to have been as 'wasteful' a
product as a *Tornado* or *Jaguar*. By criteria of commercial
viability there is little to distinguish the two, *Concorde*
absorbing from State funds more than £457 million of the
development and £205.4 million of the production costs
between 1970 and 1980. One draughtsman said to me that
the first *Concorde* was numbered 001 because that covered the
percentage of the population able to afford to travel in
Britain's first supersonic civilian aircraft. *Concorde* was
supported by State funding through all four stages of its
production: project study; design; development; and in
service. It is more common for the State not to fund the
latter stage. Negative feelings about *Concorde* co-existed with a
certain pride in the engineering excellence of the aircraft. The
duality between commercial viability and technical excellence, and social utility and wasteful production permeated
the consciousness of workers in the industry. Many had felt
a national pride in working on aircraft after the Second World
War because of the industry's technically innovative position,
and its contribution to Britain's war time defences. But this
'pride' was not very evident during my period of research,
although a boyish interest in aircraft speed and performance
was not far below the surface of some interviews.

In Britain the majority of government spending on research
and development goes on defence. Excluding spending on
space research, Britain spent, in 1979, over 55 per cent of its
total research and development spending on defence, most of
it going to British Aerospace and the two major electrical
companies, GEC and Plessey (CIS, 1982, p. 7). France spent
35 per cent of its R & D budget on defence and West
Germany, 43 per cent. The vast outlay on research and development in the aerospace industry means that as a sector it
provides a main area for technological experimentation and

development. It is the dynamic, innovative centre of capitalism, and it is frequently war or the threat of war that provides the impetus for technological change. Noble (1979) found the origin and development of numerically controlled machine tools to be totally bound up with the aerospace industry with funding from the US Air Force. Kraft (1979) traces the development of computers to the aerospace industry and the military requirements of the US Air Force during the Second World War. Cooley (1972) has shown that the application of computer-based technologies to the field of design have their origin in the aerospace industry. The Plowden Report (1965) into the aircraft industry placed considerable emphasis on the innovative nature of the industry. The report examined what it termed 'technological fall out' and listed seventy-five examples of product innovation from the industry:

> The evidence [which was not exhaustive] convinces us that the technological fall-out from the aircraft industry is important . . . . It seems probable that no other single industry would have such a pervasive effect on the technological progress of the nation.
>
> (Plowden, 1965, p. 18)

The report concluded that the innovative nature of the industry was due to the special features of flight:

> Flight demands high power/weight and strength/weight ratios in the products of the industry. Second, as a defence industry, its products are required to surpass those of potential enemies. Together these characteristics have led to engineering standards higher than in most other industries. Finally though some other industries, atomic energy, computers and chemicals, match these standards, only the aircraft industry embraces so wide a range of scientific and engineering skills. It covers aerodynamics, materials, structure, hydraulics, instrumentation, propulsion, fuels, electrics and electronics.
>
> (Plowden, 1965, p. 131)

However the report begged the question:

> It is difficult to gauge whether comparable or larger benefits
> could be achieved by deploying in other ways the 8600
> scientists and technologists who produce it.
>   (Plowden, 1965, p. 133)

Both Cooley (1981) and Melman (1981) have challenged the
assumption that only the 'war industries' can provide the
innovative dynamic the system requires. Both have pointed
to the enormous waste of capital, raw materials and labour in
an industry that gives so little directly back into the 'civilian'
economy.

The political volatility of the industry also makes for instability for workers in aerospace companies. The cancellation
of contracts, and the failure to get beyond prototype
production are both common occurrences. At BAC only *one
Brabazon* civil aircraft was built, with the government footing
£6.45 million of the costs and recovering nothing. Between
1954 and 1960 there were over twenty seven major contract
cancellations which cost an estimated £203 million (Bristol
Siddley Shop Stewards, 1969, p. 16). This did not include
the cost of cancelling, in 1965, the *TSR2*, *HS681*, and *P1154*.
Instability of employment is concomitant with the economic
waste of contract fluctuations. Many thousands of workers
lost their jobs as a result of the cancellation of the *TSR2*. At
Filton the dependency on *Concorde* production meant redundancies when the contract ended and the then *BAe 146* civilian
aircraft project was shelved. Unemployment within the
industry does not strictly follow the ups and downs within
the economy as a whole. During the boom of the 1960s redundancy was a common feature of the industry and the increase
in defence spending following the Tory election victory in
1979 temporarily stabilised the industry while most British
engineering firms have been in deep slump.

At the general level, then, the industry is subject to the
fluctuations in changing governments and government policy.
This also percolates down to trade union activity at the base.
Dey (1979) analysed the experience of fighting *Concorde* redun-

dancies at Filton in the early 1970s. What is interesting about Dey's account is that it reveals another special feature of the industry, the level of political involvement of MPs in industrial disputes. Given the dependency on the State, industrial disputes especially redundancy disputes, have a tendency to very quickly become 'political' issues, with Labour and Tory MPs vying with each other for influence and involvement in the trade union and management demands. The political wrangles over the privatisation of BL being a case in point. The month-long redundancy dispute in the company at the end of 1971, which ended with voluntary, not compulsory redundancies, had close MP involvement. Dey explains that:

> The full-time officials and the Trade Unions Redundancy Committee* met with four MPs (Adley, Benn, Cocks and Palmer) in one Bristol hotel while BAC management waited in another. The MPs then met management . . . and put to them their views on the unions' case. Finally, the MPs returned to Transport House with 'firm indications' that management would seek 'meaningful' talks with the unions the following day.
>
> (Dey, 1979, p. 37)

MPs not only act as occasional mediators, they also put pressure on government and lobby for work and contracts for the industry. During the mid-1970s redundancy dispute management supported trade union delegations to Parliament to lobby MPs over *Concorde*. Correspondence between full time officials, convenors and MPs was a regular feature of trade union activities at Filton. The TASS convenor of Bristol No. 3 Branch, which is based in the Filton factory was on the Divisional Council and had regular meetings with the Labour Party Aerospace Group (LPAG) with trips to Parliament to lobby for contracts and to brief MPs sponsored by TASS or involved in the LPAG. He told me that he had written several

---

* The Trade Union Redundancy Committee was formed after the announcement of compulsory redundancies in October 1971. It consisted of eighteen representatives of the manual and staff unions. It folded after the voluntary redundancies.

briefs for Labour MPs and they had formed the major part
of the MPs' speeches in Parliament. He once recounted an
incident when he was talking to a manager at the factory and
Tony Benn telephoned him. He commented to me on how
this had 'impressed the manager'. The tendency to use the
parliamentary arena to sort out 'industrial' issues is therefore
a common feature of the industry.

The convenor told me he had no 'illusions' about MPs
and considered industrial strength the key determinant in
industrial relations, he nevertheless 'went through the
motions' of lobbying, meeting, and writing to MPs and generally involving them in industrial issues.

He explained that he did this as 'an insurance', so that
MPs could not turn around when they were required, and
complain that they had not been kept abreast of events.
Importantly, the political character of the industry infused a
strong national ideology amongst both workers and managers.
Competition was seen in national terms, although an
increasing European consciousness was emerging due to
Concorde, and the *Airbus* programme which combined the
resources of several European aerospace companies. A
residual element of this ideology was a sense of corporatism,
most evident amongst qualified engineers and middle
managers, and discussed in Chapter 5.

The British Industry

The British industry is dominated by the once State-owned
British Aerospace (Aircraft Group and Dynamics Group);
Rolls-Royce (aero engines); Shorts; and the privately owned
Westlands Helicopters. These four large corporations account
for the bulk of aerospace production and over eighty five per
cent of the employees in the industry. But these big companies
are supported by thousands of small subcontracting firms
indirectly dependent on defence contracts. The former
Chairman of Rolls-Royce stated in 1974 that:

There are over 800 engineering companies who are either
subcontractors or suppliers to Rolls-Royce, 140 of these

each do more than a quarter of a million pounds worth of annual business with us. The amount of work we give to them is several times this figure. Their factories are spread all over Britain and constitute a large slice of the nation's total Engineering Industry.

(National Shop Stewards, 1974, p. 3)

TASS and other trade unions opposed the use and extension of subcontracting, as it removed work from within the Filton factory. Management used subcontracting to cheapen production costs and weaken trade union numbers, although this policy was not pursued with the same corporate determination as in other industries or countries (Smith, 1984). Banning subcontract work by technical workers was their first response in an industrial dispute, and proved a useful bargaining ploy as it gradually inflicted damage on the company.

During the 1960s the dominance of the big three American aircraft manufacturers – Boeing, Lockheed and McDonnell Douglas – exposed the weakness in the size of the then two British 'giants', British Aircraft Corporation and Hawker Siddeley. The Plowden Report held back at total nationalisation, but recommended the merger of the top giants, concentrating the industry explicitly against American competition. Around the time of nationalisation in 1977 the big three American operations had 84.3 per cent of the world jet aircraft sales. The Plowden Report recognised that even a fully nationalised industry would be small by American standards and therefore it recommended the internationalisation of aircraft development and production with Germany and France (Plowden, 1965, p. 434). The joint Anglo-French collaboration on *Concorde* and the *Jaguar* strike trainer in the 1960s was the beginning of the permanent international division of production of the British airframe industry. The Plowden Report favoured European collaboration against partnership with the US giants. The Labour Party has tended to favour closer links with Europe, and the Conservative Party, after Thatcher, has preferred joint European and American collaboration. So today British Aerospace participates in the *Airbus* Industry programme (which has two civil projects, the *A300* and *A310*) in collaboration with French, German and Spanish companies and is undertaking the *BAe 146* project with some degree of participation by US and Swedish companies.

The significance of the internationalisation of aircraft production for technical workers' assessment of their job identity, will be brought out in later chapters. The concentration of ownership was welcomed by most middle managers and technical staff. They thought the 1977 Aircraft and Shipbuilding Industries Act, that brought the then BAC into public ownership, a good thing. The millions of pounds poured into BAC on the *Concorde* project made nationalisation a logical step. The dependency of aircraft companies on State finance has historically meant the trade union and labour movement has been in favour of nationalisation. Many of the justifications for nationalising the industry were to do with the 'immorality' of private companies' profiting from the armaments industry.

Brockway and Mullally's (1944) *Death Pays a Dividend* characterises this tradition. A 1935 Fabian Research pamphlet on the aircraft industry called for the 'socialisation of the industry'. Beswick (later to become Lord Beswick, the first Chairman of BAe) (1955) *Plan for the Aircraft Industry* stressed the need for State ownership. The two pamphlets produced on the industry by BAC and Rolls Royce trade unionists *The Aircraft Industry and Workers' Control* (1969) and *New Approach to Public Ownership* (1975) stand in the same tradition. It was not until 1977 that parts of the aerospace industry came under public ownership. The nationalisation was not however a 'new approach' and it had little to do with 'workers' control'. Nationalisation represented the Labour Party's using the State for certain national economic and political ends which came to an abrupt halt when the Tories denationalised and reverted to partial State ownership in February 1981.

British Aircraft Corporation: Filton Site

Before examining civil aircraft production at Filton, I shall review the background to the nationalisation in 1977. As already mentioned, the Plowden Report suggested the merger of the two main airframe manufacturers, Hawker Siddeley (HS) and the British Aircraft Corporation (BAC). The 1965 Labour Government did not act on these recommendations, although committed on paper to nationalisation. In 1973 the Conservative Minister for Aerospace, Michael Heseltine, arranged that BAC and HS should combine on a commercial basis with no government stake. This fell through and the return of Labour in 1974 produced the Aircraft and Ship-building Industries Bill which eventually led to the formation of BAe. This consisted of BAC, HS Aviation, HS Dynamics, and Scottish Aviation. This was a partial nationalisation and stopped far short of the National Aerospace Shop Stewards Liaison Committee's demand for public ownership of Short Brothers, Westlands and a number of large component suppliers (Bristol Aircraft Workers, 1975, p. 8). BAC came into existence in 1960, and the history of the company indicates the monopolisation and centralisation of the industry. Prior to nationalisation the Corporation was divided into three divisions: Commercial Aircraft, Military Aircraft and Guided Weapons. The Filton site was part of the Commercial Aircraft division with Weybridge and Hurn, and also part of the Guided Weapon division with Stevenage. After nationalisation the three Divisions became two: the Aircraft Group and the Dynamics Group. The Commercial Aircraft Division site became part of the Weybridge–Bristol Division of the Aircraft Group, and the Guided Weapons became part of the Stevenage–Bristol Division of the Dynamic Group. My research was exclusively based on the Aircraft Group.

When I started my research in 1978, the Aircraft Group, Weybridge–Bristol Division employed 10 800 people. There had been a steady decline in the 1970s following the end of *Concorde* in 1978. Table 3.1 gives the breakdown of employment in the Division.

Table 3.1 *Employment in the Aircraft Group Weybridge–Bristol Division*

	1964	1976	1977 (Jan)	1977 (July)
Filton	6500	6035	4840	4060
Weybridge	9742	5205	4390	3790
Hurn	3948	2490	2090	1910
Totals	20 190	13 730	11 320	9760

SOURCE: Flicker (1977, p. 14).

The 1977 figure was half that of 1964, although in the Division as a whole, Filton had suffered much less than Weybridge. With the go-ahead on the *BAe 146* there was actually a shortage of technical and skilled manual workers in 1978. They had increased the 4060 employed in 1977 to 4600 by July 1981. The figure was between 4000 and 4500 during my research, and this approximately divided into: 1400 technical staff; 900 clerical, managerial and administrative staff; and 2200 hourly-paid workers.

When I started my research the *Concorde* programme was nearing completion. In July 1977 approximately 4000 of the 9760 workers in the Aircraft Group were employed on *Concorde*. Production came to an end early in 1978. Sixteen aircraft were produced, eight assembled at Filton and eight at the Aerospatiale (BAC's French partner) factory at Toulouse. The *BAC 1–11* was being assembled at Hurn, with some work located at Filton. The *BAe 146* was taken out of cold storage in 1978 and this was to provide most work for Filton. During the ending of *Concorde*, Filton had become, in both design, machining, assembly and services, a subcontractor for American, European and other BAe factories. One of the consequences of this turn around, from being a major contractor to becoming a subcontractor, was that the amount of timed work increased in technical areas. Additionally, work on the shop floor was changing from one-off or short-run batch work, to longer-run production work. Several technical workers I interviewed who had formerly worked on the shop floor complained to me about the standardisation of work in the machine shop as subcontract work increased.

During my fieldwork the atmosphere inside the factory was 'depressed'. There had been three waves of redundancies, in 1971, 1975, 1976–77, and although in 1978 the company was actually advertising for skilled labour, the 'mood' was still one of uncertainty and despondency. This began to change early in 1979 when the *BAe 146* project looked certain, and the 5 per cent Government pay policy had successfully been broken by a 'phoney' productivity deal. The profits, after taxation, indicated the company could afford to pay higher wages and all the unions were putting in for substantial increases in 1979 following three years of pay restraint.

Having examined the general and specific industrial context of this study, it is necessary to briefly explore the social and economic structure of the city of Bristol, which provided the geographical location for this book.

Bristol: Employment Structure and Labour Tradition

Bristol has the highest density of population in the South-West, with over 700 000 people living in the immediate locality of the city. Nearly twenty per cent of the South West's employees are located in Bristol – 306 666 of the 1 549 000. The city is the natural magnet for workers in the South West and its particular employment structure has meant it has escaped the worst of the economic recessions. However, that does not mean it is completely cushioned from unemployment. The strategic position as the chief city in the South West means that the administrative and service sectors of employment dominate the labour market. Between 1971 and 1981 the service sector grew from 57.2 per cent to 66.4 per cent of the 297 660 economically active population. Within the same period manufacture declined from 35.7 per cent to 27.7 per cent, nearly 26 000 jobs lost. Within manufacture (81 460 workers), the broad engineering group employed

41 210 (49.3 per cent) of the total, with aerospace employing 21 000 workers at Rolls-Royce and British Aerospace.

Whenever it has been necessary to write a sketch on the labour traditions of Bristol, to put some flesh on the lifeless employment statistics, one is always struck by the absence of any literature. The common-sense impression is that the Bristol working class are 'conservative' and insular, cut off from the great upheavals of labour during the 20th century. Nichols and Beynon (1977) noted the significance of '*émigrés*' from the North of England in their study of ICI and one Northern designer I interviewed also thought the absence of Bristolians in other parts of the country was an index of their relative employment security and insularity:

> Bristol people I have found, I hope I won't get shot for this, but Bristol people are much more insular, much more tight to themselves. I often say to the chaps that I work with that they would be awfully suprised to find that the world was round, and that if they went beyond the end of Filton runway they wouldn't fall over the edge . . . You don't meet Bristolians in other parts of the country, but look around this factory and you'll find people from Scotland, Liverpool, Yorkshire, Newcastle, Ireland, all over the place.

This impression of the Bristol worker was echoed again and again by the non-Bristolians I interviewed at Filton. But there is a labour history, a tradition of struggle, in Bristol. Pollert (1981, pp. 14–19) in an attempt to debunk the myth of the acquiescent Bristol worker, uncovers some of the more militant milestones in Bristol's past.

The only history of the Bristol working class from the late nineteenth century to 1939 is Whitfield's (1979). His account stresses the importance of general unionism in Bristol, but also emphasises the fragmentation of class-consciousness in Bristol and the absence of any independent shop stewards movement – which reflects the general union base. In the aircraft industry the National Aircraft Shop Stewards Movement, which helped rebuild the shop stewards movement in the 1930s under strong Communist Party influence, had no foothold in Bristol. Whitfield notes the hegemony of the full-time officials and not the stewards in the then Bristol Aeroplane Company (Whitfield, 1979, p. 287). This position may have changed during the war, and a war and post-war history of Bristol has yet to be written.

In contemporary trade union terms few of the TASS militants interviewed considered Bristol had what they would call a strong labour tradition. The three TASS officials (two of them *émigrés* from London and Birmingham) and rank-and-file representatives had a sense of place within the working class as a whole, and also within local struggles in specific factories, but there was no reference to a local tradition of struggle. Their individual experience fitted into a general context of class struggle but not a local one. The term 'labour tradition' is a problematical concept and certainly in the post-war period industrial militancy has been gauged by the performance of workers in individual companies rather than large geographical areas of industrial communities. The mobility of capital and labour, together with the decline of the traditional heavy industries have wrecked earlier notions of areas possessing in some absolute way, definite labour traditions. The experience of class struggle today is more fragmented, varied and transitory. Bristol in this sense is no different from other areas in the South West or South East, where heavy industry has been absent or insignificant in employment terms.

Politically, Bristol – or rather certain parts of Bristol – has a left-labour tradition going back to the 1930s with Stafford Cripps, and continuing until the 1983 election, with the left MP Tony Benn. One of the TASS stewards at Rolls-Royce had been Tony Benn's press secretary during elections, and many other TASS activists I interviewed supported his politics. There was certainly a strong link-up between the major shop stewards bodies, the Trade's Council, and Bennite politics. He provided a natural political gravitational point for left-wing stewards and convenors. As I have already indicated, the political nature of many industrial disputes at BAe, and Rolls-Royce, meant Bristol MPs were closely involved in both factories. Many moderate Labour voters and Liberal voters I interviewed in 1978 disagreed with Benn's politics, but thought he defended their interests during the *Concorde* rundown.

British Aerospace, being the second largest employer in the city, naturally exercised an influence on the character of the local trade union movement. That influence had been largely a moderate one. Of the three AUEW officials in the town, the only right winger had come out of BAe, the other two having been sponsored by the broad left and from Rolls Royce. The TGWU, the biggest manual union at Filton and in Bristol was not considered very 'progressive' by shop stewards and convenors from the more militant Rolls Royce. The political tradition of TASS at Filton was slightly to the left of the manual unions. Before the mid-1960s the branch, Bristol No. 3, had been outside the broad left, which has been dominant inside the union since the early 1960s. Tom James a left Labourite with strong sympathies for the Institute of Workers Control, ended fifteen years of chairmanship of the key industrial committee of the branch in 1978. The new chairman, Alan Mann, was in the Communist Party, although only a few of the six hundred and fifty TASS members at Filton were aware of this fact. He had a different approach to TASS from Tom James, and emphasised bread-and-butter issues, rather than what he considered to be Tom's obsession with workers' control. He also preferred to work through the official machinery of the Confederation, rather than the National Aerospace Shop Stewards Liaison Committee, which he thought a mere talking shop. The TASS officials within the town also changed in the late 1970s. Prior to 1977 there were no broad left full-time officials, and as explained in Chapter 8, the TASS broad left is controlled by the full-time officials. This changed in 1977 when a new Communist Party official was appointed. This was expanded to three when the Bristol divisional office became a regional office housing three Divisional Organisers. The TASS officials exercised a significant influence on the AUEW Engineering Section broad left, taking over the organisation of meetings in the late 1970s, they were instrumental in changing the political complexion of the AUEW officials. The broad left was purely an 'election machine' holding closed meetings and functions on a regular basis, but especially during AUEW elections. It did not embrace any stewards outside the AUEW and was considered to exhibit a marked degree of craft sectarianism. The existence of three Communist Party TASS officials, and a CP convenor at BAC did not mean the TASS membership was necessarily very militant.

Filton had neither a tradition of militancy nor solidarity, and there was no organised political influence amongst the rank and file. No-one I interviewed had any recollection of ever taking action or paying a levy for another group of workers, either in the factory, within British Aerospace, or outside the corporation. The two year strike of Fine Tubes in the South West, which initially obtained support from Rolls-Royce, did not have the same impact at BAe. When I asked Alan Mann about this he said, 'No one has ever asked us', and his attempts to initiate collections, did not obtain very good results. Similarly, there was no BAe involvement with Grunwicks. The one-day strikes against the Tory Industrial Relations Act organised by the AUEW did not get strong support.

TASS had sole negotiating rights for technical staff but it did not have one hundred per cent density. The TASS convenor claimed in 1981 that seven hundred out of a possible nine hundred technical staff were organised. Membership in November 1980 actually stood at 618 according to local records, and the Divisional Organiser responsible for the site put TASS density at 60 per cent in BAe and 90 per cent in Rolls-Royce, which was, as I have indicated, better organised and more militant. Significantly, TASS organisation in the design areas was low and the United Kingdom Association of Professional Engineers (UKAPE) had maintained between 100 and 200 members in the Engineering Design Organisation throughout the 1970s. This Association organised managerial and non-managerial professional engineers, and their concentration in the large Stress Engineering section (fifty one members) and Aerodynamics (eleven members) inhibited TASS recruitment into the higher end of technical occupations. The creation of the first TASS management Branch at Filton in the late 1970s, set in train negotiations that looked like accommodating UKAPE as an autonomous section of that branch. But it is significant that an anti-TASS, elitist organisation persisted inside BAe for such a long period, when elsewhere militant activity of TASS members had eliminated such organisations, e.g. C. A. Parsons. Newcastle-upon-Tyne (Armstrong, Carter, Smith and Nichols, 1986). In addition to blocking TASS recruitment, the very existence of UKAPE acted as an ideological and political alternative to TASS policies and perpetuated the elitism, separation and professional autonomy of graduate engineers.

In certain middle-level departments e.g. estimating, a closed shop existed, but in every other department I examined there were pockets of two or three anti-unionists. There had been an expansion in membership in the mid-1970s and during the redundancy disputes. Job insecurity was listed as the main reason for joining. Despite the existence of non-union members in almost all the offices, in only one, the Jig and Tool Design (Assembly), did the matter lead to a very polarised situation in the department. In the other department, TASS members justified the existence of non-TASS members in terms of their individual freedom of choice. They said they did not want to 'bully anyone into joining'. Technical workers who had transferred into the office from the shop floor, found this attitude 'very weak'. It was clear that 'hard' unionism was not in evidence at BAe and the national one hundred per cent membership campaign initiated by TASS between 1968 and 1973, which produced closed shops and eliminated UKAPE in many industrial sectors, had not resulted in TASS at Filton making major inroads into all the technical departments.

The dispute most frequently mentioned by technical staff was a strike over pensions in 1973. The dispute involved the issue of TASS representation on a pensions committee and involved sanctions which culminated in some TASS members being locked out for eight weeks, before a settlement was agreed that represented a failure for TASS, as none of their demands were conceded. The legacy of this dispute was very apparent amongst activists and rank-and-file members alike. One young draughtsman summarised the lessons of the dispute:

> you haven't got the backing of the people in this company. If you are in a dispute you just don't get support. We were

out for about eight weeks, just before I came out of my time. They were out on a pension issue and they went round collecting money from people who were still working, because we were the first office to be hit. They collected enough for about a fortnight and that was it, they were out with little funds and no support. They had union pay but that wasn't much, but no backing from other technical departments.

There had been no mass strike of TASS members since the 1973 dispute, and the legacy of this one strike and the other features of TASS organisation discussed here need to be remembered when situating my more general statements on technical workers.

The existence of two large aerospace factories, BAC and Rolls-Royce, in Bristol has recently attracted many of the new so-called sunrise hi-tech industries into the area. These new companies can readily draw on a trained technical work-force, something not present in all areas of the country. Those I interviewed were not, on the whole, aware of the scarcity of their skills, and viewed their employment opportunities within the existing aerospace companies. The long-established position of BAC and Rolls-Royce, and the paternalism that had existed in the companies up until the mid-1960s, reinforced this sense of attachment, or, to put it another way, limited the choice of employment. The various waves of redundancies during the 1970s had increased the mobility of the younger and better-qualified technical workers, eliminated those over sixty, and had left an age bulge of those between the ages of forty-five and fifty-five years. This group was too old or unqualified for the newer technical occupations, and too young or reluctant to take early retirement. The industrial and trade union contexts described in this chapter undoubtedly structured many of the perceptions and attitudes I describe in this book. This general context was mediated not only by the specific occupations and division of labour in the factory, but by the special age structure of the workforce.

4

Technical Workers and the Division of Labour

Introduction

In line with other findings on the work of technical staff, this study identified several key features typical of most technical occupations (Roberts, Loveridge and Gennard, 1972). Firstly, the craft nature of many technical jobs required practical engineering knowledge of machinery and production processes, in addition to more 'theoretical' skills. A planning engineer illustrated the problems encountered by someone without this craft background:

> We have had cases where a person's been transferred into this department and he may never have been on a machine, and he's completely lost. Because he just doesn't know what is happening. When he says [to the operator], you know, 'mill this' or 'turn that', he doesn't know what's going to happen because he's never done it himself.

The polarity between technical and manual workers suggested by concepts such as 'mental' and 'manual' labour, was more fiction than fact for the majority of technical staff at Filton. By training, background and daily co-operative practice, there was considerable mutuality between skilled manual workers and established technical occupations. Craft

126

competence and technical skill were widely considered essential components of engineering knowledge, and this provided technical staff with an identity recognised by management and manual workers.

A second feature of technical work is the high degree of job control and independence exercised by technical staff. Despite departmental variations, most technical workers enjoyed a considerable amount of autonomy over their work, in conditions relatively unfettered by either supervisory control or restrictive individual time constraints. Knowledge of a specific job usually resided in the head of the particular draughtsman or planner, and not the manager or section leader. Most workers were responsible for 'whole jobs', so for example draughtsmen and planners attached their name to their drawing or process sheet. This allowed management to identify the source of any faults that may have arisen in the design area, but it also served to integrate the technical worker and enhance his identification with the product of production. I indicate in Chapter 5 how computer-aided design is undermining this situation. Such autonomy and 'self-supervision', had however its own distinct pressures, as this new part-programmer describes:

> Down here you're really on your own. Nobody knows as much about a particular component as you do. It makes it very difficult at times . . . Most of the pressure is created because you have to get the jobs out onto the shop floor, not because you've got somebody breathing down your neck. You know your deadlines, you know when the job had to go out. That's the pressure you have.

No technical workers were working 'to the clock', in the sense of being tied to a set time for a task. I was frequently told that technical work could not be timed in the same way as the machining of a component on the shop floor. Both staff and line management in various departments said that it would be impossible, inefficient or just plain 'daft' to impose time constraints on an essentially 'open ended' operation. And yet, as the programmer makes clear in the above remarks, time pressures were not alien to the technical office.

More importantly, the intervention of computers into most technical fields was establishing more formal systems for organising work, and departmental planning schedules were increasingly itemising work tasks as a means of timing output more efficiently. Tenders for work which involved a design or technical component increasingly meant that technical areas, like the shop floor, had to be timed. Several people thought the computer threatened to introduce a new time-conscious atmosphere into the technical area. Mick Page, an electrical planner in the assembly area, said his work had been changed considerably by computerisation and, although not 'tied to the VDU' the potential for this loss of autonomy was very apparent:

> As an individual I'm not timed, I'm not screwed down by a certain time, not like an operator, they have to punch the clock when they start and when they've finished a job . . . With us we have so much time allowed for design, for planning; that means it's a block time for the whole of planning etc. . . . But there's been a little bit of a variation on that now, and this is where the computer is beginning to take over. Because the computer has a supervisory mode which can analyse the number of times you press a button, the time it takes to do a number of jobs etc. . . . The planners have resisted the computer acting as judge on their work pace, although in mass services where women are employed this is not the case and the computer monitors their performance . . . They do a lot of repetition work and there seems to be a screwing down in certain cases where they want to know how long they've spent away from the keyboard . . . You can see that if you're tied to a machine and that machine is recording everything you're doing, then it's controlling you or whoever is reading it is controlling you.

The proximity of 'mass services,' a centralised clerical function, to the electrical planning department, and the very different work paces, demonstrated to Mick, that his work was not immune from the dangers of speed-up. Other technical workers – estimators, draughtsmen, tracers – were conscious of the changes threatened by technology. The job satisfaction derived from technical work, and the sense of reward gained from accomplishing tasks independently are not stable conditions. In those areas where the computer was assisting the transformation of the pace, pattern and organisation of work, workers spoke of the mental stress, boredom, and frustration of performing an increasingly routine set of tasks.

Like clerical workers, technical staff worked in offices with an average size of twelve. However, several drawing offices were open-plan in design and this created the impression of draughtsmen working in much larger units. The office, compared to the shop floor, had little capital equipment, the drawing board, visual display unit, computer terminals, and the occasional piece of automatic drawing equipment, occupied space in technical offices. Banks of drawing boards existed in the Design Engineering Organisation and drawing offices adjacent to the giant *Concorde* hangers, in the final assembly area. In these offices a strong image of men and machines was created. Yet despite these qualifications, the overheads in the offices were lower than in the machine shop. This fact, as demonstrated in Chapter 2, provides the economic justification for transferring work, especially judgemental or conceptual work which is more indeterminate, off the shop floor and into the technical office. Taylorism has an economic, as well as a political rationale for management.

The technical offices were quiet with air unadulterated by the smells of machinery and burning metal. In general, technical staff wore collar and tie, jackets and trousers, with the occasional pair of jeans and 'T' shirt on some of the younger workers. There were no uniforms, graded overalls or other facets of a shop floor environment. All these features created a distinct office atmosphere which differentiated, in an immediate and poignant fashion, 'staff' from 'works' employees. But to get beyond these impressions, significant as they are, we need to examine the detail of technical work. This is especially important because of the profusion of unresearched generalisations about the functions of technical work in the capitalist production process. This chapter will firstly examine marginal quasi-technical functions, then established occupations and finally a relatively new occupation based on electronics technology.

Working at the technical–clerical divide

Rate-Fixers

A TASS report on membership eligibility in 1962 acknowledged that rate-fixing was becoming 'more technical', i.e. closer to the planning function. The report stated that:

> The objection to recruiting time study staff and rate fixers is that they are engaged in functions which make them the direct agents of the management in the determination of piece-work prices. Because of the nature of their work they are likely to be in conflict from time to time with workshop operators. Time study staff and rate-fixers are, however, sometimes engaged on process planning. Probably the best solution is to adhere to the practice that those who are engaged mainly on process planning are eligible for membership, while those who are engaged mainly on time-study or rate-fixing are ineligible.
>
> (DATA, 1963, p. 50)

This report, as well as reflecting the politics of TASS in the 1960s, also captured the ambiguous position of rate-fixers in engineering. Rate-fixers at Filton were not primarily engaged in the direct timing of operators, but indirect process planning. The name rate-fixer, although in common usage inside and outside their department, had changed to 'cost control engineer' to indicate their altered function. I interviewed cost controllers after visiting several other technical departments. The contrast between their department and other technical offices could not have been starker. Their office was situated on the shop floor in a small building with glass along one side. This gave the rate-fixers a view out across the machine shop. Eight people worked in the office. I arrived to introduce myself at 4.20 p.m., when the manual workers were preparing to leave. They lined the aisles in front of the office waiting for the buzzer to clock out. Several manual workers stared in at the rate fixers, pressing their lips and noses against the glass, pulling contorted faces, gesticulating with their fingers and generally mocking those inside. For their part, the rate-fixers started to chant 'boring, boring', pulled faces and cursed at the manual workers under their breath. This ritualised behaviour appeared dramatically to characterise the relationship between the two groups. I later found out that this scene was enacted on a daily basis with varying degrees of intensity. The rate-fixing office was located on the shop floor, but there was a Chinese wall separating the manual workers and the rate-fixers. Frank Barlow, the head of rate-fixing, told me, 'Some of them [manual workers] won't step inside the office, I don't know why, they just won't'.

The eight men who worked in the department had all made what one described as a 'sideways step' from the shop floor. Two were ex-shop stewards, others moved to escape the pace of work on the shop floor. The office had a relaxed, close atmosphere, fostered by its small size, isolation in a large machine shop, and the presence of only one manager, himself an ex-shop steward from the shop floor.

Rate-fixers traditionally fight for times for work with the machinist or operator. They act, as the TASS description put it, as the 'direct agents of management' when determining piece rates. Their job is to get the times as low as possible, while the operator tries to get the longest time on a job. Unlike the planner, who had no direct controlling influence over the manual workers the rate fixer can assume a very powerful position in a machine shop and determine the general pattern of authority. The fight with the operator is usually a verbal battle of wits, although it can spill over into a physical confrontation. The section leader, Dave Brown, recounted his early experiences in the office when the Premium Bonus Scheme was in operation on the shop floor:

> I had only been in the office a few days and I was very green. I was asked by my boss to go and check why one man had taken twice as along as he should have to complete a job. The guy was an old worker and I was a young rate-

fixer. I approached him to ask him why he'd taken so long on the job and he just told me to fuck off, and that it wasn't any of my bloody business, and he wasn't having no youngster telling him how to do his job. He grabbed me by the collar and threatened me. I dashed into the office and he went away. When I told my boss what had happened, he said not to worry and that he was only trying me out.

Although an exceptional experience, it demonstrates the underlying conflict between the two sides. The rate fixers are equipped with the power to reduce an operator's wages, armed with their 'objective' times, and to some extent the weight of managerial authority. The manual worker is equipped with his experience, wits, cunning and the collective power of the shop floor unions. The rate-fixer's job was unique among the technical workers I examined. He was locked into a relationship with manual workers that was carefully structured with oppositional roles and responses.

The rate-fixer's job had changed in the two years before I began interviewing. Times were no longer based on observation and barter with operators, but were pre-estimated standard or synthetic times, based on the accumulated experience of rate-fixers and methods engineers. In common with other airframe manufacturers, BAe.AG. had found the Premium Bonus Scheme inefficient and conflict-ridden. A report on the reasons for the eventual scrapping of the PBS listed the problems, including:

> inflation and demand for higher earnings owing to the rising cost of living, militant Trade Union use of the 'mutuality' clause in the National Agreement, and unrealistic allowed times involving factors of 6 to 8 × working times.

The 'synthetic times' book, the rate-fixers bible, had been compiled several years prior to my research and was considered in need of revision The standard times referred to activities such as clocking on a job; reading the drawing; obtaining tools; changing chuck; setting machine and stripping machine. At one level the 'synthetic times' book represented a further objectivication of capitalist knowledge and control which removed the manual worker from the process of deciding machine times. What Edwards (1980) would term 'bureaucratic' control. However, with the productivity of the machine shop much lower than under the mutuality of the PBS, operators had greater control over the real pace of their work. The collective strength of the shop floor unions was now central to the bargaining machinery and more effectively controlled the rate of exploitation than the traditional control battles between the individual rate fixer and individual operator.

For the rate-fixer, the inability to directly time work left a question mark over his existence. The new scheme meant that the foreman figured more than the rate-fixer on the shop floor. The foreman, and ultimately the personnel department, replaced the central role given to the rate fixer under the PBS. It was written into the new agreement between the shop unions and management which superseded the PBS, that rate-fixers and operators were not allowed to 'talk times'. The operator was allowed to walk off the job if a rate-fixer 'talked times', and the operator ran the risk of losing his union card, and because of the shopfloor closed shop, his job, if he was reported discussing times with a rate-fixer. All communication on times was supposed to be mediated through the foreman, although all the rate-fixers had their 'operators' who were willing to talk times. New timings for new operations or on new machines, were done after the manual workers had left or in test rooms. But new timing was an insignificant part of the rate-fixers daily routine, most of which was spent working out times for jobs from a book of standard or synthetic times.

The office was not unanimous in its evaluation of the eroding of direct timings. For some the mental strain of daily fights with operators was not regretted, while others actually bemoaned the scrapping of PBS because their authority and managerial control had declined with the system. Frank Barlow, the ex-shop steward manager in the department, was in the latter group. He told me:

If two men were standing around chatting and a foreman came along, they probably wouldn't move. But if a Rate-fixer came past they'd separate like lightning. Because they knew that the Rate-fixer had control over their money and that if he saw them wasting time, he would mark the job down.

Dave Kenzie, a rate-fixer who had only experienced the system from the operator's position said:

I wouldn't have liked to have done the job as it was, not on personal bonus. I wouldn't have liked that at all, because that would have been too much conflict between the rate-fixer and operator. I'm not a great one for arguments actually, but if its helping somebody, no matter how small, then I enjoy that.

All agreed that the PBS had 'got out of hand' with bonus pay eventually constituting nearly half take home pay, and therefore not strictly an additional or extra payment. Under these conditions disputes between rate-fixers and operatives were very bitter and intense. Most wanted some form of direct timings if only to relieve the boredom of the increasing paperwork. They all felt resentful about having to do 'just paper work for the computer'. Two new ex-machinists hadn't realised that there was so much 'paperwork' and they and other rate-fixers missed the practical engagement of the operator and his machine. While I was interviewing, a plant-wide productivity deal was being negotiated for all workers at BAe. AG. The deal had a 'no timings clause' and therefore did not involve the rate-fixers in any direct way. Combined with the decline in staff in the office, from twelve to eight, the future of the department looked bleak.

Their work had been appropriated by planners, central cost control and the personnel department, who had devised the end of the PBS. One further attack on their position came from the rise in the number of numerically-controlled machine tools and the advent of long-batch, rather than short-run batch, specialised machining work. The conventional machines were declining in absolute and relative terms with the rise of numerically-controlled machine tools. This affected the numerical composition of manual workers, shop supervision, and those in the technical departments supplying information to the shop floor. For the rate-fixers, the rise in NC machines had meant competition between themselves and planning engineers outside the shop floor. In the planning department there were planners exclusively concerned with NC machines, and although they had to liaise with the cost control engineers, there was an element of animosity. Historically, the planning engineers had been more involved in timing work for the shop floor before the individual bonus system necessitated rate-fixers on the shop floor. Dave Kenzie was in the machine shop as an operator when planners played this role:

> It was quite a joke really because you could end up with a job that came out onto the shop with, say a quarter of an hour on it, but the planning department would give you three hours.

The rate-fixers considered themselves to be part of 'shop floor life', more than part of 'office staff', which meant for some, acting as a direct 'service' agent to the production worker, and for others the stick to maintain shop floor productivity. All the rate-fixers had worked in machine shops, (over three quarters at Filton), and experience of the shop floor was considered a vital part of their work. Their physical proximity to the shop floor, relative to the planning engineers, made them consider that they *knew more* than the planners. They tended to regard the technical staff in the adjacent offices as a 'different breed'. Dave Kenzie described the relationship between themselves and the planners like this:

> Planners tend to keep themselves a little bit aloof. Whereas people in here, they are all ex-people from the shop floor. Planners don't necessarily seem to be so and some of the people have been to college and then they go straight in there. They have the academic qualifications to do the job, they haven't necessarily got the practical know-how. You go to a [planner] with a job, and say I'd prefer it done this

way, and he'd look at you as if to say, 'who the hell are you?'

The return to process planning of times meant it was now being suggested that planning engineers should once again be more directly involved in what was seen as a rate-fixing function. This increased the animosity between the two groups, and in a climate of declining work and redundancies, this competition assumed a major significance.

Rate-fixing is an occupation that combines service or co-ordinating functions with those of control and surveillance. At Filton the move towards a more technical co-ordinating role in the form of process planning, actually threatened the existence of an autonomous rate-fixing office located on the shop floor. This produced a reaction amongst most rate-fixers that stressed their controlling, central role in determining labour productivity. They had the 'know-how', 'the experience' and the physical proximity to better control the pace of work on the machine shop. Measured day work and 'strong shop floor unions' had reduced productivity. In claiming the right to better exploit manual workers, rate-fixers were clearly moving away from a technical or worker function, towards a managerial rationale for their position in production.

Production Controllers

The Production Control Unit (PCU), was located within a complex of four technical offices adjacent to the machine shop. Unlike rate-fixing and the 'viewrooms', which were occupied by inspection and pointsmen ('progress chasers'), the PCU was not located on the shop floor. The main work of the PCU was to ensure that every component in the machine shop was 'in the right place at the right time'. Each component had its own identity slip or 'route card' which described work already executed and that to be performed. It was part of the job of the PCU to keep a track of the route card and keep it up to date. The twelve workers in the PCU, nine men and three women, were divided between two basic functions: shop loading and shop forecasting. Both groups considered their work to be technical, although the company and other workers viewed it as clerical or at best semi-technical. Shop loading entailed supplying the one hundred and fifty machine operators in the machine shop with a continuous flow of work. They calculated processes in terms of work for 'machines' not operators, and talked about loading machines not supplying machinists. Shop forecasting involved developing medium-and long-term plans for workload through the machine shop. The PCU concerned itself with the 'most effective use of labour and machinery'. Disputes on the shop floor generally created more work for those in the PCU and this coloured their attitude to shop floor trade unions.

The PCU supplied data for the 'efficient' management of the machine shop. Wainwright and Elliot (1982) have shown that these intermediate departments were helpful in supplying data to the Lucas Aerospace Combine on management's long-term plans for production areas. The strategic importance of the Filton PCU for informing trade union strategies on resisting redundancies, was not recognised by those in the PCU, who viewed forecasting through a managerial perspective. While the PCU only *advised* on forecasting, they did make decisions on the progressing, i.e. on the short-term use of men and machines, whether a job should be worked in the machine shop or subcontracted out to another machine shop.

A lot of the work of the PCU had been formerly executed from the planning engineering office which was now close to the PCU in the offices near the machine shop. The major departments the PCU liaised with were rate-fixing, planning, NC programming, the commercial department and a battery of shop floor departments. Workers in both parts of the PCU were classified under a clerical category, although this was not wholly endorsed. Those in forecasting appeared to accept this definition, although a few wanted to be considered as technical clerks. But practically all those in shop loading wanted to be classified as technical workers because of the claimed technical knowledge needed for the job and the fact that they had to liaise with technical departments on a daily basis:

Management, technical workers and manual workers, say

we're just clerks, but I disagree. Up here on the machine side of it, we have got to know what a job looks like, we've got to be able to read a drawing, and know whether we can machine it . . . We've got to sort out technical problems and we've got to liaise with technical people and if you are too illiterate you cannot liaise with these people.

The production controller's union, APEX, were putting forward a case for reclassification to technical status. The training period for most of those in the PCU had been short, and training programmes and college courses in production control offered only a limited potential for upgrading the job. On-the-job experience for those who came off the shop floor appeared to be the primary method of training. The one college trained student in the PCU, Richard Grass, was attending one of only two vocational, one year courses in production control at Bristol Polytechnic. Six months were spent in college and six months on placement. He did not intend staying in production control, but saw it as a stepping stone into production engineering management. He estimated that it would take someone without an engineering background six months to learn his job. Fred Hoyle considered it would take a non-engineer twelve months to learn his job. Both estimates are considerably higher than the six weeks given for training a pointsman, although a knowledge of engineering was included in that estimate. Unlike the pointsmen and rate-fixers those in the PCU did not identify themselves with the shop floor workers, but with staff, especially planning engineers. But they were in a marginal role, as Fred Hoyle, an older controller, explains:

Being the intemediary you get the kickbacks from one side and also from the other side as well. You're never right . . . If I don't get the card out onto the shop floor on time they say you're at fault, whereas usually it's a planning fault. And if planning have processed a job and you haven't got it out, they say, 'What's the hold up?' And it could be because you haven't got the tools from planning or they haven't given you enough time.

Not only were those in the PCU in a marginalised manufacturing role, they were also socially estranged from technical
workers and production workers. Both machinists and technical staff thought they could absorb the function performed
by the PCU. Those in the PCU did not exercise direct control
over the operators, they had no established authority to legitimate their role (as the rate-fixers possessed on direct
timings), and they did not possess a discernible technical
skill. They borrowed authority from the foreman, who they
would invoke in any disagreement with operators. They therefore accepted, to some extent, a less than positive image of
themselves.

The thing is that planning say they can work without you
and the shop floor say they can work without you. They
say if they didn't have a route card, if they had a drawing
and a piece of metal, they could still do the job, whether
it's documented or not . . . Planners say that instead of
writing a process they could write a hand-written card
which would give instructions and they could hand it
straight to the shop floor. Well it would mean that they
wouldn't be able to cover repeat orders, when the
programme gets repeated, it would mean they would have
to do their work again. Whereas once the process is raised,
it's automatically [recorded] on the machine. Even though
they say that, I can't see it myself.

Computerisation threatened to eliminate a lot of workers
in production control, and even the section leader of the
PCU admitted that it would be possible for planners, shop
supervisors and operators to re-absorb a lot of the functions
currently being carried out by shop loading. The computer
had the facility to 'enlarge' the operator's function so he could
select his own components. A lot of the intermediate quasi-
technical and indeed technical occupations were threatened
by a further 'enlargement' of the operator's duties with on-
line editing and direct contact via the computer between the
design area and the shopfloor. However, there were other
more politically sensitive functions of the PCU, which
management would not transfer to the operator.

The rationale of the PCU was to keep the work on the shop floor moving to ensure that the programme schedule was maintained. A good relationship between the PCU and shop floor supervision was important to ensure the redirection of work (either openly or secretly), in the event of a dispute in any particular section. Although not called 'organised black-legging', this was very often the function performed by those in the PCU. During a dispute, the PCU attempted to ensure that those who were not affected by the stoppage, continued working and 'where practicable' the work of those involved in a dispute was transferred to areas that were working. Obviously the issue of 'blacking' was important and the workers in the PCU insisted that they had to be careful not to 'escalate a dispute' by 'annoying the shop floor unions'. However, they would be central to any management effort to break a sectional dispute by getting work transferred, often surreptitiously by re-labelling and re-routing it to other sections. Their co-operation with management in such an operation would in part depend on the strength of the shop floor unions. Several workers in the PCU said they would 'help production along' and refused to be drawn on the issue of worker solidarity. This productivism stems from their place in the division of labour, but also from the weakness of APEX at Filton. Richard Grass explained the dangers of 'moving work about' to maintain the programme:

> You've got to be careful how you go about sub-contracting work off the shop because if you annoy the unions they start slapping bans on and you might have strikes . . . If you've got good relations with the foreman you can go to him and . . . he will find somebody and tend to do it for you.

The production controllers needed the co-operation of the foremen on the shop floor. Nevertheless there was a conflict between the two groups, based, in part, on the division of information and knowledge. Those in the PCU claimed expertise in forward loading, while the foremen concentrated on daily or weekly loading. For example, when two components required the same machining but carried different weights or priority, they were frequently machined at the same time. Richard Grass again:

> Alright, they've put the two jobs together, they think they've done you a favour because they've saved you extra time and got some productivity out of it. They haven't. They've probably done you an immense amount of harm by not putting another job up in the right order. They don't know, they don't know what's required, and what isn't.

For the production controller his logical procedures and organisation of work flow was paramount. The 'common sense' of the foremen and operators often interfered with this 'logic'.

The lack of a career ladder into and out of the PCU added to the low status of the job. It was one place where the older or invalided operatives 'ended up', a sideways step away from the pressures of the shop floor, rather than a promotion into a respected occupation. A clear strategy or ideology to cope with this marginal position was expressed by several production controllers, who inverted their alleged non-productive status by celebrating production 'for its own sake'. The ideology of productivism is not unique to those in the PCU and it pervades the whole area of production engineering and is a common managerial ideology. But it was central to the make-up of these groups. The clearest exponent of this ideology came from a person with the least experience of engineering who had no manual engineering background but had entered the PCU as part of his course at Bristol Polytechnic. When I asked him what changes he would like to see at Filton, he did not give me the usual reply of increased wages and status, but the following:

> I would like to see machines working twenty four hours a day, seven days a week on full performance, all the time. If the unions wouldn't stand for it in this area, I would simply shift the machines to another area. This place is wasteful, it doesn't make the best of its facilities, it's just not a production shop, it never has been.

The ending of *Concorde* meant that the machine shop had moved away from small batch and specialised production, towards long batch sub-contract work for other airframe manufacturers. In addition to describing the suppressed wishes of most production controllers, Richard Grass is also articulating the teething problems caused by the changing type of work going through the machine shop.

To the operator the production controller was a 'helper' or arm of supervision, not a producer of a physical object. To the planner, draughtsman and programmer, he merely assisted the work flow; he was dispensable to production, it would continue without him. Whereas technical workers were conscious of the value that they added to production by preparing the product for manufacture proper, the same was not true for those in the PCU. And yet objectively they were part of the production mechanism, part of the aggregate of labour, (the collective labourer), necessary for the production of commodities. But subjectively, and in a relational sense, they were denied this consciousness by the social forces around them. Despite emphasising their usefulness, there was an uncertainty about their position, and without the prop of authority, technical skill, or collective strength, their defence of the independence of their position was very muted. Trevor Taylor, a pointsman or progress chaser attached to the PCU, captured this weakness:

> I could hold my own as a machinist. I could turn round and say to the foreman 'Well as far as I'm concerned that is the way it should be done and that's the way I'm going to do it'. I knew if it went wrong I was going to get a bollocking But I would stand my ground . . . and I'd have the backup . . . But as a pointsman you're attacked all round and you can't seem to defend yourself.

By embracing the ideology of productivism, these groups were clearly trying to establish their place in the control of labour, to compensate for their perceived marginality, lack of skill and real authority over manual workers. Their positions in production and social identity were radically different from those working in established technical occupations.

Established Technical Occupations

Jig and Tool Draughtsmen

The machine shop jig and tool drawing office employed eighteen draughtsmen, located on fifteen drawing boards set out in three rows. Each draughtsman tended to work at the same drawing board and referred to 'his board' in the same way that a machinist will refer to 'his machine'. The office had two managers, three section leaders, one checker, three senior draughtsmen, seven draughtsmen and one junior draughtsman. Previously it had employed more trainee draughtsmen, but redundancies and natural wastage had reduced the numbers. There was approximately one section leader to every four draughtsmen, and each section leader had his own group of draughtsmen, and there was considerable sectional variation based on the supervisory styles of the three section leaders. For example, two of the three section leaders were members of TASS and the third was very anti-trade unionism. As with the tool design office in assembly, the department was far from homogenous, although the sectionalism did not inhibit co-operation 'on the job'. Nevertheless there were real differences, e.g. Phil Burn, the anti-union section leader, was considered a 'bit of a disciplinarian' and did not allow very much 'independence' on the job, checking on the progress of those in his section at least every two days. The other section leaders allowed a greater degree of autonomy.

What then was the function of the tool design department and how had the work of draughtsmen changed? The increase in sub-contract work through the machine shop had altered the work of draughtsmen who were no longer working on one project, but a variety of jobs from within and outside BAe. The major consequence of this diversification was the increase in the amount of 'timed work' in the drawing office. It was changing the atmosphere in the office. Timed work is not new to draughtsmen; sub-contract offices are based entirely on timed work, but it was new to the experience of those at Filton. The overall contract times meant draughtsmen had a clear idea of a target date, although when it came to the quality of the job and sticking to times, Colin Luck told me, with a sense of craft pride, that 'the job came first':

> I don't worry about time, sod the time, that job has got to be right when it leaves my board. Now I take pride in my work, we all do out here, we don't want it to come back with a scrapped job. Because that's the big thing out there, we mustn't get scrapped jobs. Money again . . . But you've got times on your mind.

Over fifty percent of those in the jig and tool office had entered draughtsmanship after working as skilled machinists on the shop floor. The rest had either completed technician training courses or transferred to technician apprenticeships after studying general engineering for two years. According to Michael Philipson, the checker, it would take two years for a 'good, skilled manual worker' to reach a reasonable standard of competence at the job. Although he told me instances of a tool maker producing good drawings after only six months, and a skilled machinist after only twelve months. It was emphasised by all I interviewed that a knowledge of craft skills was an essential feature of the job.

The draughtsmen worked closely with the planning engineers. A design came from the main design organisation, went to planning and then to the jig and tool draughtsmen who highlight, detail or draw additional information. Although the designers I interviewed did not consider draughtsmen had a creative function, those in the jig and tool office emphasised the intellectual link between design and detail draughting.

> When we start drawing out the first drawing, the general elevations, the design work, once you've done that you've frozen the design, after that it's just WORK to get it out into its component parts and then get it checked and made . . . Some jobs take you longer to design than to detail and some jobs it's the other way around. It just depends.

A large part of the work of the tool designer was with modifications to existing drawings. A job may be set for production and then changed or sent back to tool design for

additional information or design. Colin Luck estimated that
between eighty and ninety per cent of the jobs received from
design had problems, some minor, some major. To the
draughtsman a lot of the blame for the high incidence of
modifications lies with the design department. This is a source
of friction and frustration between draughtsmen and designers
and flows in part from the division of labour which separates
the two functions into rigid specialisms.

> I could take you out there and show you jobs in which you
> can see an easy way of designing it, to simplify our job and
> to make the whole thing cheaper. But they don't seem to
> see it. They don't seem to be as cost conscious as we are,
> possibly because they're that far away from the production
> line, you see.

The conceptual separation of designers and draughtsmen
was compounded by a physical separation of one mile. The
muted respect for the knowledge and technical competence
of the designer was overlaid with what the draughtsmen saw
as their ignorance in the practicalities of production. They
designed things to be 'too difficult' with 'tight tolerances',
they were not 'cost conscious', or 'practical'. The designers
lacked the skills and knowledge of the tool designers who had
'got to get down to basics'. The hierarchy in technical work
is built on the principle of the overall knowledge of production
constantly floating upwards away from the direct producers
and those closely associated with them. Where unity of
conception and execution exists in an organic form, for
example, in the direct relationship between draughtsmen and
craftsmen, this unity is under pressure from forces that
threaten the work of both groups. 'Deskilling' involves a
decomposition of an organic unity of occupational groups and
a recomposition of tasks based on more formalised relations
between workers performing increasingly discrete functions.
Personal contact is replaced by the impersonal 'liaison'
through joint committees and written instructions. The
computer replaces informal conversations between two co-
operative groups. This bureaucratisation of the division of
labour means that something is lost in the relationship

between groups of workers. The tool designers around the machine shop were articulating the problems of a division of labour that falsely separates them from designers and actually creates massive problems for their own work. This will be examined in more detail in the following chapter.

A large part of draughting is concerned with mathematical calculations and geometry. The advent of the pocket calculator had speeded up this part of their work. There have always been calculators in the drawing office, the pocket calculator was simply cheaper, more accurate and functionally versatile.

> The advent of the pocket calculator has really speeded things up . . . One grumble is that we've had to pay for them, another is that the company won't supply batteries.

The calculator was considered a useful tool by the draughtsmen, an aid to the arduous routine of large-scale calculations. No one expressed alarm at the calculator removing or reducing arithmetical skill. A drawing machine in the office, used mainly for tape control drawing, was not considered a threat to skill either:

> There are draughting machines, there's this thing we call the white elephant, along there with the covers on it. That has a way of plotting a component and putting it directly into the tape. And you could use it straight into a machine. Well you could at one time. I don't know if you can now. It's now out of date. We do get the odd request from GW [Guided Weapons] to come over and use it. But that machine can't get rid of my work, it's more for tape.

Computer-aided draughting had not yet entered this area, but as I show in the next chapter, it was changing the pattern of work in design.

The job identity amongst draughtsmen was very strong. It is a universally understood and acknowledged occupation. Ask anyone in the street what a draughtsman does and he or she will be able to give a reasonably accurate reply. This strong occupational identity helped develop TASS, and gave the union a strong craft-consciousness. The history of the occupation, the nature of the job, the relationship to 'the board', the drawing and the product, and the special craft association between draughtsmen and skilled manual workers, combine to give the occupation a unique status within engineering. I will examine in Chapter 6 the implications of these features for forming co-operative associations between technical and manual workers. Before examining programmers, it's important to consider one female technical occupation that has suffered silent extinction, not from computers, but from changes in the materials and tools used by the draughtsmen.

Tracers

Tracing has existed in engineering for almost as long as draughting. As the title suggests, tracing entails copying drawings to enhance their appearance, durability and quality for the shop floor. Reid (1980) in his examination of the history of shipbuilding crafts, found that tracers were originally apprentice draughtsmen. Women were first introduced into the job in the railway workshops around Glasgow, and then into the larger shipyard drawing offices in the 1880s. By the early 1900s tracing was becoming an exclusively female occupation. The large-scale expansion in the numbers of draughtsmen during the first World War also increased the demand for tracers, who were not considered a threat or potential dilution of the drawing function. The draughtsmen *drew*, the tracers enhanced the drawings, tidied them up and made them stand out 'for the shops'. By 1922 tracers were a recognised class of members of the AESD. Tracers are now an insignificant technical occupation inside TASS, whereas when the union was in its early stages they were the second biggest category next to draughtsmen, until the rise of other technical occupations, such as planners, in the 1930s. By 1968, the union acknowledged tracing was 'a dying profession':

Tracing, whether we like it or not, is definitely becoming

a thing of the past. It is quite conceivable that in a couple
of years' time, perhaps even less, tracers will be faced with
wholesale unemployment.

(*DATA Journal*, January 1968, p. 20)

Retraining was seen as the main way of avoiding tracer unemployment. This was something that had not happened at
Filton or other large corporations.

At Filton the number of tracers had fallen tremendously.
In 1978 there were only four female tracers and two men
located in the reprographics department and not recognised
as tracers by the women. Within twenty years the number of
tracers had declined from forty to four, changing from a
large, active section of TASS to an insignificant handful of
individuals.

Tracers used to copy in ink everything the draughtsmen
drew in pencil. The draughtsmen would work on paper, the
tracer on linen. Changed materials and techniques altered
this process. The use of plastic film or foil by the draughtsmen
instead of paper allowed them to use ink instead of the
traditional pencil. This was the biggest change in the division
of labour between tracers and draughtsmen. Additionally,
reprographic techniques had affected tracing. Good hand-
writing, earlier an essential part of tracing, had also been
partially undermined by the use of Letraset and stencils.

Tracers did not possess a craft background or require a
knowledge of production to carry out their function. And
unlike the majority of technical occupations, they had a
limited knowledge of the drawing they were copying, being
unable to visualise the physical fixture or component. To the
tracer the drawing was the end product, and their stencils,
pens, rubbers and inks, the tools of their trade.

The demise of tracing at Filton was due partly to the ease
with which women workers were removed from employment
by piecemeal redundancies and natural wastage. But more
importantly was the fact that draughtsmen appropriated their
work without massively intensifying their own work pace due
to the development of inexpensive materials and equipment.
The concern for the quality of hand drawing was increasingly
anachronistic, a fact bemoaned by older draughtsmen as well

as tracers. With the progressive expansion of tape-based information between design and production, draughtsmen too
would continue to decline. However, given their versatility,
broader skill base and, it must be emphasised, the fact that
they are mainly men, extinction is likely to mean a transfer
into new areas rather than elimination from work.

NC Part Programmers

Despite the relative newness of the occupation, programmers
share with draughtsmen a currency within sociology not
shared by other technical groups. This is primarily the result
of the work of Braverman (1974). He examined the nature of
numerically-controlled machine tools to illustrate the separation of conception from execution at the heart of Taylorism,
and for him, essential to the capitalist division of labour. For
Braverman, NC machines represented the physical objectification of Taylorism, as skilled machinists (fitters, turners, jig
borers, etc.) have their skills abolished by a labour process
that centralises the creative component of machining within
a new technical occupation, and the routine manual
component in an unskilled manual operation. The former
organic unity of design and production, mental and manual
skills, is divided into office labour in 'management staff', and
unskilled manual labour on the 'shop floor'. The boldness
with which Braverman discusses NC has been challenged by
Jones (1982), and others, who have questioned the alleged
unskilled nature of NC machining. I want to argue here
that not only does Braverman overplay this polarisation, he
ignores the knock-on effect of NC for technical, clerical and
other intermediate occupations, which in turn directs attention exclusively towards the one division between manual and
office workers. Furthermore, while NC programming involves
a qualitative shift in technical language, there persists an
association between programmers and machinists which one
would not have expected given the type of analysis suggested
by Braverman's work.

The first NC machines came to the then British Aircraft
Corporation in 1964. Noble (1979) has shown that engineers

to the American aircraft industry designed these automatic tape machines with the explicit intention of undermining the craft control exercised by the skilled machinists in the machine shop. The aircraft industry in Britain was one of the first areas to use NC, and the first NC machine at BAC was an automatic jig-borer.

The NC part programming department was set up in 1963, with a small group of three engineers embracing different technical skills and expertise. The three consisted of a 'theoretical man' (a graduate in engineering), a jig and tool draughtsman and a planning engineer. One of the original three engineers, Ben Stock, still worked as a senior programmer in the department.

Prior to the introduction of NC machines templates had been, and were still, used for certain jobs. These are the equivalent of metal stencils and considerably reduce the machining skill of the operator. They have not received the same attention as NC machines because they did not entail the same qualitative reorganisation of the machine shop as did NC. The ratios of skilled to semi-skilled operators on the machine shop had changed dramatically in the 1960s and 1970s. The manager in the NC part programming department said the ratio of skilled to semi-skilled used to be 4:1, although in 1978 it was 1:1. The reduction in skilled machinists had occurred over a fifteen year period, and according to Ben Stock, who had worked at Filton since 1949, there were never more than four NC machine tools introduced in any one year. This staggered introduction resulted in the *gradual* demise of the skilled conventional machinists. Had the machine shop undergone a *rapid* transformation, opposition could have crystallised, but there had been no compulsory redundancies and more importantly, no reduction in earnings. Ben Stock told me the general reaction of the craftsmen:

> Well of course they didn't want to know. Because the idea was that you train unskilled people for these machines and skilled men realised that the idea of tape is taking the skill away from the operator and putting it in the tape office.

It would be wrong to assume that the introduction of NC

and the subsequent employment of semi-skilled rather than skilled machinists led to a dramatic reduction in the wage bill in the machine shop. Sellers of NC machines promote these advantages, but they were not realised at Filton, and neither need they automatically reduce wages in a well organised factory. What they did do was transfer some of the costs of producing a commodity from the machine shop, a capital intensive, high overhead area, to technical and clerical departments which were relatively labour-intensive with lower overheads. Neither were the NC machines simply replicas of conventional machines with tapes. They were larger, faster and capable of handling two or three components simultaneously. Furthermore, they were able to machine larger airframe sections, and perform tasks impossible for non-conventional machine. They represented a qualitative break in technology, and this enabled management to justify the necessity and inevitability of their introduction. The three technical and economic advantages management derive from NC identified by Shaiken (1984, p. 71) were partially in evidence at Filton. These were 'the creation of economies characteristic of mass production, in low-volume manufacturing; the ability to produce complex parts that could not be made any other way; and the flexibility that makes possible rapid and varied new product development'.

Dennis Smith, an NC part programmer, showed me examples of work with reduced production time and products impossible to produce conventionally. For example, a job that required eighty-four hours to produce one component conventionally, took only four hours to machine two components with NC. The planner would have spent one month designing the method for the conventional machine, whereas he spent three months planning for the NC machine. This threefold increase in 'office time' was of little significance compared to the saving in 'shop time', where labour costs, fixed capital and overheads are higher. This was one of the financial incentives for capital in introducing NC.

The NC part programming department was located in the group of four technical offices around the machine shop. There were twelve programmers in the office during my fieldwork which was the highest it had ever been. Whereas all other technical departments had declined, programming was expanding. The department had grown by absorbing, from the machine shop technical offices, draughtsmen and planners and NC operators from the shopfloor. Nationally the demise of subcontract jig and tool draughtsmen had fed NC programming, the former declining because NC had reduced the demand for fixtures, which together with vacuum fixtures had dented the demand for their skills.

What then was the function of the part programming department? The people I interviewed were called *part* programmers because they literally dealt with only a portion of the tape preparation. They worked to a system, a language, a 'software' that had already been developed by analysts in a computer services unit. The part programmers claimed that their skills were every bit as complex as those of the software experts.

There were no Computer Numerical Machines when I was at Filton, although they were being introduced across the road at Rolls-Royce. CNC machines give an operator the facility to correct tapes on the job. In 1981 there was a dispute at Rolls-Royce between TASS and the shop unions over who should correct machines, technical staff or operators. Jones (1982) has described similar disputes over the same issue and with the same combatants. The majority of the machines in the machine shop were continuous path and therefore involved a limited degree of initiative on the part of the operator. Although the part programmers worked within a standardised software language, there was still room for individuality in preparing the programme. Brian Maunders explained the variation in programming styles. He had recently entered the department after being an NC operator at Filton and in Canada.

> Ken, for instance, tends to do everything in a very complicated way because he enjoys doing it that way. It makes it good for him because it makes it more interesting. But difficult for everybody else to pick up. John Mann is another equally skilled programmer, he does it much more simply, much more basic. Maybe it takes him longer to write it out but it's much easier to follow.

The variety in programming styles, was tempered by considerations of the type of job (a one-off or a batch product), for the shop floor. Simon Gee, a senior programmer, explained:

> We do tend to standardise things if everyone's doing the same job, it's good production engineering methods. But if it's a particular job you're doing then it's on your own . . . If you're doing a batch of jobs which are all similar then we'll all try and do the same method . . . So when it goes out on the shop floor it's uniform, so it doesn't confuse an operator.

Standardisation for the shops imposed its own routines on the programmers' work. The pressures of time also generated a need for a standard product.

Programming, especially in the aerospace industry, was universally considered to be more technically demanding than draughting or planning. There were more people with academic backgrounds in the office than in any of the other technical departments around the machine shop. There were fewer people from the shop floor in the department, only three of the twelve had entered directly from the shops, two from the machine shop and one from the toolroom. The other nine had entered from other technical departments, or straight from college or technician apprenticeships. One was a graduate engineer and two were members of professional engineering institutes. When I asked the office manager, Mike Cooper to describe the training needed for a programmer, he said the ideal candidate should have ten years' experience in the machine shop; five years as a planning engineer; two years as a jig and tool draughtsman – and be twenty-five years old! The emphasis as with other technical departments, was still on craft experience. In practice the training for someone off the shop floor consisted of twelve months split between planning and tool design – 'learning the system' – and then twelve months attaining basic programming skills. All the training was 'on the job' and in-house recruitment was favoured to avoid the necessity of having to pay 'above the odds' by poaching programmers from other firms. In the

early days there was no job market established for programmers so this method of recruitment had been essential. The
method persisted because it was both cheaper for the
company, and provided a continuity with established training
patterns.

The concern with the status of NC was also evident and
two of the programmers were members of the Association of
Programmers, the professional numerical control society
which is affiliated to the Institute of Production Engineers.
The association aimed at promoting NC in industry, as Simon
Gee, a member, explained:

> I think it was to give people in NC a bit of recognition
> because, let's face it, even now in this country, it's not
> really very NC orientated. Most people think it's a sort of
> black magic as far as I can see.

These concerns with improving the status and awareness of
programming through a professional body placed the
programmers alongside design engineers, who were also
concerned with this sort of professionalism. But unlike the
professionalism of the designers, discussed in the next chapter,
programmers respected manual craftsmanship and saw it as
an essential part of an all-round engineering 'art'. The
programmers had frequent interaction with manual workers,
and an association with production; exclusive or elitist
professionalism, based on the elevation of 'mental' labour
over 'physical' labour, was no part of their ideological
relationship with the shop floor. On the tape 'try-outs' prior
to production proper, there was a close involvement between
operators and programmers. All the programmers liked the
idea of seeing the finished product, the realisation of months
of work. This was partly to check for mistakes and possible
improvements, but also out of a desire to see their 'abstract'
labour realised. As one put it, 'we're the next thing to cutting
the material, you can't get closer than that'. Like other technical workers, they had a distinct relationship to production,
they produced an object essential for the realisation of a
product; they had a close association with the shop floor and
other technical departments.

They also possessed a skill or craft that was valued by management, other technical staff and manual workers. Designers, draughtsmen, planners and NC operators, while assuring me of their own skills, also placed a high premium on the technical capabilities of the programmer. Unlike other technical departments, programming was a new and growing area, although growth was not occurring in a linear direction, as major changes were already threatening the labour process so far described. The future flow of information would remove some of the creative aspects of programming, the early preparatory stages of translating three dimensional data into geometrical form. Designers in future would send information as 'soft-ware', not a drawing, and this data would then be used by programmers to prepare their tapes. Shaiken (1984, p. 122), drawing off research conducted in the States, has shown that the designers use of 'an electronic pencil to design a part . . . automatically generates a path for an NC cutting tool, [thereby] eliminating one of the programmer's central tasks'. A new computer terminal had only been recently installed in the office while I was interviewing. This was the beginning of a computer link-up between design and programming. To Ben Stock it represented an intensification, not simplification, of his job:

> Yes, it's more intense, that's the trouble. There's sheets of your work which is boring, boring. You're three months on one job, that's purely writing the programmes. Starting off doing your drawing, yes you're interested and you do your geometry and then you start using it to make your programme, week after week after week on the same job. It really gets you down, you feel you've had enough some nights. It's a strain.

Conclusion

This chapter has identified some of the major differences between technical and quasi-technical occupations. One needs to partially qualify any generalisations drawn from these findings because of the special feature of the aircraft production. Production control, as a function, will vary considerably according to the size of the plant, the nature of the product, type of technology and scale of production. However, the core tasks of checking the progress of components, forecasting work-loads in the long and short term, remain the stable features of the job. One could make similar qualifications to most of the occupations discussed here. Notwithstanding these remarks, the broad conclusions of the chapter are as follows.

The skilled nature and 'legitimacy' of the established occupations were not under constant evaluation and so the defensive postures associated with the marginalised positions were absent from these technical workers. There were established training schemes, career ladders and a skill recognition that confirmed the technical expertise of draughtsmen, planners and programmers. By and large the ideology of productivism was not a strong current within the consciousness of these workers. It was not something that naturally developed out of the place they occupied in the process of production. Quite the reverse. The concern for quality not quantity, the sense of craft independence and the respect for engineering skill meant that these technical workers' daily routines were not bound by the fetters of quantifying and measuring the results of the labour of directly productive manual workers. The lowly esteemed clerical, 'serving' or 'helping' status, that characterised the quasi-technical jobs, was not something that haunted the consciousness of those in established technical positions. Even in planning, which had a clerical component, there was an association with production, a sense of creating the plans, drawing and processes essential for production proper. There was a sense of being necessary and productive in a direct way. Although the occupants of the quasi-technical jobs examined in section one held a belief in their work as necessary, this evaluation was under a constant questioning from manual *and* technical workers. Their subjective construction of technical skill was promoted by a desire for improved wages, although this did not sustain a stable identity as the objective parameters of skill (training, tradition, relations on the job etc.), blocked any moves towards a stable self image.

Technical change was affecting both groups. Changed

drawing techniques had almost destroyed tracing, and rate-fixers and planners were not optimistic about their future and believed the computerisation of their work would reduce staff and routinise the job. Computer aided draughting machines existed in certain departments, but there had been no large-scale introduction of computer aided design systems, although in 1982 the company were negotiating for such an introduction. Evidence of the effect of CAD from other factories would suggest that draughtsmen had few grounds for optimism (Incomes Data Services, 1982b). NC programmers were also aware that their increasing dependence on computer data may intensify their work.

The close relationship with the shop floor and manual workers, and the craft tradition of recruitment of technical staff in British engineering, persisted in the established technical areas. Threats to this craft tradition came from two sources. Firstly, the decline in differentials between trainee craftsmen and technical staff which reduced the incentive for those in manual occupations to transfer into the office – I was quoted several examples of trainee draughtsmen returning to the shop floor because of financial pressures. Secondly, for technical workers at the higher end of the technical spectrum, the craft tradition had been eliminated altogether. Although apprenticeships were down nationally in all these middle-range technical occupations, the craft connection was still emphasised and in-house recruitment of technical staff from the manual areas was the biggest source of new labour. But the expansion in technical work in the 1970s was taking place at the higher end, amongst graduate engineers and technologists. This growth has posed a challenge to existing recruitment patterns, and the craft ties between the 'office' and the 'shops', while simultaneously threatening to formalise the hierarchy within technical work itself. Professional or graduate engineers have also provided the cast for the drama between professionalism and unionism, or as it appeared in the 1970s, between professional and general white collar unionism. But before moving onto that particular debate, it is necessary to set the scene by examining the work and social relations within the higher technical area.

5

Design Engineers and the Hierarchy in Technical Work

Introduction

In previous chapters I have analysed the specialisation of design engineers' functions following the increased complexity of aircraft, the accelerated design of planes during the Second World War and the spatial segregation of production and design engineering during war-time conditions. This chapter examines the work and social relations of a group of design engineers as they relate to other technical workers and to management. It is concerned with questions about design engineers as wage labourers, employed in large numbers within the Engineering Design Organisation of British Aerospace.

There were about 300 qualified engineers at Filton, over half were organised by AUEW-TASS and a further 100 by the United Kingdom Association of Professional Engineers, a body with no negotiating rights at Filton. Tensions between these two groups have been studied elsewhere (Smith, 1986). All of the engineers I interviewed were TASS organised, (a problem of access preventing interviews with UKAPE members). The Engineering Design Organisation contained several sections, the biggest of which, a UKAPE stronghold, was Stress Engineering, and contained over 50 engineers. The average size of the departments was approximately 10, although the CAD Numerical Geometry Group and the Propulsion Technical office had only 4. I interviewed young and old designers, those in new engineering disciplines, for instance avionics design, and those in declining departments, such as electrical circuit design, those with and without managerial status and those who had worked with, or were developing, CAD systems.

I have elsewhere examined theories of the social status of British engineers (Smith, 1985). My concern here is with the relationships between engineers and other technical staff, the role of engineers in technological change and their place in the class structure.

Hierarchy in Design: The Technical and Social Elements

The hierarchy in design is based on the ranking of engineering knowledge along an abstract-practical continuum. The more abstract the function, the higher up the scale it is placed. However, this formal continuum was not 'accepted' as legitimate by those placed in low status positions. Designers celebrated their work and skill by reference to the non-practical nature of their work, but draughtsmen and planning engineers signified the importance of their work by emphasising its utility. Designers concerned with the removal of drawing through CAD, denigrated the status of drawing, and emphasised its routine, non-creative aspects. This allowed them to see the transformation of the draughtsman's role accompanied by CAD in a very positive way. Designers were, in fact, *helping* the draughtsman, making his work easier and more interesting. John Cockran, an avionics designer, told me:

> There's nothing more boring than just pushing a pencil around a piece of paper and making marks. So, as far as CAD is concerned, as long as it gives a man more time to think, it's a good thing . . . People tend to see the process of drawing as such a magical thing, [but] there's nothing magical in just pushing a pencil around a piece of paper.

John Cockran's argument about drawing is interesting. It follows the standard Taylorian practice of dividing a task into its constituent components and then reassembling them through an interaction between the worker and the machine. Draughtsmen, however, tended to see their work in a more holistic way, and had aspirations for an integration of the different moments in the design process. For example, Graham Ell, a young draughtsman in tool design said:

> What I would like to do myself is design the tool, draw it and then go out and make it, you know I think I would get more satisfaction out of that than actually letting someone else make it. I find a great deal of satisfaction when I've done the job, even if I don't make it, just to go out and have a look at it.

Design engineers tended to view design and drawing in polarised terms, while the draughtsmen I interviewed saw drawing as a process containing creative and routine elements that were difficult to separate. At least, something was lost in the process if disengagement occurred. Cooley (1981) has strongly attacked the feasibility of disaggregating design into creative and non-creative elements. The designers I interviewed wanted to monopolise the 'creative' elements, whereas Cooley argues that to even talk in these terms, is to introduce Taylorian terminology which is inappropriate to design:

> The design activity cannot be separated in this arbitrary way into two disconnected elements (the quantitative and qualitative) which can then be added and combined like some kind of chemical compound. The process by which these two opposites are united by the designer to produce a new whole is a complex and as yet ill-defined and researched area. The sequential basis on which the elements interact is of extreme importance . . . [and] depends on the commodity under design considerations. Even where an attempt is made to define the portion of the work that is creative and the portion that is non-creative, what cannot readily be stated is the stage at which the creative element

has to be introduced when a certain stage of the non-creative work has been completed,

(Cooley, 1981, pp. 101–2)

Cooley could be accused of mystifying intellectual work to preserve professional autonomy, because he is both a designer and writer on design. However, the quote reflects his radical craftism, which supports the necessity for unity between the 'mental' and 'manual' components of engineering design, something stressed in chapter 1.

I asked two young avionics designers whether they did any drawing, and they replied with an element of humour and indignation:

Bill: We don't do any drawing at all.
John: We draw pretty pictures on scraps of paper.
Bill: Yea! Very loose sketches [laughter].
[John Mulvey defined avionics as 'electronic systems which aid and control communications'. It was a branch of design exclusive to aerospace.]

The basis of their differentiation from draughtsmen and other technical workers is revealed here. They are emphasising the flexibility of their work, that design and development are creative, innovative processes. This is counterposed to the inflexible, regimented work of the draughtsman, who must draw or copy with precision and accuracy the information provided to him by the designers who simply do '*pretty* pictures' or '*loose* sketches' on '*scraps* of paper'. There were certain 'design' features performed by some draughtsmen, although Bill and John were quick to emphasise their domi-nant intellectual position in the process of design:

John: Now if you take Doug Williams [a draughtsman] now in terms of racking and basic structural elements which hold our black boxes so to speak, that is a design task which he performs so you can call him a design draughtsman. In terms of wiring, the inter-facing wiring *we tell* them [i.e. circuit draughtsmen] what to [do].

Bill: We also tell them which racks to put in, and which boxes to put in.

John: That's right! Basically the overall structural task is ours.

The design engineers evaluated others by the technical content of their job in addition to their place in the flow of instructions. John Mulvey made this observation about planning engineers:

> Planning deals with the generation of paper work for the dissemination of information to production . . . You have to have a certain technical background to be able to do it and a certain *amount* of experience . . . but the technical content of their work is a lot lower than the technical content of my own work.

The designer's perception of the functions performed by 'subordinate' technical workers helps explain why technical innovation which will obviously have negative consequences, can be pushed through. Positive evaluations of technical change were also supported by economic ideas related to the need to 'maintain market position', or substitute for the 'shortage of skilled labour'. Noble (1979) has argued that technical choices are always social in nature and technical imperatives do not override social ones. The designers saw technical change largely in straight capitalist terms of staying in the field, by keeping up with or ahead of the firm's competitors. 'Competition', 'profit', 'efficiency' were part of the language they used to explain the necessity of technical change. There was no sense of engineering and capitalist logics being oppositional alternatives. The designers were wage labourers paid by capital to improve the profitability, efficiency and performance of BAe. The 'benevolent technocracy' of Veblen (1923) was nowhere in sight. Design engineers are at one level the innovative vanguard of the industrial bourgeoisie. They pioneer new products, new methods of production and apply and modify new techniques. In fact, the old distinction between research, development and design has become blurred and a precise definition of the latter two functions is hard to sustain. The designers I interviewed concentrated their attention on translating innovations into practice and applying tested systems to new areas. In earlier chapters I discussed some of the changes taking place in the design of aircraft, outlining the way specialisation had narrowed the designers' overall knowledge of a system. However, specialisation has not simply produced a narrowing of technical conceptualisation, it has also been widely argued that *British* engineers have had their career position in management held back by a narrow attention to technique (Lazonick, 1985). Other writers, notably Armstrong (1984), have stressed the inherently open access of engineering technique, which, unlike law or medicine, is subject to a wider evaluation by non-engineers. A problem with Armstrong's attention to the abstract labour process of engineering is that it does not explain international variations in the standing of engineers. Lazonick (1985), in a comparison of British and American management education, has argued that the inevitable technical specialisation of monopoly capitalism reduces the broader vision of production and demands integration through co-ordinative and global functions of general management. While American corporations structured the education system to produce specialists and corporate career structures to turn them into coordinators, British capital left the engineer a specialist and drew off elite education institutions for the global functionaries.

In Britain industrial specialisation of engineers along product and discipline lines has fragmented the global interests of engineers. This reflects the absence of state control in the British economy, early industrialisation and the patronage exercised by employers over their engineers. Watson (1975), in a detailed historical portrait of the development of engineering institutions has revealed how rivalry between the early starters, the Civils and Mechanicals, produced a pattern of institutional fragmentation as new bodies proliferated in the 19th and 20th centuries without a global voice.

The Design of Work

It has been argued that designing work organisation is a
social process, in that jobs are not *naturally* given, but created
(Shaiken, 1984). Posing the question of design in this way, is
the equivalent of saying that everything is social. The
important thing to establish is the constraints and choices
available to groups involved in work design. Such constraints
as technology, product and production processes are well
known. A recent study of changes in work organisation in a
food factory by the author, revealed how the design
parameters of high-volume, low-skill production shaped the
perspectives of engineers, managers and workers alike (Smith,
Child and Rowlinson, 1987). In aerospace, with its different
skill structure, product and production requirements, choices
over work design existed in different parameters. It is within
the skilled, flexible traditions of aerospace that I look at the
issue of computer technology, specifically CAD. Not surpris-
ingly some of the designers see these traditions continuing
with CAD, while others see a break with existing occupational
structures. This section explores some of the social choices
designers see as being built into CAD.

I was concerned to discover how far engineers involved
in process design thought they incorporated conceptions of
hierarchy and authority into their designs and to what extent
social considerations entered their consciousness relative to
notions of engineering rationality and efficiency (Cooley,
1980; Noble, 1979; Rosenbrock, 1981). Figure 5.1 represents
Noble's model of the role of the 'social' in the design process.

Noble argues that the separation of technical and social
imperatives and interests is really a myth:

> In all technical work there is always a tension between
> technical and social determinants. In actuality, technical
> imperatives define only what is possible, not what is
> necessary; what can be done, not what must be done. The
> latter decisions are social in nature.

He lists three mediating social processes that filter the
outcome of a given technology. These are:

Figure 5.1 *The design process*

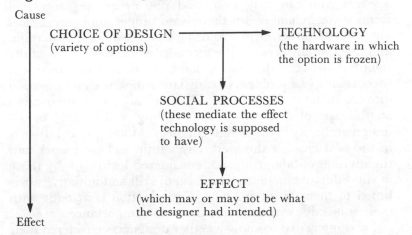

Cause

CHOICE OF DESIGN ⟶ TECHNOLOGY
(variety of options) (the hardware in which
the option is frozen)

SOCIAL PROCESSES
(these mediate the effect
technology is supposed
to have)

EFFECT
(which may or may not be what
the designer had intended)

Effect

1. The redesign of the physical technology after trial;
2. 'Adaptations' of the workers to the technology;
3. The struggle against the technology by the workers.

Noble argues that it is through these social moments 'that we find the only point of entry for labour to register in the process of technological development,' (Noble 1979, p. 41). His model applies to manual, clerical and technical workers, although his case studies have been on the design of NC and its impact on manual workers.

It may be possible that workers' struggle exists in all three mediating sequences listed by Noble, not simply in stage three, when there is overt individual or collective resistance to a piece of technology. Redesign is often a result of worker resistance, adaptation is never a stable process. Although Noble is correct to emphasise the way design intentions, which attempt to control and subordinate the workers to the rhythm and pace of the machine, are frozen in the hardware of technology. But he over-plays the monopolisation of knowledge held by designers. Following Braverman (1974), who follows too closely the intention of Taylorism and not its actual practice, Noble assumes that design engineers possess a store of knowledge and information which has been expropriated from the direct producers over the decades and accumulated into an objective power which is wielded over workers who can only *react*, and not *act* in the process of technological change. But there is no 'single store of technical knowledge', rather formal and informal flows of information, and differential access to the formal system. Regardless of the tightness between the conception of work and its execution, there is always a problem of translation of written information into manufactured products. That gap allows for innovation on the part of those who are 'formally' subordinate to the design authority of the design engineer. Moreover, as I discuss in the next chapter the hierarchy within technical work and the division of labour are not considered legitimate by those in subordinate functions. The level of skill and initiative attributed to them by their place in production is at odds with their subjective evaluation of their own importance.

I was interested to know whether designers considered their design work in social terms. That is, whether they saw their job as a technique, a means to an end; or whether, as members of the same union as those below them, they in any way believed their actions would degrade the work of their fellow trade unionists. As far as those management members of TASS were concerned, technical change, and their role within it, was inevitably good, because it relieved the lower technical grades of boring work. But what of non-managerial designers, how did they see the consequences of their work?

I interviewed two young avionics designers with different analyses of the role of the design. Bill Sweeney had worked with a manager on the computerisation of design and was very keen on technical change. When I interviewed him he had just returned from a TASS weekend education school on new technology which I had also attended. The school left me with the impression of TASS acceptance of technical change, but its determination to 'control' the introduction of new systems. Sweeney was a recent member of TASS and had had his faith in the positive importance of new technology unnerved by the school, although he was still convinced of the need for new technology. John Mulvey was the TASS representative in avionics. Both came from working-class backgrounds and entered design engineering after graduating. John was more trade union conscious and had recruited Bill into TASS when Bill would have preferred to have been in UKAPE had they had bargaining rights. Both were critical of the management structure at Filton, and believed the company to be slow in introducing new technology. John was aware that the effect of their work as designers would be to deskill draughtsmen and planners. Bill did not agree:

> *Bill:* The design motive is merely to produce a better product, not to produce something that will deskill the operator and put him in his place. That comes about, but it's not the driving force, at least I hope that's not the driving force. I'm probably being terribly naïve about that.
>
> *John:* In any interface between a machine and a human being, obviously at one end of that someone has written the instruction 'Do this' somewhere and the bloke has to follow. It is guiding the operator, therefore it must be very difficult in writing the software for that machine not to impose your view of society in some way. Even though it's a very logical process and you're trying to apply it to a whole set of procedures which are very logical. Still in the end . . . you're writing it to control somebody else, making them do what you want them to do.
>
> *Bill:* I'm sorry but that goes against what engineering is about, certainly in terms of CAD. As far as I saw my job in CAD, and I'm not a draughtsman so I don't see the draughtsman's point of view, but what I wanted to do was give the draughtsman a tool. I wanted to give him a tool that he could use and would like using. I didn't want to give him an authoritarian tool that said: 'Do this!' When I design I ask, well 'What does he do naturally? What's easy for him to do? Let the bloke drive the machine the way he wants to! And let the machine be subservient'.
>
> *John:* But you're trying to interpret *his* way of thinking.
>
> *Bill:* Yes, and that's what you should do.
>
> *John:* The trouble is that some people do like doing the little drawings and things.
>
> *Bill:* Well, yes I know.

John: [with irony] But that's a disposable skill?
Bill: That's a disposable skill, yes [laughter].

We can see from Bill Sweeney's remarks that at one level he believes he is designing in order to give the draughtsmen greater freedom. He did not want to believe that his designs are used to subordinate other technical workers to the computer. And yet, when pressed, it is clear that the designer will be part of the process of eliminating so-called 'non essential design work', the 'mechanical' side of draughtsmanship. Mulvey recognises that although the designer denigrates drawing, the draughtsman does not. Sweeney, in one sense, embodies those features of the 'benevolent technocrat' described by Elliott and Elliott (1976). He wants to aid production, for efficiency's sake, in the interests of 'progress' and does not wish to consider the negative consequences of his job as a designer. Hence, he invents a scenario of increased freedom and initiatives for the draughtsman, although recognising that this is 'cloud cuckoo land'.

There were pressures on designers to design 'as simply as possible' to account for the productivity of others. But it is also part of engineering practice under commodity production that methods should be standardised and instructions clear, precise and readily understood. Ambiguity in method – that which allowed the use of choice or initiative by draughtsmen – was deemed expensive and unnecessary. Designers did not need to think that they were actively de-skilling other workers, they were simply following engineering practice, itself invested with Taylorian ideology (Cooley, 1980). Their own assessment of the skills of draughtsmanship allowed them to justify the removal of what could be described as non-essential. This ideology of engineering practice distances them from the real consequences of their actions, although those in non-managerial positions with strong contacts with other technical workers are not unaware of these consequences.

Technical Change: Designers, Management and Corporatism

Technical change is not planned under capitalism as a system. It may be rational within the firm, but chaotic within the system as a whole. But even within the firm there is no single logical set of criteria for introducing new machinery. There is always a choice of technical alternatives and therefore there is always disagreement amongst designers, and between designers and managers about what is appropriate to a particular task. Melman (1981) has noted this choice:

> Designers are always confronted with an array of possible materials and degrees of precision for obtaining desired properties in machine components . . . Production managers must select from among production methods alternatives that are readily ranked by capital intensity, capital productivity, and total unit cost.
>
> (Melman, 1981, p. 325).

In the aerospace industry, designers' prejudices about the selection of particular materials, procedures and techniques are frequently bound up with their working experience on one aircraft, or with one airframe manufacturer. Different companies have their own entrenched design custom and practice and a lot of the conflicts between designers at BAe. reflected the 'school of design' or company, in which a designer had been trained. A second series of design prejudices stems from the place the designer occupied in the hierarchy of the firm. A manager was usually able to veto the level of initiative exercised by subordinate designers. Their argument may be technical, but rank played a major role in determining the parameters of debate and even outcomes.

Technical change in the aerospace industry is not always geared towards saving costs by conventional techniques for cheapening the commodity. The cost-plus funding of the industry lifts it, to some extent, out of the commercial pressures of the market place. Therefore there are more experiments, a greater degree of choice in materials, techniques and machines, and the criteria of cheapness in materials and machines, is not always applicable on government contracts. Moreover, the requirements of flight and military considerations frequently meant that quality, rather than cheapness of parts, was a major purchasing principle.

Many of the designers at Filton had entered during the *Concorde* programme from more commercially-orientated airframe companies and brought with them the expectations of commercial designers. *Concorde* was widely regarded as an 'open cheque book' project in technical and manual areas. This did not mean there was not an intense pressure of work pace for both technical and manual workers, but it did mean there was an absence of cost consciousness, especially in areas of design where a lot of experimentation took place that had no practical consequences. John Pill had come from A. V. Roe and had brought with him a 'cost consciousness' that provided the background for a series of conflicts with management about choices of technical designs and materials. 'Old fashioned management' and 'progressive designers' were positions that characterised some of the conflicts between the two groups at Filton. For example, John Pill had argued with middle management that solid state sensing switches should be fitted to *Concorde* instead of micro-switches which he claimed were larger, heavier and more expensive. He was told that the electrical design department had already tried this equipment for opening and closing the undercarriage on Concorde, and had found it inadequate. John Pill insisted that they had been of a different order to the ones he was proposing, but he:

Couldn't get anything out of them. So I then went to a great deal of trouble and found a current list of every American aircraft that was fitting sensory switches. Still nothing doing. I then got hold of a document that said Sud-Aviation were evaluating these sensing switches with a view to putting them onto *Concorde* and the *Airbus*. Still wouldn't budge. Finally I got a document that said British United Airways were in the process of replacing all the undercarriage micro switches on their *Britannias* with solid state micro switches and my boss wouldn't budge, and the

Britannia was his bible. After that I gave up. I gave up in disgust . . . It's just old fashioned thinking.

This view of management as 'old fashioned', 'slow to change' was echoed by all the designers and a lot of the other technical staff I interviewed, e.g. Mac Smith:

Do you want a personal view of management? Bloody old fashioned . . . It is very, very slow to change . . . They are not au fait with how things could be done if we used new techniques. Some of them don't even want to learn new techniques.

It is often assumed in the literature on new technology and deskilling, that managers are unreservedly in favour of change, especially change that enhances their power and control at the expense of skilled labour. From my research at Filton, I found this model of management-led or inspired technical change, unrealistic. Design engineers were frequently at odds with management about the necessity for changes. Managers often stood in the way of new methods and techniques in the interests of peace in their department. Unlike 'conservative' managers, design engineers personified that condition of agitated dynamism central to capitalism, which often meant battles with senior management. Much of the conflict designers experienced was with management refusing to authorise technical changes. The requirement of managerial approval for new processes tended to mean designers had to legitimate technology, to sell their ideas or the advantages of buying-in new technologies. The deskilling debate frequently underplays the division between the sellers of new technology and the buyers. The rationale adopted by the sellers of new machinery will frequently be different from the rationale adopted by those who seek to convince a reluctant management of the necessity for buying such equipment. NC and CAD are usually sold on the strength of their capacity to reduce lead time, save on labour, cheapen labour costs, increase work tempo, and replace skilled operators or draughtsmen by unskilled or less qualified staff. However, designers seeking to buy in such equipment may have to emphasise the opposite features, i.e. how the machinery enhances skill, gives the draughtsmen greater freedom, etc. in order to justify to local management that such machinery will not upset industrial relations. If a technical manager was dealing with the senior management, then saving labour may also appear as a rationale. Baldry and Connolly (1984) in their study of computer aided design in seven Scottish engineering companies, found evidence of a variety of rationales used by designers to justify the introduction of CAD. They also noted the disparity between claims made by equipment suppliers on reducing labour, and the fact that none of the firms they examined intended to reduce labour, although one manager said:

> I tell . . . the directors that it'll save on labour costs in order to get the money for the equipment. *That's the only thing the Board understands.* But I've no intention of getting rid of any of my people. I need them all. (emphasis added)
> (Baldry and Connolly, 1984, p. 13)

The importance of buyer-seller relations in explaining the different rationales for technology, has been noted by Noble (1979), Shaiken (1984) and Smith *et al.* (1987). Also of importance are internal company rules over capital expenditure, the degree of centralisation or autonomy exercised by managers or engineers in the purchase of machinery. These, together with the dominant company strategy governing variable and fixed capital ratios, provide important contextual variations which qualify notions of the inherent consequences of technology at work.

It is one of the myths of the debate on new technology that the application of new systems within the firm marches along at an inexorable pace. What I found at Filton was that new machines were frequently introduced on the advice of perhaps one designer and sold off when that designer left the company. In the electrical planning department a mini-computer stood idle for eighteen months because TASS approval had not been sought before purchase. In other areas draughting equipment stood under-utilised because of changes in demand or because projected demand was never forthcoming. The high rate of obsolescence in the high technology area means under-utilised machines are an expensive waste. The fact that draughtsmen in a tool design department referred to an automatic draughting machine as the 'white elephant' indicates their scathing assessments of the company's competence to introduce useful technology.

It is clear from my interviews with design engineers that their relationship with management was of a different order to that of other technical staff. Designers were not passively reacting to technical change, they were actively promoting it, advising management, and developing new applications for existing systems. The designers were often adaptive to technical change because they did not experience it as an external imposition, but as something they had struggled to see developed. They were all in favour of CAD. Their positions as innovators and their perspective on industrial relations often went together. Their identification was frequently with 'the company' not management or other technical or manual workers. It appeared to them that they were often the only group to be thinking about the interests of 'the company'; while management and the unions were merely squabbling between each other. This corporate identity gave them a sense of distance from both sides.

However, not all designers expressed this view and a corporate consciousness existed alongside a trade union consciousness. Trade union propaganda could feed into this 'corporate consciousness' by emphasising the need for modernisation, capital investment and a recognition of the status of engineers.

A major concern of designers was the lack of investment in BAe and British engineering as a whole. This belief united active TASS members and anti-union designers, which signifies the corporate nature of the demand that TASS has been making above all others since the latter part of the 1970s. Bill Sweeney, an avionics designer, thought investment in new technology a corporate goal for the benefit of both unions and management.

At the moment they're at loggerheads, one group is continually trying to beat the other group down and vice

versa . . . [Management] are so bloody backward and
sleepy that they ain't woken up to the technological age. I
don't go along with the idea of continuing to beat your
head against a brick wall. It used to have to be like that,
but I don't think it does now. There's too much at stake
on both sides.

The logic of Bill Sweeney's argument was that increased
investment would increase wages or 'should do' if management 'woke up to the new technological age'. Therefore
workers and managers should be concerned with the
corporate goals of increasing investment in plant and putting
aside other grievances. There was no sense in which this
investment would threaten his position, as he saw changes
occurring downstream, in the work of the planner and
draughtsman, not in his own area. He considered the 'squab-
bles' between unions and managers to stand in the way of
the *real* job of both sides which was *making* airframes. This
argument is a familiar one and not the preserve of designers
alone. John Mulvey saw an inherent conflict between management and workers, while subscribing to the ideology of corporatism promoted by Sweeney. Mac Smith, another designer,
had similar views to Sweeney's:

Mac: I'm glad to see dogma in trade unionism go.
Chris: How do you mean?
Mac: Well the cloth capped unionist. And, for that matter,
the pin-striped trousers and black jacketed engineer.
We are all part of a whole to produce something.
One cannot exist without the other.

The need for unity between management and workers, the
need for *better communication* between the shop floor and technical staff was expressed by management designers in strong
human relations terms. John Cockran, one of the 'old school'
of design engineers who had been through the shops, through
the drawing office and into design, used the rhetoric of the
'team', the 'big family' in his approach to the shop floor. He
was an active member of the TASS management branch and
led the support for a No. 3. Branch wages dispute by calling

for, and getting, a five pound levy of all TASS management members.

> It's a partnership that's not emphasised enough. I can go out on to the shop floor and talk to the operators, and I can talk to the supervision and I'm no snob, I enjoy talking to them. Having been through that path myself I know what their world is like. But there are other people who wouldn't talk to a man with a spanner or a screwdriver in his hand and that's wrong.

Cockran's view of the corporate factory meant one skilled group of workers was as functionally important as another:

> A man on the shop floor, the operator on the lathe, *if he's an 'A' rate man* he is capable of using his expertise which is of no less an importance than the expertise of the qualified engineer. I see no difference between the skilled worker and the professional engineer.

This craft-consciousness produced an egalitarianism that was not unusual in the design engineers I interviewed. John Pill echoed the same sentiments and felt betrayed by TASS, because it had diluted its former craft base by allowing non-technical staff to join. However, there was also an insistence that the skills of the designer, his expertise were under-valued relative to his counterpart in the US or France or Germany. There was a clear pecking order to this functional interdependence with the designer at the top, and the manual workers at the bottom. With Cockran, functional interdependence assumed a radical craft equality, although behind that ideology Cockran knew where he preferred to work, and was aware of the distance his ideological appeals had to bridge. Cogan, a younger professional engineer who had entered design engineering after university, applied no moral evaluation to the functional interdependence between designer, draughtsman and operator:

> They work in conjunction with each other, they are closely allied, they have two different roles to play and they play

them separately, and they are paid separately of course. A technician has a more practical approach than an engineer, and yet a more academic approach than the man on the shop floor.

In Britain – because of the legacy of craftism and fragmentation of engineering institutes mentioned earlier – interdependencies persisted as a strong ideology. Professional elitism, autonomy and the disdain for manual labour, while not strong currents, existed more amongst graduate engineers than craft entrants. This had obtained an organisational expression through UKAPE, which was concentrated amongst non-managerial, graduate engineers. UKAPE emerged in the late 1960s in response to this new professionalism amongst the growing dominance of *graduate* engineers at the higher end of the technical division of labour. However, increasing educational segmentation amongst technical workers did not sustain organisational segmentation. UKAPE failed to establish a national voice, thanks mainly to union opposition, but also to UKAPE's ambiguous conception of engineers as salaried staff, employers and professionals.

It is easy to see how a craft consciousness can co-exist with a professional elitism, a sense of autonomy and separateness that Cogan outlines. Both managers adopted different styles of management which again reflected their respective craftism and elitism – Cockran a 'muck-in-with-the-men' style, and Cogan an 'each-to-his-own' style. Both were formally united around improving the wages of design engineers, but there was nothing inconsistent in that. I have discussed elsewhere the competition between the professional engineers' trade union (UKAPE) and TASS for design engineers and shown that while the dividing line between craft protection and professional elitism is very thin, it is very important, (Smith 1986). At present it is a line that influences the potential involvement of higher technical staff in the labour movement and the struggles of other workers.

Alongside changes in the pattern of entry into technical work, developments in new technology have broken the established knowledge bases between the technical department and the shop floor. How this has affected designers themselves is the subject of the next section.

Computer Aided Design and the Position of the Design Engineer

Recent surveys all indicate that the shortage of technical labour was either a cause or contextual feature of the introduction of CAD in Britain (Arnold, 1981; IDS, 1982; Arnold and Senker, 1982). While the majority of writers accept skill shortage as a given fact, most technical workers I interviewed saw this situation in more active terms, pointing to the decline in apprenticeships, poor wages and redundancies in the industry as creating an artificial scarcity. Cooley claims that the growth of graduate engineers paralleled the decline in the traditional 7-year apprenticeship for designers, which in addition to reinforcing the hierarchical divisions discussed in this chapter, did not actually keep pace with the demand for technical workers (Rader and Wingert, 1981, p. 13). That this growth coincided in Britain with the rise in militancy amongst traditional technical workers may also explain the employers' new-found enthusiasm for indirect channels of training. Although the existence of such a strategy may be difficult to prove, I encountered evidence from Rolls-Royce, BAe, C. A. Parsons and Westland Helicopters of employers encouraging the development of managerial status amongst engineers in an attempt to block TASS recruitment. There is also evidence of the increased use of graduate engineers in sectors of engineering where the 'technical demands' are lower, to speed up the adoption of CAD. Wrench and Stanley (1984) show that at BL in Birmingham, TASS believed 'the company had brought in all these graduates (described as being "very different" from the traditional design staff) to undermine the solidarity of the membership' in resisting shift-working (Wrench and Stanley, 1984, p. 17).

Arnold and Senker (1982) see labour shortage together with the desire to reduce lead time between design and production, and the ability to prepare tender documents faster and cheaper, as primary reasons for introducing CAD. Baldry and Connolly (1984) in an examination of seven CAD-user companies in Scotland, found that personnel management emphasised the possibility for higher productivity, whilst drawing office management mentioned labour shortage and improvements in quality and accuracy as the key reasons for bringing in CAD. Managers at Filton gave similar reasons and also insisted that there would be no immediate loss of jobs although long term prospects were different (Rader and Wingert, 1981, p. 28). It was estimated by one engineer in electrical design that the application of CAD would change the ratio of designers to draughtsmen from 1:9 to 1:3, but such estimates are notoriously inaccurate and depend on the industry and degree of capital utilisation.

Baldry and Connolly (1984) argue that CAD has five major applications: as a design tool for interactive designing: automatic drawing; as a mathematical instrument for complex calculations; as an information base on materials, components etc; and as a link with Computer Aided Manufacture (CAM) to develop automatic manufacturing. It is really only with the advent of computer aided graphics that CAD came into its own. Like other computer based systems, CAD was developed for military purposes and received its first British industrial application in the aircraft industry in 1953. It obtained State support through the establishment of the CAD Centre at Cambridge in 1969. At Filton, the new generation CAD was not in use during my research period although there was some experimental equipment and a few older automatic drawing boards. Design management were nevertheless preparing to introduce CAD. Alan Cogan, a manager negotiating with TASS on CAD told me:

> Because they have been consulted and they are aware of our shortfalls in engineers and the advantages it will bring, I don't anticipate any resistance from people in the design office.

Although CAD programmes had been in existence from the 1960s, it was not until the late 1970s that employers began to introduce the technology on any significant scale. This reflects the shortage of engineers, created through low pay and the reduction in apprenticeship in the late 1960s, but also the new industrial relations climate that meant employers could introduce the equipment on their terms. In 1970 TASS successfully resisted the imposition of CAD at Rolls-Royce Bristol, on terms that challenged the traditional conditions of technical staff. Fundamental to management's aim was to get the maximum use from the equipment through lengthening the working day of design staff by shift systems. Designers associated with earlier generations of CAD, or strictly speaking automatic draughting equipment, wanted to see shiftworking, but the 'climate' (amongst technical managers and staff) did not favour this 'extreme' position. John Pill belonged to an earlier generation of designers who had attempted to get the company to buy-in automatic drawing equipment. These machines were new to Britain and John Pill had helped pioneer their introduction in Britain:

John: They were a new thing that I brought into this country, well I brought it in in conjunction with BAC.

Chris: How long ago was that?

John: Oh, that's going back to the 1960s. I had seen these machines in operation before I came to Bristol. It was always my contention that to get the best possible results out of them, and to get them down to the lowest cost per single drawing, two shifts were advisable. I couldn't convince anyone of that so consequently the machines were used seven and a half hours a day and they were idle for the rest of the time, which, to my mind, was basically wrong. The same machines were being used twenty four hours a day over in the States.

This awareness of international conditions of labour productivity, created in part by the international labour market for engineers, did not mean that these conditions could be straightforwardly transplanted into the unionised drawing offices in Britain. Baldry and Connolly (1984, p. 17) quoted one manager who said he lay 'awake at night thinking about the computer standing there doing nothing'. No other non-managerial technical workers I interviewed, except Pill, were in favour of shift working, and if a shift system was a condition of getting the full benefit of this equipment, it is not hard to see why the machinery was eventually scrapped. In favour or not, by the early 1980s employers were pushing through CAD shift working agreements. One study noted that:

> most employers want either shiftworking or some other means of extending the working hours of those who operate CAD. The main reason for this is to increase the utilisation of the expensive equipment.
>
> (IDS, 1982, p. 6)

While the ability of workers to resist the imposition of CAD was a central constraint on management obtaining the most exploitative utilisation of the machinery, there were also contextual or processual influences at work in Filton. A younger engineer who had worked with CAD in the States and was preparing the ground for its introduction at Bristol explained the company's slowness in these terms:

> Well, first of all, I think they were waiting to see how effective the system would be. Boeing have proven it, so have all the other big companies, McDonnell Douglas, Lockheed. So there is no longer a risk involved in going into new technology, because it is no longer new technology, it's at least seven or eight years old. Secondly, this country has been financially bankrupt in new investment . . . If you look on the continent, Aerospatiale and Snilma have already purchased these systems and are about to work on them, *so the message is finally getting through*. I have a document here which is dated 1972, which was when I was working with Lockheed, Georgia. That document was compiled in the late '60s and early '70s. And they were using the computer to a very effective degree then. O.K. they didn't use all the graphics, now they've gone into the graphics of it as well and, of course, it is a very formidable package. But even at that stage they were using the computer for job control,

for material ordering, and material movement, and that was a long time ago and everything's moved on since then.

Given the absence of CAD on any scale at Filton, I was not able to assess the changes the new technology had introduced. However those engaged with experimental equipment or past users in other companies, offered judgements generally favourable to a widespread increase in CAD. Managerial and non-managerial designers generally highlighted the benefits of further computerisation in the design area. It is not possible to separate the effects of CAD on the designer, without examining changes in the work of technical staff intermediate to design and production. Managers typically viewed CAD as speeding up design decisions by increasing the autonomy of the designer, as he interacts with the computer rather than other workers. They had a view of the technology as liberatory. John Cogan, an electrical designer:

> With the old system you had a design engineer produce a diagram, and when that diagram was finished it was issued to the planning and production engineering departments . . . Now with the new system these intermediate stages will be eliminated, largely, because once the design engineer inputs the original scheme onto the computer, he will have automatically created a data base which will provide him with all the answers he wants.

And an avionics manager, who welcomed the elimination of planning and production engineering functions, was convinced that this would not intensify the labour of designers:

> I don't think that it's a valid argument to say that CAD will increase the work rate. It will bring about a set of conditions, if it's organised properly and administered properly, which allow the interplay of ideas to take place far more freely and therefore it can only be a good thing.

Others also argued against intensification:

Alan: The work pace will increase, the work load will not. Because the work will be simpler by the aid of the computer, so that the output would be increased. The performance will increase, but the actual work load of the individual will not.

Chris: But what about the quality of the working day, the stresses and strains, do you see them increasing?

Alan: If handled properly, it will enable the design engineer more time to think, more time to make good decisions, more time to verify his design and that cannot be bad. I'm biased! I'm for the CAD system.

Cooley (1972), analysing the role of machinery under capitalist relations of production, and after discussing the fate of craftsmen under the impact of NC machines, views the intensification of designers' work as inseparable from the introduction of CAD under current capitalist conditions:

> The rate at which they [designers] will be required to make decisions continues to increase all the time. In the past the freedom to walk about to a library to gain reference material was almost a therapeutic necessity. The opportunities to discuss design problems with one's colleagues often resulted in a useful cross-fertilisation of ideas and in a resultant better design. As more and more interactive systems are evolved and software packages built up for them, man's knowledge will be absorbed from him at an ever increasing rate and stored in the system.
>
> (Cooley, 1972, pp. 32–3)

An illustration of this strain was given to me by one designer, Mac Smith, concerned with CAD and its relationship to Numerical Control. He worked in a small unit called the Numerical Geometry Group and was very much in favour of CAD, as were all the designers. Nevertheless he supported Cooley's assessment of the computerisation of design intensifying the working day:

Mac: I think there is more mental strain because you don't get the quiet periods. If you produce a drawing, there

> are routine and mediocre parts, which you have to do anyway, so there's a quiet time where the stress is minimal. Now, being specialists, you find that the stress is there, the mental stress is there practically the whole working day.

Rader (1982, p. 173) encountered two managerial strategies in his examination of the organisation of CAD facilities within the firm. In the first, the design staff controlled CAD, and in the other, specialist CAD functions were created. For the individual designer specialisation may change the working day in ways suggested by Mac Smith. It could also lead, given a cheapening of fixed capital, to the subcontracting of CAD design out of the firm and a new division between specialist and non-specialist designers.

Lee (1986), in a study of information technology in some West Midlands manufacturing companies, found some evidence of the buying-in of expertise from small, specialist software houses, as an alternative to in-house systems departments. However, for design, the stress was still on internal developments because of the absence of ready-made programmes and the need to integrate design and production. Baldry and Connolly found a definite trend towards specialisation within design offices. Against the desire of TASS to ensure that specialisation did not occur, their studies revealed that in most firms CAD training was not open to all, and even where it was, certain individuals tended to operate the machinery more than others. They contrasted what they described as the social cohesiveness of the Drawing Office, its light open layout and solidaristic values, with the small, dark computer rooms which housed fewer individuals and were operated by shifts of workers:

> two thirds said they missed some aspect of the traditional drawing board work, mentioning specialisation among draughtsmen (particularly mentioned by older men), identification with the drawing and the general satisfaction of putting your name on a good piece of work.
>
> (Baldry and Connolly, 1984, p. 19)

One of the big changes for the draughtsmen they studied was loss of 'ownership' over his drawing, as CAD permitted groups of draughtsmen to work on more than one drawing. Although their study concentrated on draughtsmen and not designers, their findings on the movement towards specialisation and a change in the social arrangements and conditions has parallels with trends at Filton. The Avionics Design room, the NC Geometry group and the computer room adjacent to the NC Programming department, all conformed to their description of small, capital-intensive units. However, at Filton there was considerable movement between the two environments, and resistance to both shift working and specialisation.

Designers demanded more fixed capital and the linking of CAD to NC and CAD–CAM to 'close' the gap between design and production by eliminating the labour links in production between the two areas. Given what the designers considered to be backward management, it was they who sponsored increasing the introduction and spread of CAD. The success a design engineer has in convincing management to accept his innovation, process or new piece of technological hardware, will depend on the implications of that technology. It will be dependent on management's willingness to rationalise and capitalise and on the pressures they feel from the market place.

Designers did not advocate capital investment and technological change to consciously subordinate and control the labour of other workers. They generally lacked an explicit production orientation. Nevertheless, they operated within an engineering paradigm (Rosenbrock, 1981) in which standardisation, simplification and efficiency of methods, limited the freedom of others. Noble (1977) has described this well:

> Technical and capitalist imperatives were blended in the person of the engineer and converged in his work, engineering. The engineer designed his machines with profit and reduced labour costs as well as the quality and quantity of product in mind, and with the aim of transmitting management authority into the work process (usually described merely as a 'transfer of skill' from craftsman to machine).

As the father of modern management, the engineer simply extended his efforts beyond the machinery for the same purposes.

(Noble, 1977, pp. 257–60)

The younger designers maintained a strong favourable self-image through the belief that they were 'freeing' others from routine work, although this widespread myth was not adhered to without contradictions and uncertainties. It is these ambiguities that Cooley has sought to exploit through notions of 'alternative products' or 'socially useful products' discussed in Chapter One. That the engineer's position within the capitalist relations of production permits these openings, is evidence that their class position is not straightforwardly wedded to the interests of unfettered capital accumulation for the benefit of the industrial bourgeoisie. They serve these interests because they are paid to but also through 'educated habit, ideological blindness to alternatives, social constraints (and) conscious choice' (Noble, 1977, p. 257). At BAe the chief contradiction in their design perspective was between civilian and military products (something at the heart of the Lucas Plan as well) and not between a proletarian and bourgeois design menu. Without a major assault on the capitalist division of labour and training of engineers and manual workers (Braverman, 1974, p. 443), it is hard to see how this could be any different. Craftism, which had been partially sustained by employers and the State as a barrier to the engineering institutes (Whalley, 1982; Armstrong, 1984; Smith, 1985) had maintained a more fluid social relationship between engineers and manual workers in Britain. This has made the class relations between the two groups more ambiguous in Britain than elsewhere. However, this situation began to break up in the 1960s with the growth of graduate engineers who bypassed the craft route. This formalised the hierarchy in technical labour and began in the 1970s to expose the class divisions within the membership of trade unions that recruited technicians and engineers, for instance TASS (Smith, 1986).

Conclusion

In his 1972 book on CAD, Cooley argued that the introduction of high capital equipment into the design area would 'proletarianise design staff and increase their strike power' (Cooley, 1972, p. 37).

By design staff, Cooley includes draughtsmen and design engineers. This absence of differentiation reflects Cooley's own craftism, as well as the less educationally divided nature of technical work in the late 1960s. I have already indicated how graduate barriers have grown and blocked the flow of draughtsmen into certain design areas. All the young designers at Filton were graduates. I would therefore wish to differentiate where Cooley seeks to integrate. Clearly draughtsmen as productive wage labourers, and active trade unionists, have been members of the industrial proletariat since the 1920s. Designers on the other hand have traditionally resisted union advances. Their employment in small numbers, their professional and managerial aspirations and autonomous conditions of work, have meant that they occupy a position as the technical advance-guard for the industrial bourgeoisie. How can CAD be said to 'proletarianise' them? The obviously mechanical nature of such an equation is surprising, considering Cooley has elsewhere attacked uncritical approaches to science and technology.

The application of high technology to the design function is an attempt by capital to reduce the number of draughtsmen and speed up the time-lag between design and production. One effect of this is to re-organise the intermediate technical occupations between the designer and shop floor operator. In assessing the effect of interactive technologies on their autonomy and working conditions, the six design engineers considered CAD would enhance their freedom on the job. It should be stressed, however, that no CAD system was fully operational in Filton during my interviews, and so these were based on the experience of the designers working on experimental systems or their experience in other companies. Those who had worked on experimental models described increased mental strain arising from an intensification of work, and this has been seen as a feature of design work with CAD (Baldry and Connolly, 1984). But others did not anticipate these changes and welcomed the *independence* the computer would give them; they could call up information rather than having to go and see a particular technical worker. CAD was not seen as a threat, but a necessity. However computerisation has facilitated checks on the performance and cost benefit of the design function, but would this, of itself, lead to proletarianisation? I asked a design engineer who had worked in the design area of BAe up until 1970, before leaving for N.E.I. Parsons, if new technology would change the class position of designers:

I don't think it's a matter of new technology as such, I think it's more a matter of the scale of technical involvement, the scale of employment of professional engineers. If you've got two hundred graduate engineers scattered in a hundred factories, they're much more likely to be part of management, part of capital. *They would expect to keep things going in a dispute.* But if two hundred graduate engineers are in one plant, then the attitude of management becomes quite different and the attitude of the engineers becomes quite different. And with a highly technical product you need engineers, well qualified draughtsmen in bulk, you cannot do it with ones and twos any more. And I think that's the difference between now and the earlier part of the century . . . You find that your technical staff are being treated as workers. Management adopts exactly the same attitude towards design engineers, they've become a unit of production.

This 'massification' of the job conditions of design engineers opened up the need for them to defend themselves as a group against the company. It did not objectively secure their commitment to the working class. Their grievances were largely to do with pay differentials and the demand for a grading scheme reflecting their desire for clear direction to their career. They did not, on the whole, consider their conditions of labour would be eroded by CAD, and issues of freedom of movement were considered to be organisational rather than technical, that is to do with the style of management rather than technical features of CAD.

There was little pressure on designers or rationale from their work situation to identify their interests with those of manual workers. They had little contact with manual workers and a distant interdependence. Their relationship with technical staff was, as noted earlier, mediated by their evaluation of the 'technical' content of their work and the perception of their creative role. Organisationally, engineers were divided between TASS and UKAPE, but even those in TASS felt swamped by planning engineers, a large section and one that had provided the key leadership positions at Filton. Design engineers had not yet 'found a voice' in Bristol No. 3 Branch as the following conversation indicates:

> *Bill:* No. 3 Branch is predominantly planners. Even if the draughtsmen and designers got together, we wouldn't be able to do things differently, we really haven't got much of a say.
>
> *John:* We don't really exercise our voting right properly. Engineers in general around here haven't really got together.
>
> *Bill:* Because they're apathetic . . .
>
> *John:* They joined the union and assumed it was all going to happen. But without any collective or group emerging that is going to fight the engineers' case nothing's happened.

The designer's relationship with middle management was close. Most of the younger designers, who were not at a managerial level, expected to achieve that status at some time in their careers. But, above middle management there was a distancing based on the perceived backwardness or conservatism of management *vis-à-vis* technical change. There was also a feeling amongst non-managerial designers that all managers were out for the quiet life and were an impediment to technical change. Managerial status was being 'devalued' and used by technical companies that employ a large number of senior design staff as a way of keeping TASS out of the area. The level of specialisation amongst design staff meant their skills were often company or industry specific and their livelihood was completely bound up with large aerospace firms. Many of the older draughtsmen I interviewed, who were hostile to TASS, had been employers and/or managers of small subcontract drawing offices. This route out of the large companies, the opportunity to 'go it alone' did not exist for the highly specialised design engineers, such as avionics designers, and had not been an option for other designers and general technical staff because of the capitalisation costs in the design area. But this was also changing; new technology was permitting spatial decentralisation, pushing management into embracing subcontracting to cut rising overheads and designers' wages (Smith, 1984; Labour Research, July 1984).

There has also been a growth in self-employment, which blocks unionisation. Watson (1975, p. 50) noted that in 1960 only 2 per cent of engineers were in private practice, compared with 33 per cent of principal accountants, 25 per cent of architects, 27 per cent of surveyors and 62 per cent of solicitors. The absence of a client–practitioner relationship for engineers has fostered a bureaucratic identification with a single employer. However, this may be changing. Lee (1986) notes that whilst self-employed and consultant engineers constituted only 2.8 per cent of the membership of the Institute of Electrical Engineers in 1977, this figure had increased to 7.5 per cent by 1985.

One of the TASS Divisional Organisers, reflecting on the difficulty of unionising INMOS workers, said that 'a lot of these new technology firms are very difficult to crack. All the engineers have got a vision of themselves as entrepreneurs and think they're going to make a packet out of it'.

The individualism and autonomy associated with those technical groups who had experienced self employment was, however, in decline during my fieldwork. *Concorde* had both sucked in labour and supported many small subcontractors. The ending of the programme meant the rapid demise of these firms and forced individuals back into the larger firms if they could get back in. Amongst the designers I interviewed, I found a strong ideological commitment to 'the company' or 'progress' or 'efficiency'. They were integrated into the 'logic of profitability' which was considered as part of working as a designer. Their views reflect their experience at Filton and other aerospace firms they had worked in. From this particular experience, and from conversations and interviews with design engineers at BAe Guided Weapons, Lucas Aerospace, Rolls-Royce Bristol, and N.E.I. Parsons, most of what I have here described seems universal to the work of engineers in large, technological companies.

The success of the United Kingdom Association of Professional Engineers (UKAPE) response to the awakening of the professional engineers 'need for a voice', in the early 1970s has varied. Its intrusion into the design field was strongly resisted by TASS nationally and at factory level. I compared the handling of UKAPE at Filton and N.E.I. Parsons and how the influence of different trade union leaderships in the two plants had conditioned the views design engineers had towards UKAPE. Objectively the conditions in the two plants, the aims and aspirations of design engineers were similar, but the trade union response was very different, leaving a different legacy for designers in the two plants. At N.E.I. Parsons, the unionisation of designers into TASS was forced through after a protracted battle with UKAPE in the early 1970s. At BAe Filton the failure to tackle UKAPE as an organisation, meant separation was an open option, allowing a strong body of anti-trade union opinion to develop and weaken TASS organisation in several design departments (Smith, 1986).

I have shown in this chapter and Chapter 2 that design engineers are very removed from manual production workers, and the avenues into design are now predominantly through universities and polytechnics. The ending of the craft tradition at the higher end had not, however, percolated down to middle-grade technical occupations and in the newer computer-based technical jobs. I will now analyse in detail the work relations between technical workers and manual workers and the implications for consciousness and working class unity of these relationships.

6

The Craft Tradition Under Threat: Technical Workers' Relations with Manual Workers

Introduction

My analysis of the class position of middle-range technical staff has emphasised the tremendous importance of the craft tradition in technical work and the close association between skilled manual workers and technical workers. I have rejected any ideas of technical workers belonging to a new middle class, and have said that, through their waged labour, production of surplus value, craft tradition and association with the labour movement, technical workers in British engineering are a section of the working class. In the last few chapters I have indicated the persistence of this craft tradition in the newer as well as the established technical occupations. The two groups that are marginal to this tradition are those at the higher end of technical work for whom the craft tradition has all but ceased, and those in quasi-technical areas in production control. In this chapter I will elaborate on the daily factory relationship between technical staff and manual

192

workers and examine the areas of co-operation and conflict between these two sections of the working class. I am particularly concerned to examine the extent of a control or power relationship between the two groups and the extent to which the 'knowledge' of technical staff dominates manual workers. This is continuing my empirical assessment of Mallet (1975), Gorz (1976), Poulantzas (1975) and Carchedi (1977).

The particular work experience I examine will in part reflect the trade union and political traditions at Filton discussed in Chapter 3. It is difficult to establish in any precise form the weight that should be given to these organisational features. However, from discussion with TASS officials in Bristol, TASS activists at Rolls-Royce (Bristol and Coventry), Lucas Aerospace, and especially N.E.I. Parsons in Newcastle, I am reasonably confident that the relations I describe here are typical of the on-the-job association between technical and manual workers. They reflect the likely relations between the two groups in a large corporation, producing a very 'technical' product. The relationship between the two groups would be different in small-and medium-sized engineering plants, where technical staff would more likely be incorporated into more managerial or supervisory functions. It would also be different in firms producing a less sophisiticated technical product, where technical staff would more likely be in a production control function. Where technical workers are not unionised, where they are a small elite or fraction of the work force, and where they perform supervisory functions their relation to manual workers will be very different. Technical work has this flexibility. It should be remembered, however, that the majority of technical workers work in large units of manufacture. TASS membership reflects this concentration: sixty per cent of members are located in sixty combines.

The Division of Labour in Practice

Technical workers have worked out their own relationship to management and manual workers through their daily work practice, trade union experience and involvement in the labour movement. Although technical workers are placed in definite social relations of production with manual workers, these objective relations are not sufficient to indicate the relationships in process at the factory level. The objective division of labour needs its counterpart, the experience of these relations in the real factory setting.

The apparent monopoly of knowledge held by technical workers and used to exclude and dominate manual labour, was for Poulantzas (1975) the basis for a class divide between the two groups. Braverman (1974), sharing much ground with Poulantzas, saw technical labour as internally divided between those with a proletarian polarisation, draughtsmen for example, and those closer to the bourgeoisie, for instance, qualified engineers. This gave technical labour a degree of duality, with 'one foot in the bourgeoisie and the other in the working class', a point theoretically developed by Carchedi (1977). For Braverman, the potential unification between technical and manual workers was only possible if there was a substantial re-integration in the existing division between mental and manual labour. Gorz (1976) argues a similar position, that a major *ideological* transformation was necessary to secure the support of technical labour for socialism. These writers implicitly project a French or American pattern of training and relationship between technical and manual labour, where qualifications obtained indirectly through higher education institutions heavily structure the labour force. Cooley is the only writer to articulate the craft tradition and under-development of graduate engineers characteristic of British technical labour until the mid-1960s.

Two absences are apparent in this literature: a dearth of empirical research and a neglect of the unofficial experience of the division of labour between technical and manual workers. Cooley is the only writer with any direct experience of technical work, which, as I have shown in Chapters 1 and 5, he uses in his analysis of the changing division of labour within technical work, and to support his commitment to craftism. Braverman, despite using empirical data for his discussion of clerks, relies exclusively on his own work experience for his discussion of technical labour. Gorz uses a single technician as a prop for a one dimensional line of argument. The lack of attention to the *subjective* relationship between technical and manual workers reflects for some writers – Poulantzas, Carchedi, and Wright – its irrelevance to the question of class placement. For Braverman it is a noted absence, but not one which would seriously qualify his assessment of the objective division of labour.

My intention here is to examine in detail the concrete character of technical workers' relations with manual workers. Particular stress is placed on the continuity of experience through recruitment from the shop floor and common craft tradition. Within this tradition, far from oppressing manual workers, British technical workers share many common experiences, based on continuity of training, class background, cooperation, mutual interest in the product and productive labour – experiences which make them part of the working class. This was not the case with higher technical labour discussed in the previous chapter, where a rigid educational divide, lack of cooperative contact with manual workers and an elevation of mental over craft skills, placed qualified engineers within a 'new middle class' position.

The division of labour within the technical area flows from the abstract to the concrete, from the designer to planning engineers and draughtsmen. Providing there is some degree of movement of personnel between these different moments, then its functional interdependence will be legitimated through a shared understanding about the relative weight and worth of different occupations within the technical hierarchy. Traditionally in Britain there has been a degree of fluidity between the shop floor and drawing office, and within the drawing office from draughtsman to designer. This led to a diffusion of common values, collective solidarity and trade union principles. But this sense of mutual respect and understanding is under strain, and a shared legitimacy for the hierarchy is being replaced by a forced interdependence. The break between the middle and higher level technical positions was described in the last chapter. The continuity and change from shop floor to office floor is the subject of this chapter.

Central to my analysis of the relations between technical and manual workers, are the contradictions of the craft tradition in engineering. C. Wright Mills (1953) in an early attack on the 'romance of labour' now associated with Braverman (1974) and the deskilling debate, argued against comparing modern wage-earners' levels of job control and craft skill (unity of planning and performance) with a portrait of craftsmanship of the nineteenth-century skilled worker.

> We cannot compare the idealised portrait of the craftsman with that of the auto worker and on that basis impute any psychological state to the auto worker . . . For the historical destruction of craftsmanship and of the old office, does not enter the consciousness of modern wage-worker or white-collar employee; much less is their absence felt by him as a crisis as it might have been in the course of the last generation; his father or mother had been in the craft tradition – but statistically speaking they are not. . . . Only the psychological imagination of the historian makes it possible to write of such comparisons as if they were of psychological import. *The craft life would be immediately available as a fact of consciousness only if in the lifetime of the modern employees they had experienced a shift from one condition to another, which they have not; or if they had grasped it as an ideal meaning of work which they have not.* (my emphasis)
>
> (Quoted in Eldridge, 1973, pp. 194–5)

Whilst a useful correction to ahistorical writing on craftsmanship, Wright Mills underplays the coexistence of different 'generations' of workers within the same setting. The increasing velocity of technical change can deskill one 'generation' in five to ten years. But more importantly for my purpose, he misses the point that those who have been involved in the transfer of skill can act as a craft memory, and bring a 'psychological import' into the relations with the new generation of manual workers. This was the case at Filton, as the older planners and draughtsmen were not only aware of the continuing slide of craft pride out of the job, but also the gap between the two generations of operators. For the older technical workers, this structured their relations with the shop floor.

I divide the technical workers into three groups, based on the frequency of their direct contact with manual workers. I also discuss indirect communication between technical staff and shop floor supervision. Ideally, I should have interviewed the manual workers in addition to technical staff to examine their experience of the relationship. However, the company would not give me access to shop floor workers for financial reasons. Despite this, I managed to interview two electricians and three NC operators. Hardly a representative sample, but it allowed me a limited opportunity to gauge the work relationship from their perspective.

In Chapter 2 Figure 2.1 lists technical occupations by their location in the cycle of production. Distance and proximity to manual workers reflects technical workers' location within this cycle. Basically, those in design, product support and flight testing have little or no contact with manual workers, whereas those in production engineering and maintenance are more likely to have a closer direct engagement.

Technical Workers with no Contact with Manual Workers

Tracers and commercial technical staff, located in technical publications, estimating and customer liaison had no contact with manual workers during their working day. The lack of craft tradition in tracing meant a different evaluation of the relationship between the two groups. Estimators needed craft skills to perform their work, but this was not essential for technical clerks, laboratory technicians, tracers and designers. The old-school design engineers had worked through from the shops to the drawing office and into the design department. But the craft experience was absent amongst the designers I interviewed and experience in the drawing offices was dying out. This lack of contact meant these technical workers were not in a position to evaluate manual workers. Quasi-technical workers in production engineering were linked to manual workers through an evaluation of their work performance, that is through a quantitative relationship. Technical workers proper who provide instructions and information to manual workers had a qualitative relationship, but designers had no direct relationship at all. Mallet assumed that such a distancing would create the opportunity for new unity:

> Standing apart, often some distance away from the place of production, they no longer have much contact with the workers, and the feeling of superiority with which tradition-ally the white collar workers looked down on the blue-collar workers, disappears with the loss of physical contact due to distance.
>
> (Mallet, 1975s, pp. 67–8)

I found no indication that this was the case with designers. Their professional (and craft) elitism prevented them from feeling a sense of unity with manual workers. The lack of contact or limited contact in some instances, meant the designer had no real need to consider the skills of the shop floor. Ideologically, the designers either believed in the 'team' or 'partnership' perspective at an abstract level, but saw no relationship in their daily practices; or they considered that a broad engineering background should involve a consider-ation of the importance of manual skills and recognised that the shop floor was still the main area for recruiting technical staff. Mac Smith, a designer:

> If you liaise with the shop floor you do it not with an authoritative, patronising manner. That man [i.e. the guy on the shop floor] is just as skilled as you, in a different field, obviously, but there are things he can do that you can never do, in the same way there are things you do that he could never do. But there's never any doubt that there's some on the shop floor who, given the right opportunity, will become staff personnel.

Alan Cogan, a designer, saw the world of the designer and the world of the electrician in the assembly area as totally separate:

> There is a difference which is recognised by the people who work in the hangar [assembly area] and the people who work in the design office. It may be narrowing ... but

basically they know one is doing a job which is completely alien to the other and they can't mix them.

This difference is based on the complexity of the task, the pace of work, and the attitude to work. From my discussions with designers it would be difficult to sustain Mallet's thesis on separate development and unity. It would have required a real leap of consciousness for them to identify their interests as workers with those of manual workers.

Technical Workers With Some Contact With Manual Workers

The electrical planning and tool design departments in the assembly area had limited contact with manual workers in the hangar and toolroom. As I explained in Chapter 4, planning engineers and draughtsmen tended to come from the shop floor, and even where workers had entered via another channel, craft skills were considered extremely important for the job. This craft tradition was central to their relationship with the shop floor and their assessment of shop floor workers.

Jig and Tool Draughtsmen in Assembly

Traditionally the jig and tool or tool design department maintained close links with the toolroom in engineering factories. At Filton the departmental manager and many younger and older draughtsmen were ex-toolmakers. Even where the draughtsmen had not served as toolmakers, experience in the machine shop during training was considered essential for the job. The close contacts of their apprenticeship days were maintained during the working day, and went beyond 'company work' as both groups exchanged materials and information for 'homers'. Graham Ell, a young draughtsman explains:

I know quite a lot of people on the floor here . . . you can go out there and say 'I want a bit of metal, will you cut it

out?' And yes they will do it. You know, if they come in
here and say they want something or 'will you draw this?'
Fair enough, you do it. It's help them and they'll help you.

Unlike estimators and designers, the job of the
draughtsman permitted the opportunity for such unofficial
mutual exchanges of services, and gave an additional intimacy
to the relationship between the two groups.

Formal communication between draughtsmen and toolmakers went through shop supervision, although in practice
there was a lot of contact between toolmakers and
draughtsmen. Neville Green, a draughtsman in his fifties told
me:

Neville: You liaise through the foreman but you end up
talking to the toolmaker and he listens to what
you're telling him.
Chris: But that comes through the foreman?
Neville: Not necessarily.
Chris: I see, so you talk directly to the toolmaker?
Neville: We can talk directly to these people on the shop
floor.
Chris: And does this happen quite often?
Neville: It happened a lot on the *Concorde* programme.

Direct liaison was a product of the division of labour
between the two groups and this reinforced common craft
bonds.

Neville spoke of a 'basic, indefinable respect between the
two groups' and this was something most of the draughtsmen
emphasised. But this craft tradition was not totally stable,
neither was it a totally equitable relationship. It was generally
regarded that the toolmakers were less skilled and technically
proficient today than they had been ten or twenty years
earlier, and with the perceived lowering of the craftsmanship
in the tool room, mutual respect was being undermined.
The tool designers based their assessment of the lowering of
toolmakers' expertise on the increasing volume and quality
of instructions required to give the tool room. All the
draughtsmen I interviewed spoke about the decline in crafts-

manship in the tool room. Some thought new machinery and specialisation had made the work of the toolmaker easier, and therefore less skilled:

> Now you've got machinery up there where, if the chap wants dimensions from his datum, he turns the handle on his machine and how far he's moving comes out on an electronic read-out, so it's quite easy.

Together with specialised machinery there has been a fragmentation of tasks leading to skill loss:

> toolmaking is probably broken down into more groups than it used to be, like fitting, turning and milling. I mean, in some shops people used to work on all sorts of machines to do their own job. But now they are a bit more specialised.

Graham Ell, a younger draughtsman, put it this way:

> With modern engineering, it seems to have become so technical that they are taking the actual design aspect away from the toolmaker.

And Peter Hill, a well-established draughtsman who had worked in tool design since 1960 and at Filton since 1953, said:

> Oh, I think with the older toolmakers you could leave things and they would use their own initiative, but these days you've just got to leave a very minor thing and they ring you up and want the drawing altered.

The draughtsmen's perceptions of reduced toolmakers' skill was not simply something abstract and universal, but also reflected the organisation of design and the system or method of engineering practised by the particular company. Eric Ham, an ex-supervisor explained:

> *Chris:* In terms of the instructions you've given to the tool-

makers, do you think you are giving them more
detailed drawings than was previously the case?

Eric:　Oh I think so – because it's necessary with modern
NC machinery and different techniques, although it
probably cuts both ways. You take the Preston
system, on the Preston system, the military side, we
don't have to call up or show how things are bolted
together, how the jigs are bolted together, that's a
standard practice which the toolmaker does himself.
But on our own system in this office we always do.

Peter Hill told me that there had been a change in the type
of drawings coming from the Engineering Design Organisation, and these had increased the amount of information.
The drawing system had become more fragmented, instead
of one drawing containing a lot of information, there were
now many smaller detail drawings with large amounts of
direct instructions. This had reduced the toolmaker's opportunity to see where his individual detail fitted into the overall
plan, and eliminated the sharing of information through the
interchange between toolmakers around one large drawing.
Peter Hill:

I think from the point of view of the tool room it is actually
easier for them to have a pile of drawings. They can take
one specific drawing which has the total information on
and give it to one person to go away and make that bit.
Whereas before there was one drawing and everyone would
have to sort of pore over it. Certainly from a production
point of view it's better and I suppose that's really the
overriding factor.

If the non-managerial draughtsmen explained the changing
skill composition by reference to engineering methods, and
the specialisation of the toolmaker, then management in the
tool design office places the responsibility for change squarely
on the shoulders of the modern toolmaker. Keith Saw, the
deputy manager of the department:

Ten years ago it's true to say that we did not, whatever

the complexity of the job, produce drawings which said: 'When you are loading this large assembly fixture', diagrammatically, 'this is the sequence you will go through'. We did not do that because it would have been worked out by the shop floor supervisor and some of his leading men . . . Ten years ago there was a certain extra degree of skill, that's all you can put it down to, they certainly weren't better educated or anything like that. It was just a case of know-how, general experience, skill . . . Without being rude to the present day toolmakers, we generally find that we have to draw more and more detail today than we used to, in order to eliminate queries.

I was unable to obtain access to the tool room and so could not examine these claims through the eyes of the toolmaker. I was naturally suspicious because there is always a tendency to assume more craftsmanship in the past, and project forward from a situation where the product was less complex. One way of judging these claims was to examine old drawings from the 1950s and 1960s and to go through them with a designer – because the changes were said, by Peter Hill, to have originated in design – and ask him to compare the old with the new. In one sense, of course, the reality of the draughtsmen's claims was secondary to their perceptions of them as accurate. I was concerned with the symbolic value technical staff attach to their communications with manual workers. But I thought it a useful exercise, particularly as draughtsmen set such store by the relationship between the quality and quantity of instructions given to the toolmaker and his skill.

Bernard Mild was based in the Lofting department in No. 8 Design Office in the main Engineering Design Organisation. He had worked as a design draughtsman at BAe since the early 1950s. He talked his way through the old drawings with me. We went back to 1953 and found that as all the draughtsmen had claimed, there were large amounts of information left to the 'shops' – although it was not stated if the foreman or operator jointly, or individually, analysed the drawings. However it was believed by others I interviewed, that the individual operator read the drawing himself. Phrases like 'tool where necessary' appeared again and again, whereas on the later drawing the most common phrase was 'tool where shown'. On the older drawings individual items of machining were frequently not detailed, whereas on the new drawings every item of machining and assembly had its own detailed drawings: the welding, finishing, cleaning, coating, painting, were all detailed. On the new drawings every main drawing had between twenty and thirty detail drawings elaborating on the main drawing. In the 1950s there were far fewer detail drawings from the main drawing – between two and five. Drawings as late as 1969 still had 'tool where necessary' and not 'tool where shown'. The early 1970s appeared to have been the turning point when the method changed and the volume of details and directions increased.

These drawings would appear to support the draughtsmen's assessment of declining skill on the shop floor. However, this is really only one interpretation of the information. Bernard Mild put a different slant on the changes and suggested four major reasons for the growing quantity and quality of instructions. Firstly, sub-contracting and the increasing national and then international division of production of airframes over the period meant a demand for greater standardisation of parts, designs and production methods. What was called 'interchangeability' of parts required more standardised information, and this enlarged the level of detailed instructions going to the shop floor. Many of the changes in drawing practices had come from sub-contract work for Boeings. They demanded more detailed work for *their* shops, and Bernard said Boeings were the pace-setters in the industry on production methods and safety standards. The ending of *Concorde* produced a larger volume of sub-contract work into Filton, and this occurred during the mid 1970s, and earlier for the design areas, which would support the changes in the drawings during this period. The international division of labour imposed itself on those parts of the British industry that were changing from being independent producers of airframes, to sub-contractors on a large scale. This was the case at Filton, Bristol.

Secondly, the increasing costs of products, materials and labour meant that an enormous effort went into avoiding scrapped jobs, and consequently problems were increasingly smoothed out and detailed in the technical and design areas before going into production. Given the overheads on the shop floor in terms of wages, power, machinery and mainten- ance costs, it was considerably cheaper to eliminate 'error' in the office rather than the tool room. Thirdly, government safety requirements increased over the period and they demanded that airframe manufacturers keep complete sets of drawings and more detailed records of work. Again, many of the designers I interviewed emphasised the increasing strin- gency of safety standards with the growing volume of air passenger travel. Finally, he thought the increasing volume of instructions may partly reflect and partly create decline in skill. It was a 'chicken and egg' situation: changes in design method, because of the other pressures, established a new custom and practice on the shop floor. The designers did not put it down to skill loss, but tended to explain the changes by reference to the growing complexities of airframe manufac- ture, the 'tighter tolerances', the increase in inspection, the obsession with safety or simply '*Concorde*'.

Draughtsmen had no authority relations over the shop floor workers and the decline in respect for the 'word' of the draughtsmen described in chapter 3, meant liaison was largely a question of an individual's approach. Consent had to be won, it could not be imposed, the gaining of co-operation was something the draughtsmen considered an achievement. Neville Green stated for example:

> I'm very proud of the fact that I can go out onto the shop floor and if someone starts swearing at me about the job I can answer them and use similar swear words which I wouldn't use in the office. You've got to be able to talk their language, you haven't got to talk down to them.

Neville's language and overall approach to the shop floor workers reads like a standard management textbook on good communications. Although Neville was not in a direct auth- oritative relationship with the toolmakers, he was compelled to adopt managerial 'skills' of shopfloor liaison. This is indica- tive of the 'real' separation that exists, even in a technical area with a strong craft tradition. It reflects the largely one-way information flow between the two sides.

There was no animosity from tool designers to toolmakers despite the above changes, and draughtsmen expressed considerably more hostility towards the planning department. The toolroom was not considered a 'battle field' as the machine shop was for quasi-technical workers. The craft tradition continued to structure the relationship between the two sides and placed a premium on manual as well as technical skills. Although the craftsman 'wasn't what he used to be', this was not necessarily 'his fault' but to do with objective changes in the product and production process. The one hostile encounter described to me, was between a fitter and a draughtsman, and was not the fault of the draughtsman, but a mistake from the planning department. The involvement with the physical commodity unites the two groups, although mutual co-operation was something that the draughtsmen had 'to win', it was not built into their status.

Wage differentials between draughtsmen and toolmakers had declined. In 1978 the toolmakers were on a higher basic wage. TASS caught up in 1979, and 1980, but toolmakers remained slightly above. This was a source of tension and fuelled militancy in the department which was noted as a well organised office. Ironically, the lowering of the differential threatened the craft tradition directly, because without any financial incentive toolmakers would not bother undergoing retraining to enter the office. This had happened in other corporations where the differential had declined.

Despite the absence of any animosity, draughtsmen, as the 'originators' of the toolmakers' work, inevitably reflected this structural difference in their relations with toolmakers. Draughtsmen were not in an 'authoritarian' position, but being within mental labour, toolmakers stood in a relationship of formal 'dependence', and this filtered relations between the two groups. The lack of two-way communication and the reduction of transfers from shop floor to office, was weakening the mutuality that had historically characterised their craft relationship. 'Deskilling', although not the 'fault' of individual toolmakers at Filton, nevertheless affected the respect between the two groups.

Electrical Planning Engineers and Electricians

Electrical planning, like tool design, was part of the Production Engineering Organisation, not the Engineering Design Organisation. They were the next stage down from electrical design and up from the electricians in assembly. They were located in a large office near the assembly hangars, and close to the electrical design offices.

Like the tool designers most of the electrical planners had come off the shop floor into planning. Some had come through the inspection department. Many had been electricians and they now gave instructions to electricians in the assembly hangars. Although it was considered important to have had manual experience, it was not essential.

Indeed, it was increasingly the case, with the computerisation of the electrical planning area, that craft skills were no longer necessary. This was in contrast to the experience in tool design. The contact between electricians and electrical planners was not as frequent as between tool designers and toolmakers. And unlike the association between the latter, planners tended to confine their liaison to the electrical supervisors.

There were liaison planners located in an office close to the assembly area, and they dealt with any immediate queries on the drawings and processes. The electrical planners divided between computer and manual planning. Computer planning was done via a visual display unit, and it was considered that work was becoming more routinised and boring. All the planners admitted this. Planning via the VDU had increased productivity by 28 per cent, and removed two clerical workers. Although not tied to the machine, they were aware of the more intense atmosphere the change from manual planning had created. The computerisation of planning had reduced the amount of physical liaison between electrical planners and shop floor supervision and inspection. It had also allowed the entry of staff who lacked an electrical background. Hugh Evans had moved into planning from a clerical department. He was the only ex-clerk in the department and he admitted that he found the work difficult. His lack of electrical knowledge meant he believed the computerisation of electrical planning and the increased volume of instructions going to the electricians, had reduced them to a semi-skilled status. Despite it being difficult for him to assess the skills of the electrician, he believed that computerisation had:

> bred a new breed of electrician. 'Cos all they've got are tabulations, A and B ends, that's all they've got. How they ever managed I don't know [with heavy irony]. Idiots could cope. It looks complicated from the outside, but they're just working off this tabulation, the tabulations prepared by this office.

I was fortunate enough to be able to interview two electricians who received instructions from the electrical planners. This gave me a limited, but important opportunity of gauging some of the remarks about the decline in shop floor skill made by the planners.

John Stone and Ken Towers had both worked at BAe for at least twenty-five years. They had both worked as electricians all their lives and were therefore in a good position to assess the changes that had taken place. I firstly discussed the relationship between themselves and the planners. John Stone:

> With regards to technical workers, I think basically we appreciate their position and they know our position because most of the technical workers were once manual workers.

The electrical planners' argument that the increasing volume of instructions creates a feeling of superiority between the two groups was not considered very accurate. Ken Towers, emphasised the mutual cooperation between the two groups:

> Basically the broad consensus is, you know, a commonsense approach, as John says, most of the technical workers were once manual workers, so they know what the situation is. I don't think there's any feeling of superiority. I think everybody accepts the role of the others and respects their various positions. I think some years ago there was more

of a feeling of them and us, you know the staff and the works, but I think, particularly over the last few years, that these edges have become blurred and these divisions are much less clearly defined.

Both electricians considered the equalisation of conditions to have broken down many barriers between the staff and manual workers. The technical division of labour, the fact that the flow of information originates in design and passes down to the shop floor, was considered 'the optimum way an industry works', i.e. it was seen as a neutral arrangement for the best way of producing airframes. John Stone again:

The nature of the job is that aircraft be built in a certain way, you know the Design Stage, the Planning Stage and the Production Stage, the Inspection and so on. And people who have worked in the industry for only a matter of six months become very quickly aware of the set up they are working in. And there is a coming together, particularly in *Concorde*'s early days, of the Design and Planning and Production sides to iron out problems that arose in the development stage. That has also helped to bring a more harmonious working arrangement across the workforce.

Neither electrician considered the division of labour illegitimate, it was simply the traditional form of organisation in the airframe industry.

I questioned both on their interpretation of the growing volume of instructions passing to them from electrical planning. Could these detailed instructions be considered to be reducing the skill content, initiative and creative aspect of their work? John Stone:

I think a lot of the content of our work is becoming more and more technical. Whereas before it was *a lot simpler in approach where there was a local custom and practice approach*, all the cable terminations, for instance, were practically standard and you used one tool or maybe two or three tools for the making of all the cables. But nowadays, there are so many different terminations and so many different points of construction that have to be observed, you have to *really consult* these manufacturing processes, to follow the job through and in fact, inspection demands that you work to these processes. The designers stipulate that a certain order and procedure are followed. This has all evolved, particularly with *Concorde*, which was a real watershed.

The full paradox of the relationship between planner and electrician is now clear. To Hugh Evans the planner, electricians were no longer reliant upon their own knowledge for the job, but the very detailed instructions supplied by the planner. The electricians were technically dependent on planning. For Hugh Evans this dependency could only mean one thing, a loss of independence, a loss of skill, initiative and control for the electrician. However, from John Stone's perspective, the ending of 'custom and practice' and its replacement by 'a more scientific and disciplined approach' increased the technical competence of the electrician. The intervention of written procedures, which *must be* followed, elevates their manual skills into the technical area. No longer did he consider himself a standard custom and practice electrician, but someone performing a technical skill dealing with complex tools, layouts and inspection methods. Hugh Evans' ignorance of the electrician's work, further compounded his belief in their deskilling at the hands of himself and the computer. The translation of written instruction into practice was judged 'automatic', 'simple', and therefore the electrician's work was unskilled – 'Idiots could cope. It looks complicated from the outside but they're just working off this tabulation'. When I examine technical workers around the machine shop, I will show how their more frequent involvement with the shop floor and solid craft background rubbed against the kind of elitism expressed by this planner.

Apart from Hugh Evans' remarks I did not encounter any derogatory attitudes towards electricians in the planning department, yet I would argue that lack of contact and practical experience led him to evaluate the electrician's work on the basis of the instructions and tabulations prepared by the planners. This is a distorted relationship which equates the electricians' labour process to the written, formal process

worked on by the planners. Abstractly this planner was celebrating the importance and dominance of his mental skills
over the mere copying manual skills of the electrician. This,
as we have seen, is an important component in the division
of labour and relationship between manual and technical
workers.

In other relations, such as between draughtsmen and toolmakers, what has tempered any polarisation purely along this
mental/manual continuum has been the craft tradition. But
for electrical planners the more they are recruited from non-
electrical or craft areas, the greater the opportunity for a
polarisation between planners and electricians, because the
former will take literally the belief that they are doing all the
'work for the electricians to copy'. The craft bond, given the
way computerisation had expanded the clerical nature of
planners' work, was loosening faster in the electrical side than
between draughtsmen and toolmakers.

Technical Workers in Regular Contact with Manual Workers Around the Machine Shop

Chapter 4 described in detail the work of staff around the
machine shop. Although not all the technical staff interact on
a daily basis with manual workers, there was a much greater
frequency in contact than in either the design area or
production engineering organisation in assembly. I interviewed six groups of workers: pointsmen, rate-fixers,
production controllers, planners, draughtsmen, and NC part
programmers. These were divided into two categories: quasi-
technical workers and recognised technical grades. Those in
marginalised positions in production had a daily engagement
with the work of machinists – while the technical workers had
less of an intimate contact with the shop floor but concentrated on the planning, drawing and programming of work
for future production. The quantitative, managerial monitoring role performed by rate-fixers and production controllers was detailed in Chapter 4, and I do not intend to examine
these groups again here. Instead I will look at machine shop

tool designers and NC part programmers to indicate the contrasting relationship they have towards manual workers.

Jig and Tool Draughtsmen Around the Machine Shop

The draughtsmen in jig and tool, like all draughtsmen I interviewed at BAe, had no supervisory power over manual workers. They had a strong craft identity and an affinity with manual craftsmen, and over fifty percent of those in the office had entered the office directly from the machine shop. As with the two groups of planners and draughtsmen in assembly, I encountered the same account of the draughtsmen having to supply an ever increasing amount of detailed information to the operators. This was again interpreted as signifying a loss of craft pride and skill on the part of the operators. However there was again a general feeling that their interdependence and close contact with the shop floor ought to engender a sense of co-operation and unity and not disunity and animosity.

There were three non-union supervisors in the assembly tool design office who spoke, with regret, of the loss of status and authority of the draughtsmen. In the machine shop tool design office the two individuals, a section leader and a checker, who regretted their lost status, were very anti-TASS and saw themselves as having no common ground for unity with manual workers. So in both departments there were small pockets of anti-unionism, although respect for craftsmanship had nothing to do, necessarily, with a belief in staff/manual union co-operation or even on-the-job co-operation. The most solidly anti-union figure in the office, Michael Philipson, identified craftsmanship with individualism, autonomy and conservatism. Hinton (1972) identified similar qualities in the engineering labour aristocrats of the nineteenth century, although insisting upon the unstable nature of that craft tradition. Philipson's position as checker placed him in a supervisory role in the department and he viewed himself very much as the custodian for draughtsmanship. He may have acknowledged the skill of the manual worker, but did not see himself on a par with craftsmen.

Amongst those who had entered the office directly from the machine shop there was a sense of both draughtsmen and skilled conventional operators being simply skilled men. Two of the younger draughtsmen, one of whom had recently left the machine shop for the office, and the other who had transferred to a technician apprenticeship, emphasised the need for unity, while acknowledging the divide between 'staff' and 'works'. Steve Silver had only worked in the office for just over a year, and still felt very attached to the shop floor. He had not joined TASS, holding onto his TGWU membership card, although it meant nothing in the office. He had been an active shop steward in the machine shop and moved into the office for personal reasons. He based the division between the two groups squarely on the relationship to production.

> It's definitely us and them I think between shop floor and staff, because they feel they could manage quite well without us, without staff in here, but staff couldn't manage at all if they stopped work, you know . . .

It was clear from my interview with Steve that he was firmly convinced of the central place of direct production workers, although working in the technical departments had made him appreciate 'the other side':

> There's some good blokes here, and especially a couple of the chaps on the tape programming and a couple of section leaders on jig and tool, *they really know engineering* . . . Obviously technical staff are necessary, I mean, somebody's got to design the bits and pieces that go into the aircraft. It's alright for the lads to say 'well we make 'em', but somebody's got to sit down and decide what the bloody thing's going to look like in the first place.

Colin Luck was thirty-four, had worked at BAe. since he was sixteen and as a draughtsman for approximately thirteen years. His view of manual workers was that 'ultimately they're the ones that earn the money for the company, we're the back up'. He considered his own work necessary, but not productive. Another source of differentiation between the two groups was the relative pace of work. The ending of individual piece rates in the machine shop, and the introduction of company-wide productivity deals had ended one major difference between the two groups. The increase in timed work through the technical departments with the growth of subcontracting and capitalisation of the offices, was also changing conditions of work. Nevertheless, what one ex-machinist described as the 'entirely different atmosphere' of the two worlds remained:

> On the shop floor I think they've got a lot better idea of how long something should really take to produce. But in here, I think everything is so vague, they don't really know how long it's going to take to plan a job or provide the tools. Nobody's ever given me a job in here and said there's a week to do this, whereas on the shop floor, basically it's got a time to do it in. Not that the blokes worry about it out there anymore 'cause they don't.

When I interviewed the draughtsmen in 1978, the machine shop unions were involved in a wage dispute following three years of Government wage restraint. Part of their action involved sporadically picketing the gates for two and a half hours once a week. I found near total support in the technical departments for the manual workers' action, TASS backed the shop floor but had no direct involvement in the dispute. Management advised office staff not to attempt to come in to work while the pickets were on the gate. The dispute provided a useful background against which to explore the relationship between the staff and manual unions and workers. Colin Luck, by no means a militant in the department, told me:

> On the TV last night one phrase stood out when the manual workers were asked why they'd shut the gates. They said: 'To stop the pen pushers getting in'. So there's still a basic hatred if you like, between the people out there and the people in the office. They still think that we don't do a decent day's work, I'm certain of it. Yet some of them who have recently come in here off the shop floor they now realise what we do for our money and they are changing

see, they've changed their whole attitude. When you go over the line you can see how the other half lives and you know what they do.

The entry into the office to see the other side, was not an option open to the majority of manual workers. It was not part of their apprenticeship, although working on the shop floor for two years was an integral component of the technician's training. Colin Luck resented being placed amongst the 'them' category, in the manual/staff division, largely because he had started a craft apprenticeship, came from a manual working class background and considered himself to be a working class bloke.

Steve Silver also came from a working class background, and because he had only recently entered the office he felt torn between the 'us' and the 'them'. Other features such as the hobbies and social activities of those in the office forced him to see the shop floor and office as worlds apart:

> There was more fun on the shop floor, it's a different atmosphere in here. They are a bit more extrovert on the shop floor . . . they're a bit more withdrawn in here. Up until a few years ago you couldn't wear jeans or checked shirts . . . I couldn't work under those conditions, I don't believe in stuffed shirts anywhere. Well I tried to run an interdepartmental football team, it was just for a laugh, but you were struggling to raise a side, and there are quite a few young lads in here and they just weren't interested. Now on the shop floor, I know you've got more to choose from, but I could have signed on a hundred if I'd wanted. I thought perhaps we could have a game of cricket, an interdepartmental cricket competition, but still not interested.

The difference in leisure pursuits was mentioned by others, although in NC part programming, a table-tennis table was rected every lunch time and most of the department, including the manager, participated. While abstentia from collective sports activity may have symbolised the more individual and private family nature of the drawing office, as an ex-steward,

Steve Silver attributed the key division to bad union relations between the staff and the works. Steve also refers to the shop floor action which prevented staff entering work until 10 am and again a comment from one of the manual workers appeared to sum up the distance that divided both groups:

> I don't know if you saw the television last night, well they showed the lads and the interviewer said, 'You're stopping your fellow workers coming into work' and somebody said, 'they aren't our fellow workers!' Well, I think that is sort of typical of the attitude out there. Like, you know, a lot of it stems from the fact that we've had disputes up here where the issue has been something that involves everybody. But the action against those issues comes mainly from the shop floor, even though it's been on our behalf as well.

'When it came to fighting redundancies . . . they let the side down'. The opportunity for organisational unity persisted despite the divisions discussed above, and this introduced the quality of trade unionism on both sides into the equation. At Filton, joint committees had not endured, although their necessity was highlighted by the separate action of the two groups. In other companies such joint activities had been sustained, (Wainwright and Elliot, 1982). The importance of trade unionism as a potential leveller of division is discussed in chapter eight.

Placed within the wider debate on class, the perceptions of social relations by these draughtsmen indicate their inherent ambivalence as a 'conceptual' component of the collective labourer. The opportunities for individualism, the autonomy of the job, the different pace and atmosphere within the office perpetuate everyday distinctions between the two groups. These material differences inevitably filter social interaction and create barriers to co-operative integration and solidarity.

NC Programmers and Operators

Objectively, the relationship between NC operator and NC part programmer should reflect the polarisation of engineering knowledge described by the literature discussed in Chapter 4. However, at BAe, I found a very complex relationship which defied neat dichotomous categorisation. The relative newness of NC meant programmers did not in any sense bemoan the decline in operators' skills, because there was no base-line of craftsmanship with which to compare these skills. If anything, it was felt the NC operators working in 1978 were considerably more proficient than those in 1968. The common assumption in engineering of NC machines only requiring the operator to 'bang in a tape and press a few buttons' was vigorously denied by both operators and programmers. Far from the part programmers complaining about the decline in skill, they were cast in the role of defending the 'skills' of the operator against attacks from conventional machinists, foremen, and other staff workers. The division between operator and programmer was not so rigid as to prevent operators transferring into the office. As I described in Chapter 4, a quarter of the programmers had entered the department directly from the machine shop. I will describe the relationship between NC operators and conventional machinists, and then examine the association between programmers and operators.

Brian Maunders had worked as an NC operator in a Canadian engineering company and at Filton before moving into programming. He defended the alleged unskilled nature of NC work against criticism from conventional machinists and others unfamiliar with NC. He was aware of its lowly status.

> They're looked down on a lot by the conventional machinists. The skilled miller looks down on the NC operators, I've had a lot of arguments with them in that respect. They say, 'you've just got to press buttons'. Obviously it's not as easy as that. You *can* go out there and just press a button and probably turn out a job, but the quality of the work is low. This is where the skill comes into it and separates the good operator from the bad one . . . I was careful, I had pride in what I was doing even though it was only being churned out on the machine.

Skill as defined here is wrapped up with a 'pride in the job', with 'taking care' to avoid expensive mistakes, and not necessarily with control over the job. In fact, though, the flow of work and expertise was not straightforward from programmer to operator. I asked Mike Cooper, the NC manager, if the idea behind NC was not to replace time served machinists with unskilled machine minders:

> *Mike:* It was originally said that you could take anybody, literally off the street, and get them to operate an NC machine.
> *Chris:* Do you think that's the case or not?
> *Mike:* No I don't! Because I think what wasn't taken into account in those early days, was, particularly in the aircraft industry, the value of the machine tool itself, which has increased in price and also the value of the piece of material the guy's working on.

Mike went on to explain that machinists without engineering experience were no longer employed at Filton. Here the distance between the publicity for NC by manufacturers of NC machines – ('anyone can do it') – and users is significant. Like Brian Maunders, Mike identified skilled NC machinists with those who 'take an interest in their job' and 'think':

> You've got to have people who've got to think, with machining experience. He needs to be on the ball . . . an operator can change a cutter one hundred times and he makes one mistake on one occasion and he's got a scrapped job on his hands.

The major conflict for the programmers was not with the operators but the shop supervisors. The foremen, as individuals, had seen their authority, which was largely based on their technical competence as conventional machinists reduced; Mike Cooper:

> Whereas in the old days a foreman could go on to the machine to show the guy how to correct a problem or overcome a problem, he can't do that anymore. He's solely

in the hands of the tape, and as soon as he's in the hands of the tape he's in the hands of the programmers. *He has less control over his destiny shall we say.*

I interviewed three NC operators after finishing my interviews in the technical departments. I had intended to interview others but was prevented. The three were interviewed together, and this afforded a useful exchange of shared and differing views on the relationship between staff and their status as NC operators in what was once a predominantly conventionally skilled machine shop. There were two grades of operator, 'A' grade who set their own machines and 'B' grade who did not. All the operators I interviewed were 'A' grade, or 'skilled' machinists, and had, on average, worked at Filton for twelve years.

   Billy: Most of the skilled people on conventional machines, they think of NC and they think of a tape, they think of a cabinet, you put the tape in the cabinet, press button B, sit down and everything's done for you. Well in theory that is the way it should be done. But it's a long way from reaching that.
   Andy: It depends on the job. You can have a straightforward job, no problems. You get another job with lots of problems.
   Billy: Let's face it, 95 per cent of the jobs out there now have got problems. They don't come out right, tapes are wrong. I think you'd have to be a genius even as a planner, for the work involved to take cutters, feed rates and everything like that into consideration and come out with a tape, say twenty-one hours long and be right first time around. Half of the time they haven't got time to go back in and modify the tapes, so you carry on until they can. Most of the time you've got to put those problems right by off-setting the machine to suit the tape.

NC operators had to off-set the machine – that is directly intervene – anticipate problems with tapes and advise the programmer about these difficulties. This creative input by

NC operators is confirmed by other studies, both in Britain and the US, (Jones, 1982; Noble, 1984; Shaiken, 1984). All the operators had sufficient rapport with the programmers to do this. However, there were examples of arguments between programmers and operators. None of the operators I interviewed gave me any specific cases but Brian Maunders, a programmer, described an incident when he was an NC operator in the shop. He saw that what had been prepared by the programmer was wrong, and would result in a scrapped job. This was clear from reading the planner's sequencing of the job. He told the programmer, who was somebody who had entered the office from the shop floor, but he would not listen. So Brian got the opinion of three other machinists, whose machining knowledge he respected, and they agreed with his assessment of the job. Brian takes up the story:

> I came in, I saw the guy again and I said: 'look, I've checked with these guys'. He said 'I don't give a shit about that', so I said 'Fuck it, I'll let the job go then, if it's a scrapping issue, that's it. I've complained about it, I've checked with others and you're wrong'. And he comes storming up afterwards and says: 'Give me those fucking sheets', and he tore them up and went storming back into the office. And I thought, you stupid arsehole. But it doesn't usually happen like that, most of the guys in here [office] are very, very reasonable. He was an exception in that respect.

The job was scrapped. Responsibility for the job rested with both operators and programmers, although if the tape was correct, the operator carried the responsibility of avoiding mistakes. The above example illustrates the difficulty for an operator challenging the opinion of a programmer, all he can do is advise, (something also mentioned by Shaiken). Their 'subordination' to the technical competence of the programmer was not something that the operators spoke of, but they were aware of the reason for the programmer's 'superiority'.

Chris: Are technical workers indirectly supervisory? Do you
see them like that?

Sean: Some of them like to think they are.

Andy: You get this superiority creeping in.

Sean: Well it's obvious like. If they think they're starting
off the job like, they think, well I'm before you,
therefore I'm a little bit above you. It's always been
like that, and it always will be.

Although mainly attacked by conventional operators for
their lack of machining skill, NC machinists were also aware
of the premium placed on 'abstract' knowledge under capitalism and how their association with direct production
placed them in a specific manual category. But the operators
did not accept the mental/manual division and insisted upon
the responsibility of their work and the physical *and* mental
strain of machining. The typical assumption about 'mental
labour' requiring a greater degree of anticipatory planning
and forethought to 'manual' labour was also rejected:

Sean: . . . Obviously there's more concentration got to go
into looking after a machine where, if you do something wrong, you can end up being killed. If you
break a pencil in an office you can't get killed for
that.

Billy: I don't think in the office you've got to think so far
ahead. On the shop floor you've got to think ahead
all the time because thinking ahead involves your
own safety and other people's.

Andy: If I make a miscalculation on paper that can be
altered . . . but if I make a miscalculation on the
job then the job's scrapped. I'm saying you're more
responsible.

These remarks echo Mike Cooper's earlier comments. The
high cost of the NC machine tool and the component have
compelled management to be concerned about the engineering competence of the operator. The operators did not feel
'put down' or subordinate to the programmers or other staff
workers because their direct engagement with the commodity,

not only required responsibility, 'skill' and forethought, but it also conferred on them a strong identity as productive workers. They used their 'productiveness' to demand higher wages and rebuff aspersions about their subordination to staff workers. This direct engagement with the physical commodity formed the basis of a sense of superiority common to all direct production workers. As Andy Gray put it:

> The thing is if you make it, you should be paid for making it. I know there's the build-up to making it, *but you actually do the job*. At the end of the day you put in the total work content to produce the product and you should get paid for it.

Technical staff are productive workers, they are wage labourers and create surplus value for capital, and are consequently exploited by capital. But their indirect place in production relegated them to this commonsense 'unproductive' status in the eyes of manual workers. This assumption was so strong that some technical workers believed they were necessary but unproductive. To some extent the NC operators were compensating for the allegedly unskilled work by celebrating their productive powers.

The NC operators' grievances against staff workers in general had less to do with skill differences, than with conditions of employment. The apparent freedom of movement, freedom from supervision and general autonomy of staff workers was contrasted to the highly supervised, constrained working conditions of the operators. Their consciousness of being the producers of the physical commodity was reinforced by the contrast between the conditions of work in the two areas. If they were constrained by time it was because they were producing something; therefore it followed that staff, because they were autonomous, were not producing anything. One argument reinforced the other, despite the awareness that without the technical staff they would not be able to start their work.

> *Sean:* What you want to do is before twelve o'clock walk out onto the shop floor and look at the foremen

standing around watching the blokes that are leaving early. And at 12.45 go out to the main gate and have a look at how many staff are filing out. They're coming out in droves. Now that is the difference. If we're caught doing that, well!

Billy: The main point being that everybody wants to know everything about the shop floor worker. Has he been to the toilet, has he clocked in on time, did he do this, did he do that? Nobody wants to know anything about the staff, oh they can't do anything wrong.

Chris: What, they've got more independence, they can move around more freely?

Billy: They're not challenged at all.

Andy: Because they're not actually producing anything. A planner doesn't come in in the morning and produce something by twelve o'clock. At the end of the week he might get something done, but he doesn't produce a component, so there's nothing there. So I don't think it's the same kind of pressure.

The division of labour, in addition to promoting illusions about productive and unproductive workers, closed the operator to the reality of hierarchy and control in the office. Unbridled freedom did not exist, and discipline in several departments was very tight. Although in comparison with the machine shop most technical departments were environments for individual autonomy and job control. Direct control was both unnecessary and impractical given the longer time deadlines for jobs. It was this absence of close supervision that the operators resented or rather envied.

As far as NC was concerned objectively engineering knowledge had moved from the shop floor to the office, but this had not been accompanied by elitism or craft sectarianism on the part of the programmers towards operators. Programmers defended the 'skills' of operators against attacks from conventional machinists and other staff workers uninvolved in N.C. The skills of the programmer were not in doubt, and the necessity of their work was not questioned by the operators. There was a close relationship on the job between operator and programmer, and although the flow of information was from programmer to operator, there were cases when the operator could challenge the decisions of programmers and had to 'offset' the machine because of problems with the tape. The absence of CNC machines from the shop floor meant there were no demarcation disputes between TASS and manual unions, over editing tapes, as had occurred over the road at Rolls-Royce. This room for 'initiative' was considered by both operators and programmers to be evidence of the 'skilled' nature of the work. The grievances between operators and staff in general revolved around the conditions of work, the difference in the freedom of movement, and supervisory restrictions.

The Craft Memory: The Link between Technical and Manual Workers

Technical workers' location in 'mental labour', and their political role in supervision over manual workers created, for Poulantzas, a class gulf between the two groups of workers. For Carchedi, advancing a more complex model, there was a constant recomposition of those intermediate workers whose work is characterised by a combination of capital and labour functions. Some elements were driven into the proletariat through a loss of capital functions, while others are drawn into the new middle class by absorbing displaced capital functions. In both models subjective and historical relationships between technical and manual workers are ignored. This makes for a 'purer' model, but one which lacks room for explanations of national variations in class structures. Mallet, and the school of 'new working class' writers are at once more empirical and idealistic, projecting on to the formal inter-dependencies between sections of the collective labourer a *necessary*, not *contingent* cooperation and unity. This chapter has sought to qualify both schools by examining the importance of the craft tradition and the informal relations between technical and manual workers. Both these factors make for a more complex relationship between the two groups. The threats to the craft tradition are simultaneously a threat to the relationship between the two groups.

Technical workers in established areas had a craft consciousness and sense of tradition that filtered their work relationship to manual workers. Unlike those quasi-technical occupations in production engineering, they did not have a political and quantitative interest in manual workers' labour power. Training programmes maintained this craft association. In the older technical areas – draughting, planning, estimating – over fifty per cent of the staff had entered directly from manual areas. In the newer technical departments, such as NC part programming, only twenty-five per cent used this entry route. So the craft tradition persisted but to a lesser extent, in the newer computer based technical areas.

This craft tradition is very double-edged. Technical staff frequently appeared to act as the custodians of craft skills, as the memory of past generations of craftsmen who appeared to have exercised a greater degree of initiative, skill and sheer engineering 'know how' relative to the living generation of operatives. This qualitative relationship, on the one hand, placed these technical workers in a more co-operative position and closer identification with manual workers. On the other hand, it meant that there was a loss of respect for manual workers in certain instances. This did not apply in the case of newer technical areas, like NC part programming, which grew out of the deskilling of craft functions, and the transfer of engineering knowledge to the office. Skill hierarchies are constantly changing as new generations enter with differing expectations of what constitutes skill. The socialisation of craft workers indicates a constantly changing level of skill expectation (Singh, 1977).

Technical workers did not have any direct power over the manual workers, they had to work out their own individual relations in a fairly unstructured setting. To do this, they drew on their common social background or their common engineering knowledge to develop a non-authoritarian relationship. The craft tradition and elevation of manual work created a degree of deference to skilled manual workers because of their direct engagement with production, their pace of work and their craft skills. In some instances technical staff, without shop floor experience, appeared to be very intimidated by manual workers. If they went on the shop floor, they were aware that they were entering, as individuals, a collective environment where they may be treated with mistrust.

Those who had regular contact with the machine shop or assembly areas did not express this disquiet. Yet the 'us' and 'them' ideology persisted: it rested upon the division of labour and the different conditions of work. As one NC operator put it, 'they think, "well I'm before you therefore I'm a little bit above you". It's always been like that and it always will be.' While the wages, hours, holidays, and level of sick pay had been equalising due to the manual unions' pressure, the apparent freedom of office workers appeared to the manual workers to be unrestricted.

There are pressures and counterpressures delimiting the degree of co-operation and mutual respect between technical and manual workers. Despite animosity from manual workers – ('keep the pen pushers out') – inter-union solidarity had featured in the course of redundancy struggles at the factory in the 1970s. But this had been short-lived, and some believed its failure compounded the sense of difference each side felt. Having said that, staff were not identified with management in any sense and therefore the potential for *worker unity* always existed.

In the concluding chapter I analyse the importance of trade union leadership and politics in enabling the co-operative tendencies within the collective labourer to undercut the competing and antagonistic elements discussed here. But before examining trade unionism amongst technical staff, however, I turn to the work relations between technical staff and management.

7

The Work Relations Between Technical Workers and Managers

Introduction

To manual workers the technical office did not appear a place of hierarchy and control. To Weberian sociologists, notably Lockwood (1958), Giddens (1973) and Bain and Price (1972), the office (technical or clerical) is an area for sharing authority, a place where staff workers borrow from the authority of management by virtue of their close working arrangements. We saw in the last chapter that technical staff worked out their own relationship with manual workers, and did not follow structurally determined patterns of behaviour allocated to them by abstract categorisation. This chapter argues that the proximity to management is only one influence on technical workers' assessment of their class position. Moreover, the relationship is not one-way, and given the ratios of managers to staff, it is not surprising that management are also influenced by the technical workers of their office.

Crucial to the authority relationship is the task control and autonomy exercised by technical workers. Individuals tended to work on whole processes, and to know the job better than anyone else in the department. This determined the pattern

227

of control and meant authoritarian, external or direct supervision was unnecessary. It was neither necessary nor feasible
to stand over a draughtsman, planner or programmer who
could spend up to one year on a single job. Neither were
technical staff on the whole subject to technical control or the
objectification of authority in the technical means of
production, although, as was discussed in Chapter 5, the
increasing use of computers did threaten major changes in
this respect.

I interviewed nine technical managers at departmental
level and one group manager, responsible for four technical
departments. The main focus of this chapter will be on middle
or line management, i.e. those heads or deputy heads of
technical departments who deal with the grievances of technical staff and work in close physical proximity to a group of
technical workers.

The contact between middle managers and technical staff
varied across departments. In NC Part Programming there
was daily contact because the manager sat at a desk in an
open plan room. In all the other departments the manager
and deputy manager had their own separate offices, and made
trips into the department to talk to the staff. Technical
workers were usually conscious of the absence of the manager,
although this did not appear to alter the atmosphere of the
office, as it was the section leader who acted to ensure the
continuity of work. Each department had one manager (chief)
and usually one under manager (deputy chief) who, if unionised, were members of the Bristol Management Branch of
TASS. Below the two managers were two or three section
leaders who were the supervisors on the job. Section leaders
were organised by Bristol No. 3. Branch of TASS. Below the
section leaders were the non-supervisory senior, ordinary and
junior technical staff. There were extra supervisors in most
of the technical departments due to the decline in the
workload with the run down of the *Concorde* programme.

In each department there were one or two people who had
formerly been supervisors but were now 'on the board' as
rank and file technical staff. The number of section leaders
fluctuated with the workload, but on average there was one
for every five technical workers. The size of management

also varied (two being the optimum figure) and in some departments of equivalent sizes, there was frequently a difference, for example in NC Part Programming there was one manager to eleven programmers, while the estimating department had two managers to eleven estimators.

Apart from programming, the other technical departments I examined had seen better times! In Tool Design (Assembly), at its peak there had been between thirty-five and forty draughtsmen and only two managers – compared with eighteen draughtsmen and two managers when I was interviewing. Redundancies had eliminated not middle-aged managers and supervisors, but a lot of younger technical staff.

A TASS survey of staff turnover at Weybridge BAe.AG discovered that twenty-four to twenty-six was the most likely age group to voluntarily leave in an unstable period. The net result of the three phases of redundancies in the company during the 1970s created what was described to me as a 'middle aged bulge' in most technical areas. A common remark was that there were 'too many chiefs and not enough indians', and the spread of the redundancies meant that such a statement had a good deal of truth in it. In terms of career prospects, the age structure meant that several people in each technical area were 'waiting on dead men's shoes' for promotion opportunities. This again acted as a spur to the movement of younger technical staff out of the company. They had no chances, or felt they had no chances of 'getting on' in the company and so they left. The dominance of older managers also affected the perceptions of rank and file technical staff. Many saw management as a conservative dead weight on technological change, sitting out the last few years of their industrial life until retirement or a 'golden handshake'. Their age meant 'they didn't want to rock the boat'. Such contextual features obviously influence authority relations and I interviewed 'young' and old managers and technical workers to obtain a fair spread of views.

From Company to Corporation: BAC to BAe

There's a lot of apathy in this company due to the redundancies and the fact that we've changed hands several

times. We've come from a small company, Bristol Aeroplane Company into a big company and then into an even
bigger company. And you feel a lot more anonymous, like
a cog in a wheel. And you don't feel that management
appreciates you so much as they used to.

This description by a young draughtsman is a familiar
enough tale, not only to workers at this company but to all
those working in large companies in Britain. The rate of
concentration of British manufacturing in the 1960s and 1970s
has meant that a growing proportion of workers experience
the sense of anonymity described by Colin Luck. In Chapter
3 I outlined the changes in ownership and size of BAe. Basically, within two decades the company had moved from being
the Bristol Aeroplane Company, with a paternalistic managerial structure and a capitalist-owner manager, to the larger
British Aircraft Corporation and then the even larger British
Aerospace. From being a single company the site at Filton
was now just one site of one division of an enormous, multi-
divisional corporation that employed 68 950 in January 1978.
Technical workers were not alone in feeling the growing sense
of estrangement and anonymity. A manager who had worked
at BAe from when it was the Bristol Aeroplane Company
explained the changes he had experienced:

> This Company started off with the old paternal structure,
> with the boss, Sir George White. But that has gradually
> gone away. We went into partnership with Vickers and
> made the British Aircraft Corporation, so we are gradually
> getting away from the paternal image, and gradually
> converting into a normal, everyday, run of the mill type
> industrial set-up, and of course when nationalisation came
> that was the final straw. We are now like any other
> commercial organisation. The paternalism has gone, we
> recognise that fact. We are adjusting ourselves. I don't say
> we've adjusted to that.

What Cockran is describing is the bureaucratisation of
management and the loss of contact between middle management and 'the boss'. Carter (1985), in an extensive review of

the literature on the changing work and market situation of managers, highlighted the progressive loss of control junior and middle management exercise over their working environment. He showed that budgetary control of departments and decentralised management organisation place a tight grip on the independence of managers. This loss of control is closely associated with the growth of the multi-divisional, multi-product corporation and the specialisation and differentiation of the management function (Hannah, 1976; Armstrong, 1984). Managers at Filton had to account for their departments' efficiency and contract deadlines, and budgetry or financial control was increasing with the application of new technology and sophisticated estimating techniques to tendered contract work.

The functional differentiation of management also affects their behaviour and Storey (1983) paraphrasing Mintzberg claimed that managers of manual workers in production roles, 'experience greater fragmentation in the role activities than other managers. They spend more time in *decision* roles of disturbance-handlers and negotiators. In contrast, the managers of staff specialists spend more time alone, more on paperwork, more on their own speciality and generally, therefore, more on the information roles of monitor, spokesman and disseminator' (Storey, 1983, p. 82). I found that technical managers, while conforming to some of the above characteristics, were equally cut off from the overall co-ordination and control exercised by senior management.

The loss of decision-making power had meant a decline in the ability of department heads to 'look after' their technical staff. This in turn had stimulated trade unionism amongst those individuals whose illusions in the 'power', 'paternalism' or authority of departmental managers to safeguard their interests had been wrecked. There was a crisis in management at Filton and technical staff commonly complained that it was impossible to find managers who 'managed' – who made decisions for all to see. This was not a demand for a more truculent style of managing, it rather expressed the need to feel those above were 'in charge' of something, and responsible to somebody. The move from a paternalistic to a bureaucratic structure had caused this confusion about where deci-

sion-making power lay in the corporation. A designer saw
great problems in plotting the structure of management:

> You investigate the family tree of the authority coming
> down from above, start at the bottom and try and work
> your way up to the top, I don't envy the task.

It was as if middle management had become isolated from
senior and executive managers, leaving staff in a state of
limbo about their future, and the future of the company.
The redundancies in the 1970s, the ending of *Concorde* and
uncertainty within the industry compounded this sense of
managers having no direction or power.

The 'defeatism' of middle management in not fighting for
the future of the company, but only their own selfish careers,
was a frequent comment on management's interest in the
company. Technical staff wanted to see an expansion in the
number of technical apprenticeships, in training and
retraining programmes. Middle managers tended to argue for
investment in fixed capital rather than labour, on the grounds
of a decline in the availability of skilled labour. The high
average age in the Engineering Design Organisation worried
the draughtsmen who feared closure without new recruits.
During a wages dispute in 1978, TASS operated a subcontract
ban, and corporate management threatened to close the EDO
if the ban was not lifted. To the TASS activists – and the
rank and file members I interviewed – this was considered to
be indicative of management's short-term interests in the
Filton site. They preferred to subcontract work out of Filton
rather than expand the number of apprenticeships. The ban
remained, without positive sanctions from management.

The nationalisation of parts of the aerospace industry in
1977 raised certain expectations that communications
between sites and divisions would improve. But no-one I
interviewed felt any more involved in the running of the
company. There had been some union proposals for a 'demo-
cratic' company structure, but this had not been implemented
in any form (Bristol Aircraft Workers, 1975). One of the bitter
complaints from technical workers was that the divisional
management at Filton had been unable to get work trans-

ferred from other sites when Bristol was short of work. TASS *had* secured work, and it reflected badly on management's organisation and communication that they were unable or unwilling to get work, and perform what were widely regarded as managerial duties. Mac Smith, a designer, and Peter Cox, a draughtsman, were both critical of management for not 'pulling their weight'. They said that before nationalisation there was extreme site rivalry, and this had not changed under State ownership. They told me about the failure of management to secure work for Filton.

Mac: That was before we were BAe, but things don't seem to have changed. You see the line of communication within that hierarchy of BAC was sadly lacking somewhere. You see, when you refer to *the company*, we've had this argument in the past, what is *the company*? For there was Warton up to their eyes in work and there was us, here, running fast out of work and never the twain met. We were the same *company*, the BAC.

Peter: It was the union, the bottom end again. We put out feelers through our union representatives and they put out feelers there about work coming down to us. Now that is how it started off. Of course management would say otherwise, but it's perfectly true that it started from Bristol No. 3 and the equivalent up there. Now we've got so much work we can't see.

Mac: Bearing in mind that if we hadn't done that work there would have been a bigger redundancy programme. Where's the communication? Where's the co-operation? Where's the management?

There was a corporate expectation amongst the technical staff that the company should 'look after' their workers and the failure to secure work, what they saw as the most basic function of management, at a time when TASS was able to do so, called into question the legitimacy, organisation and power of management. Peter and Mac were criticising executive and senior management, although they were also critical of the stolidness of middle management in certain areas.

During the redundancies many departmental managers did secure work 'off their own bat' and there was a joint effort in many departments to avoid redundancies. This was the case in the Tool Design (Assembly) office. Redundancy disputes have the ability to create a collective interest in saving jobs, although my evidence from Filton and other research sites suggests that management are less at risk of redundancy than staff or manual workers – but they are still vulnerable (Fryer, 1977; Chamot, 1976).

The experiences of the 1970's redundancies had taught the technical workers at BAe something about the inadequate channels of communication between the sites and divisions, and the short-term nature of management policies. To others, it had revealed the common interest the two groups had in maintaining their position as wage labourers. But what of the daily working relationship between managers and technical staff? How did the two see each other? While line management's structural vulnerability appeared to be projecting them into a position as simple wage labourers, these conditions were not straightforwardly accepted, and departmental heads had 'not adjusted' to those changes. There was no real pattern to middle management's reaction to the changes but unionisation and staff solidarity, as opposed to isolation and professional autonomy, were the two main options that surfaced in the research.

The Job of the Technical Manager

The social position of the manager in the technical department was described by one electrical planner:

> *Nick:*   They're only a higher level of employee than what we are. They've got a job to do, they get a salary, they're working for somebody, so what's the difference?
>
> *Chris:* But what about their authority?
>
> *Nick:*   But that's part of their job isn't it? I appreciate that you've got to have somebody to direct people. I think that there's a gap between what we can call

higher management and middle management. In a
big company I think you're bound to get this.
Whereas perhaps forty years ago, they were more or
less an elite class and not looked upon as employees
so much. I think today, there's a different attitude,
which is probably a good thing.

The co-ordination of work flow in the department, the
planning of future work loads, liaising with other departments
and managers, all figured as part of the functions performed
by the department manager. They also negotiated with
department representatives and took individual grievances
through the machinery up the managerial hierarchy. Many
other managers at Filton were more like 'leading hands' in
manual areas, in that they did not directly supervise or co-
ordinate the immediate working environment of other
workers, but were heads of small design teams, or research
groups. They were typically the most experienced, qualified
or skilled member of their section and gained their position
by virtue of these qualities. Many technical department heads
also shared some of these qualities, while performing global
functions of capital. All possessed a technical background in
the section they managed and the typical entry point had
been through long service in the one department. But they
were also very different from leading engineers of the small,
typically research or experimental groups, in that they were
responsible for the productivity, discipline, conduct and
working time of staff within their department. They were the
first line of a managerial hierarchy that co-ordinated work
and controlled the output of technical staff across the site.
They were therefore not straightforwardly a higher employee,
but an employee of a qualitatively different kind – agents of
capital (Poulantzas) or members of the new middle class
(Carchedi).

Technical workers' assessment of department heads was
based on their ability as workers, their ability as managers
and their ability as good communicators. There is a contradiction for management at this level. Technical staff wanted
open and visible management, which was non-authoritarian
and rational. So, the secrecy of decision-making, the closed

meetings and lack of worker involvement, both acted to shore up managerial prerogatives but at the same time indirectly threatened the managers' claims to employee status, and more importantly their status as skilled technical workers. Skill and secrecy go together, but management make decisions behind closed doors to preserve their power not their skills. Although all the technical managers had entered management through the office and were all technically competent in their particular fields, none of the technical workers I interviewed relied upon the manager's technical judgement to guide their work. Management were therefore not required to exercise their technical abilities on a daily basis, which undermined the workers' confidence in the managers' technical skills, although the managers believed they could still draw, design, programme, prepare a route card as well as ever. Technical workers considered the job of managers as largely clerical and administrative functions that did not carry the same value as technical skills.

The manager's position as 'worker and boss' was unstable in the technical departments. If the duties required of the manager were purely administrative, then the status of the manager was low in the eyes of the technical workers. Brian Maunders, a trainee programmer explained:

> Somebody could co-ordinate all the departments which is really all you need. It only needs a co-ordinator. A boss in here can't tell you anything about the job really. So he's not really a boss in that respect . . . I reckon a boss should be somebody you can go to with a technical query and he should be able to help you on that technical query, and John, who's only a section leader, he's a mate, a work mate and also a guy you can go to with technical problems. *You don't need a boss.*

Mike, the department manager, was 'only good for a paper-work query', technical advice was available from Brian's workmates. The removal of the manager's function as technical adviser in the office relegates his status to a clerical category, and makes him an irrelevant figure in many respects – 'you don't need a boss'. Technical staff who had got beyond their apprenticeship and had been working in an area for a number of years, also questioned the need for supervisors or section leaders because of their irrelevance to the task at hand, Peter Win, a draughtsman in his late twenties:

> In some cases the boss is not needed. We've got a job to do, we plan and then that is fed straight out through the system to the shop. No-one else looks at it. No-one else reads it through and says 'you've made a mistake here and there' – except in the very early days when you're going through your training. But after that no-one sees your work. So in a sense your section leader is no more than a person who receives and has to make decisions on different things, but as far as your work is concerned, you just get a job and that is it.

Carter and others have discussed the problem of quantifying the work of management. Capital measures the success of managerial labour by the output it is able to gain from productive labour in manufacturing, or the volume of sales in distribution. Management are the productive factor in the upside-down logic of capitalist rationality, although they only obtain recognition by default, from other people's productivity. Marx (1976, p. 450) argued that the hired manager was indirectly productive as part of the collective labourer, but as a 'special kind of wage-labourer' his function is to direct and supervise and extract the best results out of those he manages. In the technical area this meant obtaining a higher throughput of plans, drawings or programmes by carefully managing the labour of others. Lacking the tools of authoritarian and technical control, management of output was down to the manager's 'ability to deal with men'. This stress on style or individual managerial ability is obviously not confined to the technical area. However, the very difficulty of directly measuring and pacing the work of technical staff seemed to place leadership abilities high up the list of technical workers' perceptions of management. This inevitably meant some managers were good and some were bad at the 'personnel side' or 'people management'.

In addition to judging management by the yardstick of the

job, technical workers' involvement with trade unionism gave them another set of criteria with which to measure management's action. This was often trade unionism experienced on the shop floor as well as the office. We have already seen that work obtained through the trade union network threw into question the behaviour of corporate management. The experience of being a shop steward or office representative involved technical workers in a style or practice of leadership quite different from what they observed around them in department heads and group managers. Steve Silver, a draughtsman, had been an active shop steward on the shop floor. As a steward he always reported back to the membership, listened to their problems and fought for them if he judged the grievances to be legitimate. The Group Manager of the four technical departments around the machine shop was considered by Steve and many others in the departments to be a hopeless manager. Steve was prepared to believe that he performed a necessary function as a group manager, although the secrecy of the decision-making process made it impossible to assess whether this was actually the case. But his social actions as a 'leader' damned him in Steve's eyes, because he did not report back and keep the staff informed. Steve described an example of the manager's poor leadership:

> Well, he set an example of his leadership qualities yesterday when there was a bomb scare. He came out of his office with his hat and coat on, and all our chaps were there asking what was happening, like, and somebody said to him, as he was going through the door, 'Excuse me, but what's happening?' And he said, 'There's a bomb scare, you've got to evacuate'. And he was gone, like, you know. Marvellous leadership qualities, everybody was aware of what was happening like, you know [laughter]. It was pathetic.

The following things can be said about technical workers' evaluation of middle management. Firstly, structural changes in the ownership and size of the corporation had reduced the power and therefore the authority of middle management. This left the managers in a situation where they felt they had to join TASS to preserve their voice within the firm. To some technical staff, management's loss of power meant a decline in their ability to act decisively and to manage in an open and individual way. It was within these structural constraints that 'good' and 'bad' management was defined. A good manager was somebody who took an interest in the working and non-working lives of those in the office. Secondly, it was widely accepted that middle management had no contribution to make to the work tasks of technical staff. Although managers were considered to require a technical background – otherwise 'they get the wool pulled over their eyes' – this knowledge was not exercised in their daily dealings with their staff. The third feature of management was that their skills, *vis-à-vis* the technical workers below them, were categorised as clerical and administrative. These skills are held in a low esteem by technical workers, and where there was absence of open leadership on the part of a group or section manager, then he lacked the respect of his men.

I found different elements in technical workers' evaluation of middle management. Fundamentally they wanted leadership but not of an authoritarian kind. Technical staff wanted managers to act for *their* interests as staff in their dealings with senior and executive management, but this was increasingly impossible. Their work was autonomous and self-regulated, it was therefore unnecessary for managers to have any involvement in the daily labour process of technical staff. Management's main priority as far as technical workers were concerned, should be to relay decisions in a clear open way, fight for their department when work was slack, try to get improved wages or conditions according to the needs of the office, and try to get more apprentices into the department. To manage in this sense, should be simply a way of communicating, through the hierarchy of the company, the interests of his staff. Any attempt to 'control' the work of the technical worker was resisted. But there were pressures on managers to improve productivity, and this inevitably meant interfering with job autonomy.

The creation of BAe had hastened the demise of managerial paternalism but there remained a search amongst older and some young senior technical staff for a pattern of paternalistic authority that could accommodate the recognition of individual worth or merit. Within any hierarchy, those at the bottom desire to have their work and value recognised by those above. Up until the mid 1970s a payment system had institutionalised this individual ideology. Merit payments were awarded on an annual basis as a 'bonus' for individual effort in the course of the previous year. In the technical departments around the machine shop the size of the bonus was determined by the Group Manager in consultation with the three individual departmental managers. The current group manager was considered to rely too readily on the word of the office manager because he 'didn't know his men personally'. Ben Stock, an older programmer who wanted to see greater managerial involvement in wages, said of an earlier, more authoritarian Group Manager:

> Jim Denny knew pretty well what his programmers were doing and what his planners and Jig and Tool Draughtsmen were doing. *He knew pretty well what everyone was worth. Whereas now the respect isn't there.*

Clearly the ability of management to determine merit payments in this form encouraged individualism and secrecy amongst technical workers, while enhancing the authority and control of individual managers. Programming was a department where secrecy about individual's wages was only challenged by younger, trainee programmers in the late 1970s. They came from the shop floor and were amazed at the secrecy surrounding wages in the technical offices. At C.A. Parsons merit payments were part of the formalised bargaining structure, which served to weaken their individualising effect.

'Us and 'Them' in the technical area

Restricting attention to the analytical 'class' position or functional placement of department managers, we can make the following observations. Firstly, along a managerial axis, office chiefs acted as:

  i direct co-ordinators of the labour of those in their depart-
    ment through control of the office hierarchy, not by direct
    supervision of subordinates.
 ii administrators of overtime working, attendance, absences,
    minor negotiating issues, working time and other issues
    which affected the conditions of those in the office.
iii representatives of the first link in the managerial command
    structure of subcontracting. (Several section leaders were
    also responsible for specialist subcontracting in
    departments).
 iv staff not engaged directly with the product and not called
    upon to assist the direct labour in the department.

By these criteria managers represented the unproductive,
supervisory authority in the department. Along a different
axis they were closer to the condition and place of those below
them.

  i they worked as wage labourers.
 ii they were relatively powerless in terms of (a) influencing
    the wages and major working conditions of their staff
    (issues handled by central personnel and the Industrial
    Committee of TASS); (b) determining their own individual
    wages and conditions (negotiated by the TASS manage-
    ment branch); (c) controlling the flow of work through
    their department (some managers appeared to have more
    control over this activity than others); (d) influencing
    capital expenditure (negotiated centrally); (e) determining
    size of the department (some influence, but not executive
    power).

In other words, on a whole series of strategic issues, line
management was relatively weak.
    Functional ambiguity and the lack of a sufficient material
differentiation from technical workers, ensured that managers
had an uncertain self-image and were perceived in far from
clear-cut terms by workers in the offices. Some managers
stressed their proximity to their staff, others the importance
of differences. By and large if managers emphasised factors
considered along their managerial axis, they were more likely
to be identified as 'company men', as belonging to a different

group or class from those below. By emphasising their status as wage labourers and their relative powerlessness, they were more likely to identify with technical workers. But this analytical division lacked any predictive power, and like all abstract statements on social relations, ignored the role of individuals, the contextual situation, the nature of particular events and the historical circumstances within the factory and the wider relations between capital and labour at large. These contextual or historical conditions do not 'overcome' the lines of functional differentiation that separated managers from technical workers, but they ensure that over-drawn dichotomies of the kind generated by structural Marxism, will rarely be encountered as universal class characterisations.

Office managers exerted a considerable influence on the 'atmosphere' and social relations in the department. They also influenced trade union activity. At the level of the office, the manager exercises, according to Weberian literature, a conservative influence. TASS activists I interviewed thought the strength and political affiliations of office managers, together with the presence or absence of TASS militants and the social background of staff, were major determinants of militancy. But Weberian literature on office staff borrowing status and authority through association with management ignored the converse of this relationship that managers are put under pressure from those below them in the office. Middle managers stood uneasily between those above and below, increasingly estranged from senior and executive management and therefore more likely to identify with those below. More importantly, if the manager was on his own in the department, he was more vulnerable to the group pressure of the technical staff. Perhaps for this reason, I only encountered one technical department where the manager was isolated. Mike Cooper, a young manager of the N.C. Part Programming department. Brian Maunders, a programmer, explained his ambiguous position:

> Mike's in a very difficult position really. Because he likes to be one of the boys but he feels a little bit of strain. There's been instances when we've gone out on a night and we haven't asked Mike along. It's wrong, you know. They

say he's so stiff and formal, but on the couple of occasions
we've been out, he's mixed in quite well , . .   I gave them
a bollocking last time because they didn't invite him out . . .
He's a company man and a stickler for the rules and this
doesn't sit very well for a lot of people.

During the lunch hour Mike joined in a regular game of table
tennis played in the office. This sort of social interaction was
alien to shop floor workers and managers and not encountered
in other technical departments. Exerting discipline and
control directly was also harder where a manager was isolated
and subjected to individual and group pressure.

Within each department there were individuals who desired
a closer working relationship with management in general.
These individuals were not a homogeneous group, but were
roughly divided between corporatists and anti-unionists, and
tended to come from a background of self-employment or to
have experienced downward mobility in the course of their
working lives. They emphasised the importance of working
together and were dismayed at signs of division between staff
and management. The technical department contained a mix
of ideological positions. It combined reactionary 'traces' of
past occupational identities now dis-possessed of authority.
It held individuals who had been former managers or petty
proprietors. And it contained the high fliers, with managerial
ambitions for corporate glory, although it must be admitted,
such individuals were few on the ground. This, as much as a
narrow functional relationship to manual workers, explains
the diversity of competing ideologies within the technical
departments.

Practically all the technical workers I interviewed identified
their interests as distinct and separate from those of management. In the abstract it was also true that most technical staff
judged local management as another grade of wage labourer.
But, given a situation where there was a practical reason to
hold separate interests, such as the issue of a subcontract
ban, a wages difference, a disciplinary problem and/or an
argument over time-keeping, then opinions often polarised.
In the main, working conditions did not give rise to conflict
on a daily basis, and although managers had their own offices

Technical Workers

and facilities, both groups started work at the same time, and there were no company cars for middle managers. Differences in conditions were rarely mentioned as important, more typically the functional separation of interest was highlighted. Others mentioned wages, although these were secondary to the lack of good communication between managers and staff. Fred Hoyle, a production controller:

> Unfortunately there's an 'us' and 'them' situation, partly because of the money difference, although it comes back to the question of personal relationships. How many of the bosses demand a job to be done and if it's done satisfactorily the person who's done that job doesn't get the necessary, I won't say praise, but acknowledgement for doing that job. Whereas if the manager could go down to that level and say: 'Alright chaps, you've done a good job', he would be closing the differential that way.

Relations between technical workers and managers were not altogether based on structural antagonism. This was because of the autonomy of the technical worker on the job. One index of the absence of objective structural conflict was the stress all technical workers placed on the personality and managerial style of the chief for determining the atmosphere in the office. Whether there existed an 'us' and 'them' situation in the office, or a situation of mutual co-operation was down to how the manager *acted*, whether he took an interest in the job, was a disciplinarian or indifferent and a recluse. Their proximity to management, the long-term engagement with one department, their assessment of management in general, was considerably influenced by the character of the particular office manager. This may not be different from the skilled operator's assessment of shop management, although skilled and unskilled workers may have a clearer structural sense of their interests and management's interests, and fewer corporatist illusions in regard to managerial duties.

There were no major disputes across the factory while I was interviewing so it was difficult to examine relations between management and staff in conditions that may have supported polarisation. However a wages dispute illustrates some of the ambiguities in social relations. In pursuit of a general wage claim, TASS had imposed a subcontract ban that operated for six months. TASS Management Branch endorsed this wage claim and levied all two hundred and fifty members to the tune of £5. TASS members maintained that middle managers had a vested interest in seeing technical staff achieve a good wage rise because their own differential would increase pro rata:

> If we put in for a big wage claim, they would say 'Oh well, No. 3. branch has got such and such, and therefore in differentials we want such and such'. Therefore to help themselves, they would help us.

Carter (1980), arguing from evidence gathered at a medium-sized engineering factory, maintained that manual workers judged staff to be parasitic upon their activity as wage increases were frequently automatically passed on to staff following a successful dispute or claim by manual workers. Smith, Child and Rowlinson (1987) found similar grievances amongst process operatives who considered tradesmen to be dependent upon their labour and action for their own wage increases. In large organisations such as BAe, there were no automatic wage rises between manual and technical workers, but both groups supported the others' wage battles. TASS activists said the tradition of the company passing on wage increases disappeared with the rise in the number of staff. Indeed TASS wage militancy is a response, in part, to the company's general abandonment of established differentials. Management as a group, however, were *very* dependent on technical staff because of their reluctance to engage in industrial activity. The management branch levy for the 'draughtsmen's' dispute had changed a lot of minds about the importance of unionising middle management. This action was hailed at the TASS annual conference as indicative of the way managers change, once organised, and the practical benefits TASS can gain from their membership.

This interdependency and the material support between the two branches surprised many people I interviewed. But the solidarity was extremely uneven. In departments who experienced TASS sanctions, like tool design, relations between management and workers had actually become more hostile and polarised as a result of TASS action. In other departments e.g. Jig and Tool Design (Machine Shop) local management did not endorse TASS activity. For some TASS activisits, the wages dispute increased the 'us' and 'them' situation by making members more aware of management intransigence. A conflict situation meant all managers were identified as a hostile, unitary mass, or separate class.

The contradictions and ambiguities of managements' social position and the uncertainty in relations between technical workers and managers were undoubtedly compounded by the unionisation of middle managers. This produced a mixed response amongst technical staff, while the majority of managers would have preferred not to have been part of a trade union. They felt compelled to join a TUC-recognised union to safeguard their voice in the nationalised British Aerospace Corporation. Unionisation changed relationships and 'the atmosphere' in several departments, while in others it was deemed irrelevant to the established pattern of relations. It was a sufficiently important change to warrant separate analysis.

The Unionisation of Middle Management

Most of the literature on unionisation examines engineers and managers together, because it is claimed 'most engineers are also managers in the sense that they supervise subordinate staff' (Bamber, 1978; Prandy, 1965). My findings at Filton did not support this assumption, as the TASS Management Branch and its predecessor the BAe Management Staff Association, limited entry to managers. Non-managerial engineers could either join the United Kingdom Association of Professional Engineers, which had no bargaining rights, or Bristol No. 3. Branch of TASS which had bargaining rights in their area. In other factories professional engineers and managers were organised by TASS in a Professional Engineers and Managers Branch.

The growing body of literature on managerial unionism

has explained the origins and dynamics of the trend towards collective organisation amongst managers by reference to three basic forces. Firstly, the political effect of Government legislation, which covers the nationalisation of companies (McCormick, 1960) employment and industrial relations legislation (Purcell, 1976); and government incomes policies (Clegg, 1976; Metcalf, 1977). The second influence has been the attitudes of employers. It has been a central tenet of the industrial relations approach to white-collar unionism that the employers exercise a critical influence on unionisation (Flanders, 1970; Bain, 1970; Clegg, 1976). The influence of the employers is obviously crucial to unionisation, but whether their encouragement is the central determinant of white-collar unionisation is open to question. In Chapter 8 I highlight the 'struggle to organise' in non-managerial white-collar areas where employers did not encourage unions. With managerial unionisation the attitude of senior management may be more critical. McCormick found in the mining industry, and Bamber in steel, that the encouragement of higher management was an important ingredient in middle management unionisation. At Filton, senior management abandoned serious negotiations with the British Aerospace Management Staff Association and this helped push the middle managers towards joining a TUC-affiliated union that their bosses would listen to. This was encouragement by default. The third force behind unionisation is the advent of redundancy amongst management (Fryer, 1977; Chamot, 1976; Bamber, 1978). This insecurity undoutedly acted as a spur at Filton and several managers commented on the general insecurity of the aerospace industry. The cancellation of government support for the *TSR2* project in the 1960s stuck in the minds of managers and staff and the rundown in *Concorde* had generated redundancies, encouraging the unionisation of technical staff and management.

More systematic application of structural Marxist analysis to the question of unionisation of supervisors and managers has stressed the central concern with regaining *control* threatened by manual union power. This literature is reviewed in the next chapter. Certainly at Filton, this was one issue, but the process of unionisation was more related to the change in ownership of the company. Unionisation was not an active response or indication of a shift in the class position of managers. But rather, as Carter (1985) has argued, an attempt to arrest the process of proletarianisation. Managers rejected the 'leftist' politics of TASS, and other indicators of what Prandy, Stewart and Blackburn (1974) have called 'societal unionatness', that is, a union's external connection with the wider labour movement. Unionisation should be seen as an attempt to preserve a *separate voice* to a corporate management increasingly deaf to the interests of the swelling ranks of salaried managers.

Recent survey research in Western Europe on management's motives for joining trade unions emphasises the decline in differentials and the effect of government pay policy, (EAPM, 1979). These were certainly major grievances at Filton, as Alan Coggan, a design engineer and representative in the management branch, argues:

> Because of the financial situation the country finds itself in at the moment, we find ourselves in the middle of the sandwich and we don't like it. The financial implications of the various pay freezes are such that the upper levels, the executives and so on, have been held down while the shop floor workers have advanced and we are the jam in the middle. We're getting squeezed up from the bottom and we can't push up because of that ceiling there.

At Filton, nationalisation was the primary reason for management unionisation. Bamber has traced the changing fortunes of SIMA (the Steel Industry Management Association) with the ebb and flow of state and private ownership of the steel industry. His account is about the 'struggle to win recognition' by middle managers. There was no 'struggle' on the part of middle managers at Filton, quite the opposite in fact. Had legislation appeared to offer managers an alternative to unionisation, they would not have strayed from the confines of their management staff association. This reason for organisation was seen by many TASS members to be hypocritical and weak. All the managers told me that if the industry was denationalised and they were given a choice between TASS and their company-specific staff association, (with guarantees of equivalent negotiating machinery) they would have no hesitation in leaving TASS. The continued membership of TASS after denationalisation in February 1981 may indicate that the company was unwilling to re-establish the old negotiating arrangements.

John Cockran, a manager in his late fifties had been active in the developments that led to managers forming the TASS Bristol Management Branch:

> Written into the Nationalisation Act was the clause that only those members of a recognised TUC-affiliated union would have any voice where that voice could be heard. We took the only course open to us as managers, we were forced into it, we didn't want to become members of a TUC affiliated union . . . We were quite prepared to go muddling along the way we were going . . . TASS wasn't the only union the Management Society approached, *but TASS was the only union that offered us an autonomous branch and that suited our purposes right down to the ground.*

There was in fact no legal obligation to join TASS in the Nationalisation Act, and in the shipbuilding industry the Act sent managers into SAIMA (Shipbuilding and Allied Industries' Management Association), a professional engineers and management only 'trade union'. SAIMA transferred their engagements to the Engineers' and Managers' Association (a TUC-affiliated union) at the end of 1977 and eventually, after battles with TASS in several yards, persuaded the British Shipbuilders Board to recognise them. The management at Filton could have transferred the staff association to the EMA and fought TASS for recognition by the company, but at Filton there was a resigned opinion amongst middle management that it was either TASS or ASTMS. As TASS offered them political and organisational autonomy, they opted to join. Alan Cogan again:

> If the Company had told us that they would discuss our problems and act on our problems without the need for joining a trade union, then I am sure that almost one

hundred per cent of managers would not have joined
TASS. . . . We must be able to speak to our bosses and if
they won't listen to us as a group which they recommended
we should form, then obviously we had to look else where
to get our voices heard. . . . Many of the Management
Branch do not agree with the basic principles of trade
unionism, and the policies of a leftist dominated union like
TASS. And it is a really unusual union for us to join, *but it
was only because they gave us the assurances that we were completely
autonomous. We were sure that we couldn't be dictated to, that if
they went on strike we would not have to strike too.*

How then, did technical staff judge the entry of managers
into their union? Those who held union positions, especially
positions on the branch council or negotiating committee,
that is more senior positions in TASS, were generally much
keener on management's joining TASS than those who were
ordinary members or office represenatives. The reasons for
this are not hard to find. Not only are they more influenced
by TASS policy, which was heavily in favour of broadening
the recruitment base, but they are also likely to experience
the effects of belonging to the same union because they deal
with managers at a formal level. Ordinary members were not
really in positions to assess any change in the manager's
behaviour, because his union membership was generally irrelevant to the work of the department. Neville Green had
worked in the tool design since 1959 and had recently joined
the Industrial Committee of TASS after representing his
department for many years. I asked him to comment on the
interests of workers and managers:

> I would say, basically we're a unit in this office, more so
> in the last two years, without doubt, since managers joined
> the union. Some people wouldn't agree with me mind. I've
> got a special relationship with the chief, and as I've been
> in the office for twenty-seven years, I can speak to him very
> straight using four letter words if necessary. But whether
> he accepts it is another matter. But I'm in that position.

The 'special relationship' Neville had with the 'chief' and his length of service in the department added to his desire for a corporate association. Nick Page, the office representative from the electrical planning department, agreed with Neville's assessment of the unionisation of management aiding worker-management relations. He was aware that structural changes in the corporation had divided management into clear groups, and judged the unionisation of middle managers to be a natural progression of the expansion and evolution of management:

> There will definitely be more understanding now we're in the same union, from the evidence of what's happened in his office there's better communications between our union, managers, and the men. And better relations are bound to be a good thing.

In general then, those who held negotiating positions within TASS supported management unionisation for reasons of increased communication, understanding, or in support of corporate policies. Managers too, adhered to these goals, but by and large did not associate trade unionism with 'better communication'. Only one of the managers I interviewed saw trade unionism as positively enhancing industrial relations. Tony Read, the chief in the estimating department reasoned that if everyone was in a union, the sense of an 'us' and 'them' would wither away. This too, is a form of the same corporate outlook I have been examining. Joining a union did not involve any distinct ideological commitment, it was simply acknowledging the realities of working in a large corporation:

> A lot of management weren't in anything at all and they could see that there was going to be trouble if they didn't join. And I think it's a better thing. You were just talking about a situation of 'them' and 'us', well this fosters 'them' and 'us' if we don't get in a union. Today it's not a family business. You know, you used to know everyone and there was the feeling that you were working for *a boss*, you know, up at the top, George White, R. S. Brown, and all them. But today it's just the faceless ones, you can't give your

old-time loyalty to these people 'cos they don't give a damn
in any case, you see. You know, you could be dripping
blood for them and they'd just pass you in the street or
probably walk over you.

The motive of self-preservation appeared somehow
unsavoury to some managers and those technical workers
who were hostile or sceptical of management being in trade
unions. Mike Cooper, the manager in NC Part Programming,
was known as a staunch 'company man' and bitterly regretted
joining TASS. Yet he was prepared to reap any benefits of
improved industrial relations that union membership
brought. He explained his feelings at being in a trade union:

> I found it a bit unacceptable really. I felt that we had to
> join a union for our own self protection, because we were
> getting sniped at from union members below us and not
> supported by the Directors above us, it's as simple as that.
> I thought it totally wrong that we should have to join a
> union.

He acknowledged that membership of TASS had helped his
relationship with Jim Andrews the office representative.

> We're all *brothers* together I suppose [cynical laughter].
> We've got a very straightforward union man who works on
> this section, who calls a spade a spade, you know exactly
> where you are with him. But I've found him a little bit
> more forthcoming once he's realised I'm in the union and
> I think from that respect it's probably helped.

Such cynical remarks about the 'brotherhood' between staff
and management upset many rank-and-file TASS members
and office representatives who were both unsure about
management's motives for joining a trade union, and luke-
warm about TASS opening its doors to the 'opposition'. Mac
Smith, a designer, and Peter Cox, a draughtsman, both took
a keen interest in the union, although they did not hold any
union   positions   when   I   interviewed   them.   They

both considered management's motives in joining TASS dubious:

> *Peter:* On this question of the Management Branch, I would have preferred the CBI to organise the manager-type people, [for them] to have their own type of organisation rather than the TUC. It is a 'them' and 'us' situation, there's no question in my mind about that.
>
> *Mac:* Which has been furthered by the creation of 'super TASS' [i.e. Management Branch: C.S.]
>
> *Peter:* I went to a meeting the other day and two of the hard nuts, I would say, of management were there, trying to get Bristol No. 3. to break down barriers, which have been created over the years, and not without reason too. And we were very suspicious of these two people. We were running the meeting and one of these chaps prefaced his remarks by saying, 'Oh well, we're all brothers aren't we? ha! ha! ha!'. Now that to me was — well what I expected of him, to be perfectly honest, because he's only using it, using the language without any meaning.

Managers were not only 'playing at trade unionism' but belittling trade union practices and procedures. The emphasis on their use of trade union terminology in a shallow and cynical way, indicates not simply the outrage of an established trade unionist confronted by a 'new unionism', but also his conviction that managers were unwilling unionists and not really 'workers'.

The strongest criticism of management joining trade unions came from two individuals who for very different reasons were not members of TASS. Steve Silver had transferred into the drawing office from the machine shop where he had been an active shop steward:

> I think it's a bloody farce myself. I think it's just a wangle to get over company problems, the subcontract ban, etc. I don't think their trade union cards count for much. If it comes to the crunch and there was a dispute I don't think

their cards would count for anything. Mike Cooper's company loyalties would be struggling against the trade union.

In contrast to Steve Silver, Michael Philipson was a staunch anti-unionist, who had crossed many picket lines in the course of his working life. His position on trade unions was that 'it was impossible to serve two masters, the company pays me, I therefore work for the company not the union'. Management's membership of TASS appeared to him as a reversal of commonsense – 'it seems to me a fairyland, a fantasy world, how can you possibly have managers and bosses in unions?' As for the majority of technical workers they were initially surprised by management's decision to join TASS, but had accepted their unionisation.

The TASS Management Branch, when I returned to Filton in June 1982, was more entrenched than in 1978, and had been involved in industrial action – although not strike action. To a large extent the unionisation of management did not affect the daily relationship between the rank and file draughtsman or planner and the department chief. What counted in this relationship was the personality of the manager, his style of management and his commitment to the department. The reluctant unionisation of middle management at one level signified their increasing powerlessness. It did not increase the 'visibility' of management decision-making, but further formalised the relationships between the different levels of authority in the company hierarchy.

Internal and external pressures explain why middle managers were pushed towards trade union organisation, but why they chose TASS is also relevant. Its broad left tradition made it, in the words of one manager, 'a really unusual union for us to join'. TASS, which had shunned rate-fixers in the 1960s because of their connection with capitalist prerogatives, began to actively recruit management staff from the mid-1970s. Between the two periods the union had been through major political, ideological and organisational changes, in part a response to the growing heterogeneity of technical labour described in other chapters. The abandonment of craft exclusiveness in favour of general multi-level unionism, was fashioned out of much debate and political engagement between different factions of the active membership. It was not a straightforward or linear progression from one membership base to another. In the final chapter I explore these developments in more detail.

8
Technical Workers and Trade Unionism: TASS in the Post-War Period

Theories of White-collar Unionism

Two areas of research have dominated the post-war interest in white-collar unionism: the quantitative issue of union *growth* and the qualitative question of union *character*. Why white-collar workers join collective employment associations has largely been studied by focusing on objective variables such as employment concentration, the decline in staff status, collectivisation of employment relations and the policies of employers and the state. The issue of union character has centred on the differences and similarities between manual and white-collar unionism. On both issues there is a division in the literature between what has widely been called the industrial relations orthodoxy and the social stratification perspective (Crompton, 1976; Carter, 1979; Armstrong, 1986). The former has sought to deny the association between changes in the class structure and unionisation, while stressing the similarity of 'goals and methods' of manual and white-collar unions. The social stratification literature, although divided between various Weberian and Marxist positions, has exhibited a degree of unity in emphasising a 'relationship' between changes in the class structure and the issue of unionisation.

These two camps are obviously not completely autonomous. Roberts, Loveridge and Gennard (1972, p. 283) draw from the industrial relations position on aggregate data on union growth, while emphasising the importance of organisational and inter-personal factors in explaining the *process* of unionisation in different employment contexts. In a different mould, orthodox marxists, such as Allen (1971), share with the industrial relations orthodoxy the view that, while manual and white-collar workers are in different market situations, their unions are basically concerned with the same ends.

Growth factors for the social stratification tradition have, from Lockwood (1958) onwards, been connected with the decline in individual control over employment conditions due to the process of 'bureaucratisation in the workplace'. The standardisation of payments, equalisation of non-wage benefits and decline in authority between white-collar and manual workers are part of this process in the work situation. The emergence of distinct labour markets for white-collar occupations, mentioned in my earlier discussion of Braverman (1974) (see page 39), have been put forward as reasons for the emergence of collective rather than individual bargaining amongst white-collar workers. These work and market factors have been linked to the proletarianisation of condition, explicitly suggesting a shift in the class situation of white-collar employees in the course of monopoly capitalism. However, this has not meant any straightforward homogenisation of the relations, consciousness and union structures between manual and white-collar workers. Weberian writers have continued to emphasise both the importance of market differences between white-collar and manual workers, together with the sharing of authority between middle class labour and capital.

Against the above, the industrial relations tradition from Bain (1970), has tried to disengage class and unionisation. Bain, in rejecting the relationship between social class and unionism, has suggested instead that unionisation is the 'outcome' of employment concentration, employers recog-

nition policies and government action. Armstrong (1986) has
noted that Bain's approach conceives of white-collar workers
as 'passive beneficiaries' of a benign state and employers'
goodwill. The absence of process or subjective dynamics in
Bain's model has been noted by several writers (Roberts *et al.*
1972; Carter, 1979; Child and Partridge, 1982). The clearest
sustained early critique of this approach was made by Adams
(1975). He noted that Bain's attention to employment concentration shared common ground with the established connection between bureaucratisation and unionisation discovered
in the stratification literature. Moreover when the three determinants of union growth are placed in an historical perspective, they frequently coincided with more active social
processes. Government policy favouring unionisation, for
example, parallel periods of economic prosperity or national
crisis, which may support union growth. The issue of
employer recognition begs the question of what pressures
operated upon employers to persuade them of the benefits of
unionisation. The Association of Engineering and Shipbuilding Draughtsmen for example, achieved national recognition from the Engineering Employers Federation after a
protracted period of industrial activity (Mortimer, 1960,
p. 106). Moreover, in the take-off of unionisation amongst
white collar workers from the mid-1960s, it is difficult to
abstract employer strategy from union pressure and power.
At C. A. Parsons, for example, while the granting of TASS
provision to recruit higher technical groups has been interpreted by Dickens (1972) as evidence of the centrality of
employers' policy on recognition. But my own interviews with
senior stewards involved in the process itself, indicated the
contradictions and uncertainty in the employers' position,
which was only maintained under pressure from below
(Smith, 1986).

Dunn and Gennard (1984), in their examination of union
closed shops, noted the emergence of management's interest
in corporatism as a factor encouraging general spread of
unionisation from the late 1960s. Carter (1985, p. 173),
drawing from the work of Panitch (1976), suggests that state
support for union recognition should be judged within the
broader policy of welfarism as a corporatist control strategy.

In Britain support for unionism has also been a quid pro quo
for wage restraint. It is the *interaction* between national class
struggles and government policy, and not the independent
attitude of the state which is important. Carter has also
argued that white-collar worker unionisation and militancy
follow patterns in the economic business cycle and the general
strike trend amongst manual workers. In periods of prosperity, when the opportunities for individual economic
advancement, promotion and mobility pertain, white-collar
workers are less likely to adopt a collective response.
However, in periods of rising expectations and failing opportunities, such as the late 1960s and early 1970s, white-collar
workers are more likely to adopt collective solutions to their
economic problems (Carter, 1979).

Union Character

While the question of growth has aroused controversy, most
of the debate on white-collar unionism has actually concerned
the question of union character or the extent to which white-
collar and manual unions are different. Growth and character
are not unconnected. Unionisation can be conceived as merely
a question of headcount and quantity. But the question of why
some people join trade unions and others staff associations is
also related to the nature of institutions themselves. Of central
interest in the early British Weberian writing on employment
organisations was the dichotomy between professional associations as *status* institutions and trade unions as *class* bodies
(Prandy, 1965). I have noted elsewhere, that such a simple
dualism has long been seen as ambiguous for engineers
(Smith, 1986). Yet some Weberian writers persist with this
crude dichotomy, for example McLoughlin (1983). Within
the Weberian stratification tradition writers began to find
more rigorous differentiations *within* trade unions, rather than
between unions and non-unions. Most influential in this area
has been the work of Blackburn and Prandy (1965). In a
review of the literature on unionisation, Blackburn (1967)
suggested that as the 'significance of membership size depends
on the type of organisation joined . . . unionisation, the
measure of social significance, cannot be understood indepen-

dently of union character' (1967, p. 10). Blackburn found it necessary to have a measure of unionisation that combined *character* with some typology of what constituted a 'whole hearted trade union'. The term *unionate* was used as a measure of classifying 'proper' unions from non-unions. Features of union character were its external 'policy, practices, associations and the public image it has created', combined with its internal organisation and structure. Unionateness, as a measure of a 'whole hearted trade union', committed to the general principles of trade unionism and the ideology of the labour movement, was based on seven characteristics: i. the commitment to collective bargaining as a core activity; ii. independence from employers; iii. use of all forms of industrial action; iv. declaring and v. registering as a trade union; vi. affiliation to the TUC and vii. to the Labour Party. In later writing, Prandy, Stewart and Blackburn, (1974) differentiated between enterprise unionateness (items i. to iii.) and society unionateness (items iv. to vii.) They noted that enterprise unionateness, 'refers to those aspects of behaviour of an organisation which are concerned with the pursuit of interests of its members as employees through collective action'. While society unionateness covered 'those aspects of an organisation's character which concern its relation with other, similar organisations and its behaviour in the wider society' (Prandy, Stewart and Blackburn, 1982, p. 153). But this distinction between economic/instrumental and political/ideological interests, does not qualify the earlier model, but formally articulates its intrinsic division. The criticisms of the model given below therefore retain their validity.

The fact that it is possible to construct a model of what constitutes a 'proper' trade union, and one which is based on industrial economism and narrow political affiliation, reflects the peculiarity, homogeneity, stability and dominance of manual workers in British trade union history. At one level the concept of unionateness has a common-sense appeal, and reflects strongly held ideological divisions between manual and white-collar workers. However, it is also a crude scale, and one which says little about the class differences between manual and white-collar unions. A number of criticisms have been made of the model. Firstly, the metaphor of 'union character' implies a degree of unity, cohesion and individuality which does not fit with the tensions within trade union organisation. Carter (1979), drawing off the well-established tradition of writing on trade union bureaucratisation, has shown that Blackburn does not differentiate between the structural divisions between full-time trade union officials and rank-and-file members. The features of unionateness are exclusively drawn from the official structure and policy. To talk about a trade union as an object with given or pre-formed interests and policies, introduces what Hyman (1975) has accurately described as a reified approach to trade union organisation.

Secondly, the model of manual union practice informs the seven features of unionateness, without allowing for disparities between the two groups and the possibility of white-collar unions having independent and distinctive – but equally 'proper' – trade union practices. Crompton (1976) observed that the concept was based on a simple continuum, 'organisations are "more" or "less" like manual unions', something which made it hard 'to conceptualise different modes of representation as *alternative* strategies'. TASS members had to pioneer *distinctive* forms of industrial activity because of their distance from the point of production. Many of these tactics were not carbon copies of manual workers' industrial struggle, but were clearly evidence of their working class location. The assumption that there is only 'one' model is dubious. Unionateness is not ranked along a scale of importance, we cannot, therefore, assess what are the core differences between white-collar and manual workers' unions. In particular, it leaves the question of class relations of membership isolated from the issue of organisation.

Unionateness, is essentially a measure of the integration within organisations, not of division based on the different class relations of the membership. To approach the link between class position and unionism, we need a different theory, and one which begins with class relations in production, followed by analysis of the policy and practice of organisations. We need to integrate some of the insights from this British Weberian tradition which has sought to retain an 'objective' measure of what constitutes a trade union, with

new Marxist writing on the relationship between social
relations in production and union 'character'.

The New Marxism of White Collar Unionism

The diffusion of structural Marxism within Britain in the
1970s, created a 'new marxism of white-collar unionism'.
Against older marxist orthodoxies, this new writing did not
see unionisation as a major *break* in the consciousness of
foremen, engineers and other middle class labour, a sign of
immanent proletarianisation. It rather stressed the *continuity*
with unionisation and the place occupied by middle class
labour in the social relations of production. Earlier Weberian
writers, such as Strauss (1954); Roberts *et al.* (1972, p. 249),
had seen continuities in the status-consciousness of white-
collar workers and trade unions, but this new writing stressed
the *class* basis of the connection between unionisation and
social position. From this analysis, both the class structure
and trade union movement are increasingly complicated by
the growth of new middle-class labour and unions. Against
the evident stress on homogeneity in Blackburn, and the
widespread optimism of writing in the 1960s which saw the
evolution of white-collar workers and organisations into a
manual, proletarian mould, the new writing sees increasing
fragmentation and division between competing models of
what constitutes a trade union practice. Unions are seen as
either, progressively dividing into working class and new
middle class organisations, or, in the case of ASTMS, TASS,
NALGO and many other white-collar unions, as exhibiting
an internal bifurcation between a working class and new
middle class membership. In either case, the notion of a
'whole hearted trade union', as an organisational embodiment
of certain essential qualities towards which white-collar
workers are inextricably drawn, has gone. ASTMS and TASS
recruitment documents in the 1960s drew heavily on sociological studies of the proletarianisation of white-collar workers
to encourage recruitment (Carter, 1979; Smith, 1986). These
studies were by no means Marxist, but reflected a strong
current of homogenisation produced by the class struggles of
the 1960s. Today, it is the Marxist writers who speak of

division between white-collar and manual workers. And this is reflected in the analysis of white-collar unions which I will now examine.

Crompton (1976) represents an early attempt to apply structural Marxism, specifically the work of Carchedi, to the sociology of white-collar unionism. Fairbrother (1978) is in the same tradition. Crompton's work has primarily been concerned with the situation of clerical workers in the service sector. My review below considers later writers, and those who have specifically focused on middle-class labour within the manufacturing sector.

Armstrong (1986) represents one tendency within the new Marxism of white-collar unions. He has argued for examining white-collar unionisation more through the *capital function* of middle-class labour than through labour functions or the proletarianisation of condition. In a review of the literature on unionisation amongst foremen and management, he concluded that there was strong empirical support for the thesis that organisation was, in part, an attempt to restore or reinforce the control function of capital. Foremen in a variety of unionisation case studies, refer to increasing power of shop floor unions as a threat to their interests and a reason for collective organisation (Armstrong, 1986, p. 120). Similarly, the establishment of trade unionism amongst middle managers has, in part, been identified as the outcome of increased shop floor power in consultation and participation schemes of the mid-70s (Marchington and Loveridge, 1983). Armstrong observes that the 'demand for unionisation amongst managers and supervisors, is essentially a demand for *separate* representation'. He concludes from this, that it does not represent a bid for worker solidarity, but conversely, a strategy for maintaining class power derived from the control function of capital. The provision of an independent branch was the main reason why managers at BAe opted for TASS membership.

More controversially, Armstrong claims that white-collar workers' interest in restoring economic differentials in 'relation to manual workers as a whole, may be seen as just reward for discharging the control functions of capital as well as for knowledge or specialised skills' (Armstrong, 1986,

p. 121). While not wishing to claim that differentials are only what Wright (1977) has called an economic 'return to control', Armstrong's review points very strongly in this direction. While this line of reasoning has some relevance for inducement of recruits into management or supervision, the meaning of differentials for technical staff is, as I later show, explicitly tied to their productive and craft consciousness. Armstrong also ignores the *process* of wage bargaining. Engaging in industrial activity to support differentials may, in itself, be qualitatively distinct from the individual process of 'buying off' groups to undermine trade unionism or activity. Finally, I believe the confusions Armstrong encounters in discussing this issue, indicate the difficulties of talking about the meaning of wage differentials for white-collar workers as a group. It is necessary to carefully separate payment for specialised skill, strategic power, industrial power or control over labour for particular sections of white-collar workers.

Armstrong emphasises the *capital* function of white-collar labour as determining a set of differences between their organisations and those of manual groups who perform pure labour functions. Those who 'participate in the control function of capital cannot receive payment through the cash nexus, but only from revenue, and therefore indirectly from the labour of the 'proletarian proper' (Armstrong, 1986, p. 122). This remains the case even where capital functions are shared with the discharging of labour functions. The duality, which is central to Carchedi and those who have sought to apply his analysis, Crompton (1976) for example, is only partially present in Armstrong's work. He places more emphasis on the consequences of engaging in capital functions, rather than more equivocal statements related to the ambiguity of the position of foremen or managers.

Carter (1979; 1985; 1986), while close to Armstrong at one level, constantly stresses the *inherent duality* between the capital and labour functions within the new middle class. He has said:

> In so far as the new middle class perform as part of the collective worker, producing surplus value or surplus

labour, they are paid from *variable* capital. In so far as they perform as agents of capital, they are paid out of revenue.

(Carter, 1985, p. 66)

For Carter there are no pure capital organisations for new middle class labour. Both trade unions and staff associations combine the elements of division and duality within the new middle class:

Staff associations do not represent a simple identification with capital, nor do trade unions represent a simple identification with labour. The movement from one sort of organisation to the other merely reflected the fact that not only do the majority of managers not have economic ownership of the means of production, but they have diminishing powers over day-to-day decisions and their own conditions of work.   (Carter 1985, pp. 201–2).

For Carter, unionisation is simultaneously representative of the proletarianisation pressures on new middle-class labour and an attempt to retain a collective voice inside the capital function:

In contrast to the claims of certain sociologists, notably Prandy and Crompton, membership of organisations unambiguously declaring themselves trade unions does not simply reflect in managers a proletarian orientation. It also reflects an attempt to arrest the process of proletarianisation. In other words the contradictory problems of middle class labour, arising from its role in production, are also manifested in the policies adopted by its trade unions.

(Carter, 1985, p. 182)

Examining the distinctive features of new middle class unionism, Carter emphasises differences in industrial activity and representation, which flow from economic and social *condition*, rather than differences which flow from Armstrong's attention to *relation*. In other words, he does not dwell on demands against the shop floor or the issue of separate representation, but rather the content of bargaining and the

relationship between the official and local levels of middle-
class trade unions like ASTMS. He claims that middle-class
unionists are less strike prone; have fewer disputes over
working conditions, because these are 'under less attack'; and
have a greater tendency towards official disputes, with more
official involvement. The central issue in Carter's thesis is the
greater disjuncture within white-collar unions between the
consciousness and experience of officials and the 'average'
member. Any attempt to read off something about the
consciousness of white-collar members, from the official union
structure and policy, is questioned by Carter. The Blackburn
thesis, examined earlier, is therefore strongly rejected. Carter
claims, in an almost Weberian fashion, that:

> Most of the time groups of members do not have the same
> consciousness of conflict as their officials, tending rather to
> see management as a reserve bank of authority from which
> they can draw to reinforce their roles in the work place.
>   (Carter, 1985, p. 180)

The new Marxism of white-collar unionism has re-estab-
lished the primacy of the connection between class relations
and collective organisation. Its strength has been to stress the
class basis of white-collar union practice and the distinctive
pattern of formation relative to manual unions. One of the
problems with Carter's work is that it could be interpreted
as saying there are no basic differences between staff associations and trade unions. This, given the Tory legal attacks
on trade unions, could be a dangerous position to hold. The
difficulties with structural Marxism examined in Chapter 1,
also apply to the literature on unionism. There are dangers
in reducing trade union practice solely to functional class
relations. Other problems have arisen because of the tendency
to extrapolate from the situation of foremen and management
to all white-collar workers. In addition the importance of
trade union leadership, structure and the characteristics
identified earlier by Blackburn, are not simply reducible to
the social function held in production.

Having said that, I would emphasise the need to separate
white-collar organisations by their broad functional position,

while retaining the contradictory relationship between class position and trade union attachment. Three categories of white-collar unions can be identified: those performing deskilled clerical functions; those in supervisory/managerial positions; and specialised technical groups. I am in agreement with Armstrong on the position of managerial unionism, as discussed in the last chapter, but disagree with generalisations made by both writers from that group to engineers and technical staff. This chapter is a bid for specificity in the new Marxism of white-collar workers. In line with the rest of the book, I stress the importance of the craft identity to the history and position of technical trade unionism.

Technical Workers and TASS

In Chapter 1 I tried to clarify many of the misconceptions about technical workers' industrial activity, including those propagated by 'new working class' theorists of the 1960s (Mallet, 1975; Gorz, 1967), and contemporary notions about the increasing strike power of technical staff (Cooley, 1972). I also looked at the organisation of industrial disputes at the local level. Here I am interested in changes in the formal organisation of TASS. Essentialist ideas about trade unionism and class, i.e. the belief that trade unions embody in some absolute, ahistorical way, class ideologies, in contrast to professional associations which supposedly embody status practices (Prandy, 1965; McLoughlin, 1983) are strongly rejected. A trade union may be a predominantly working-class form of organisation, but it is the nature of its policies and the practices of the members that determine the class content and political character of this form in specific historical circumstances. The internal politics of a union, the dominance of certain ideas, and the entrenchment of certain factions, has a considerable bearing on the activity and consciousness of the membership at the factory level. This is especially the case with small unions that have a strong craft background, and a tradition of central organisation and direction at national and local levels.

TASS was built on craft principles with a strong single-

occupational base in draughtsmen, who formed the bulk of
the membership until the growth of 'other technicians' and
graduate engineers in the 1960s (Mortimer, 1960; Roberts *et
al.* 1972). The craft association between British technical and
skilled manual workers, discussed in this book, formed, from
the origins of the union, a continuing source of occupational
and ideological association between skilled manual unions
and TASS. This differentiated TASS from other white-collar
unions (Reid, 1980). Technical workers have relied upon their
productive and *craft* status to sustain their position as
productive labour alongside manual workers. The importance
of wage differentials for white-collar unions, is evidence, in
the TASS context, of *labour function* rather than any claim on
decision-making, responsibility or other evidence of capital
function mentioned by Carter and Armstrong. Technical
workers at BAe emphasised their contribution to the physical
commodity and distance and disdain for unproductive,
clerical work when assessing their wages. A dispute over wage
differentials at the power engineering giant, C. A. Parsons
in 1979, illustrates the productive consciousness of technical
labour in engineering.

The dispute arose after management had agreed a 27 per
cent increased earnings to manual workers and had only
offered technical staff 12½ per cent. This disturbed the
pattern of differentials which technical staff had struggled to
maintain for over ten years. This meant reduced margins for
craft apprentices transferring to technician apprenticeships,
a wage cut for craftsmen promoted from the shop floor into the
technical office and a small difference between the earnings
of young graduate engineers and skilled manual workers.
Management, in breaking established policy, claimed that as
technical staff were not subject to work measurement – TASS
opposed any such moves – they could not be considered
productive in the same way as manual workers. Moreover,
they saw TASS's claim to be included in the Works
Productivity Scheme as evidence of technical staff 'seeking to
improve their position by climbing on the backs of manual
workers' (NEI Parsons, 1979, p. 46). The TASS leadership
at Parsons rejected this view and provided evidence of the
direct and indirect productive status of technical staff, the

improvements in productivity in the technical area and the actual decline of productivity on the shop floor. After a limited dispute, the matter went to arbitration, and my information was obtained from the TASS submission to ACAS.

Wage differentials were defended by TASS, because of 'the knowledge, experience, responsibility and creative thought' technical staff brought to the productive process. The report indicated the productivity improvements in technical labour and their direct production of materials, techniques and commodities. The report quoted from 50 companies in the district where part of a technical worker's wage was production-based. These primarily included bonuses for productivity increases and contributions to production. Examples came from several Vickers' establishments, Plessey Tele-Coms, T. I. Churchill, Baker Perkins, Rose Foregrove and many other well-known names. Some of the manual workers at Parsons who had been included in the shop floor productivity scheme were indirect workers. The TASS submission to ACAS said:

> It goes without saying that technical staff make more of a contribution towards production than certain groups covered by the Work Productivity Scheme, such as security men, canteen staff and cleaners. We go further and demonstrate . . . that a substantial proportion of technical staff are equally or more directly involved in the production process than certain groups whom it would be unthinkable to exclude from the Works Productivity Scheme; such as millwrights, electricians and fitters in certain areas.
> (NEI Parsons, 1979, p. 46)

The report described the productive role of various technicians, engineers and designers, both close to and independent of manual workers. The report also dealt with the 'contribution of technical staff to shop floor productivity'. This involved, for example, draughtsmen using 'their experience and knowledge to simplify the production of components as far as possible, thereby enabling them to be produced as quickly as possible'. Technical skills also entailed making decisions on modifications to avoid expensive scrapping of components and assisting in the progress of parts through the shop floor. In over 150 pages the direct and indirect involvement of technical staff in production was illustrated.

The reason for dwelling on this issue of productivity is to emphasise that in wage bargaining it is the centrality of the independent productive function of technical staff that is stressed, and not their function of control, surveillance or supervision over manual workers. Interestingly, to further their claim, TASS leaders also drew on evidence of several government and engineering institute studies of the comparatively poor pay and position of British engineering workers. This universal orientation to wage bargaining again points to the centrality of a craft or occupational consciousness as distinct from the managerialism of supervisors and middle managers discussed in Armstrong.

The craft base, homogeniety and craft practices of TASS began to break up under the impact of political and economic forces operating in the environment in the early 1970s. Recruitment was changing to include, in addition to the skilled worker transfer and apprentice route, a more indirect, qualified route via higher education. Union expansion into graduate engineers initially followed the proletarian, craft practice of recruitment applied to 'other technicians'. However, from the mid-1970s this policy was changed towards accommodating managers and engineers as a separate class of membership, cut off from the working class base of middle-range technical staff. Carter (1985, p. 193) has shown how ASSET, the forerunner of ASTMS, initially orientated their recruitment strategy towards what the leadership identified as increasingly proletarianised middle class labour. However, 'such a view was firmly superseded by one based upon organising white-collar workers as a middle class'. TASS, given its closer ties to the shop floor, and absence of supervisors and other new middle class labour, only arrived at the ASTMS position in the mid-1970s when recruitment of managers began (Smith, 1986). This chapter explores the issues and factions within TASS that helped create the reorientation of the union away from a craft to a mixed-class base. While drawing from the new Marxism of white-collar unionism to assess the relationship between the class of the membership and union policy, I also attempt a broader integration of wider environmental factors, and internal political processes, in shaping the union structure and policy.

Wages Policy and the Broad Left

The reputation TASS earned in the 1960s as a 'fighting white-collar union' was built on wage militancy. This militancy did not flow *naturally* from technical workers' experience of declining wage differentials, their work situation or changing production methods. It was developed and organised by a particular style of leadership with particular types of policies. There are, as discussed in Chapter 2, inherent limitations in techical workers' industrial independence and industrial power, and the right wing inside the AESD relied on these objective weaknesses to justify not halting the dramatic decline through the 1930s, 1940s and 1950s of the 'traditional' differential between draughtsmen and skilled manual workers (Wooton, 1961; Smith, 1982). Against the right wing who controlled the official union, a 'broad left', based in the bran-ches and vocal at conferences, emerged from the end of the war and argued for a militant wage policy, a minimum wages campaign nationally orchestrated and supported to restore squeezed differentials (Mortimer, 1960; Wooton; 1961; Woodley, 1973; Parkin, B., 1974). The rise of the broad left in the union and the minimum wage policy were inextricably bound together and it is this development that I will now examine.

As discussed in Chapter 2, TASS members emerged from the Second World War with the differential between draughtsmen and skilled manual workers shot to pieces. From 1945 the union established a policy for minimum wage rates for draughtsmen at thirty to equalise the differential. This policy was, however, not implemented until the early 1960s. Before that period, industrial activity had been shunned because of the assumed backwardness and industrial weak-ness of the membership. Following the 1958 Conference, the broad left, initially an alliance between members of the Communist Party and the Labour Lefts, achieved an unstable majority on the Executive Committee responsible for running the union. This was consolidated in 1962 and thereafter the broad left have dominated the union. The Communist Party has always been the strongest partner in the alliance and is central to the changes in TASS during this period. The broad left was built up by arguing for industrial action to restore the differential in wages between draughtsmen and craftsmen.

Economically the period was very favourable to wage militancy. The shortage of skilled labour meant technical staff were in a strong bargaining position, but the weakness of technical workers' strike power and their industrial inexperience inhibited industrial action. To encourage this, dispute benefit was set at 100 per cent of net pay in 1960. A minimum wage campaign (MWC) began in 1960 and culminated in a series of National Agreements between 1965 and 1970. This militancy restored the differential, as discussed in Chapter 2. The CP was the dynamic force, behind the MWC, in the union. Mike Cooley, a member of the CP between 1961 and 1970, recalls the MWC:

> It was certainly the CP that developed the notion of the minimum wages strategy (and) an extremely effective strategy (it was). I remember being in CP meetings discussing this. And then it assumed a national dimension because we used to pick on employers in various parts of the country in order to give them a hammering, (particularly Federated firms). And get a wage level in that company higher than the minimum wage agreement with the Federation. Then having done that with key firms around the country, go for a national wage agreement with an employer where you consolidate that upwards rather than downwards. And that was a very, very deliberate industrial policy, and the whole idea of a minimum wage policy was highly successful.

This policy, described as 'pattern bargaining' (Roberts, *et al.* 1972) meant a continuous leap-frogging in the federated companies to keep ahead of the minimum. It was the wage drift of the manual unions, but organised on a centralised, not piecemeal, basis. It combined a high level of local militancy with substantial national direction and encouragement. Against the individualism and bureaucracy of merit payments and job evaluation, pattern bargaining encouraged a wage consciousness that had a unifying effect on the national membership. At the level of the firm it was in the interests of all sections – planners, draughtsmen, etc. – to achieve improvements in the basic rates. Within a local area the actions of workers within a specific factory had a direct bearing on the wage rate within the area. The stability of the reference groups around which the wage rates were measured, permitted meaningful national comparisons to be made and this represented the cornerstone of the union strategy.

The policy was built on the homogeneous occupational structure of the union. One of the consequences of the policy was a reduction in the distance between the national and workplace structures of TASS, which, in turn, meant a greater degree of branch involvement in the national conference. This challenges the views of Carter (1979), who, as I have shown, considered a disjuncture between the official union structure and the membership to be an inherent feature of white-collar unions. TASS in the 1960s exhibited a high degree of integration between the different levels of the structure, together with a high incidence of lay member participation in union procedures and duties. Mike Cooley, President of TASS 1972–73, told me:

It was the proud boast of the union that one in every seven members was an officer of the union of some kind, either a branch secretary, office representative or corresponding member. A massive level of lay member involvement.

Terry Rogers, a broad left member from the 1950s and later a 'left oppositionist', explained to me how the policy integrated the structures of the union:

Once conference made a decision, or in between conference once the Executive made a decision, [it] was publicised and there was a whole campaign behind this activity. And so you had at district level a minimum wage sub-committee or an Industrial sub-committee which met and discussed how to co-ordinate activity to put the propaganda about on wages. People were very, very wage conscious, and even within a branch we'd get statistics collated relating to the various firms in the branch and people watched to see what movements were taking place. And when you had a minimum wage campaign then the more militant or better organised firms would take the lead and everybody would be watching and going in behind.

Mike Cooley agreed with this analysis:

It did give a sense of national unity. If there was somebody fighting in some factory you knew it was in your interests, in the most basic sense, to support. Because they were pushing up the base, which affected everybody . . . It certainly was a unifying thing as far as the membership were concerned.

The strategy involved a large amount of industrial activity amongst the membership, as one delegate observed in the discussion about wages policy at the 1974 conference:

The publication of minimum wage rates had never enabled the members to achieve those rates. It was only industrial action and organisation that had given minimum rates any meaning whatsoever.

(TASS, 1974)

The rates themselves rested on two occupational categories, draughtsmen and technicians. The unprecedented development of new technical occupations, in the 1970s, many not related to draughtsmen, inevitably altered the relevance of the campaign. The campaign rested on both industrial action and national agreements with the employers. Hours and holidays were also negotiated nationally and fought for in the plants. In 1970 the employers ended national wage agreements although, according to Mike Cooley, TASS was also looking to end them:

In the Engineering Section as well, there was a movement

towards the ending of national agreements with the Employers Federation. The whole significance of dealing with the Employers Federation seemed to be diminishing. Also, in my view, the union was already moving away from a combative position. It did sound very 'grass rootish', you know, to say every division should do its own thing. But in fact it was taking the onus away from the Executive Committee in giving any kind of leadership by synchronising and co-ordinating.

Minimum rates were agreed at TASS Conference in 1970 and 1971 but they were never achieved with the employers. The ending of the traditional scales and the minimum wage campaign left the union with no effective national strategy on wage bargaining. Ken Gill, TASS General Secretary and leading member of the Communist Party, blamed the strength of the State and employers for TASS 'backing off' on the wages front:

Although the union's wages campaign had not been a total success, where there had been failures these had been due to massive State intervention, the rallying of the forces of the Engineering Employers Federation, which had instituted a special solidarity system to outwit the union; and a financial limitation on the number of strikes the union could support.

(AUEW-TASS, 1973)

In effect, after 1971 there was no longer any national policy on wages, and plant bargaining without co-ordination or heavy financial assistance from the national union became the norm. Despite this changed reality, the debate, continued about getting wage scales which reflected the 'new membership' firstly with a system of bench marking for a wider number of technical occupations, and later a system of 'salary targets'. For both policies the gap increased between the discussion and action on wages.

Job evaluation and grading schemes began to replace national action on fixed rates. From 1974 this was acknowledged by the leadership to be 'inevitable':

Trade unions must adjust their strategy to keep up with developments. The wage-for-age system had been fought for but was almost obsolete . . . The majority of members were now paid according to wage systems based wholly or partially on job evaluation.

(AUEW-TASS, 1974)

At both Filton and N.E.I. Parsons the national wage policy was irrelevant to plant bargaining from the beginning of the 1970s. The TASS annual salary census was used by the Parsons *management* in 1979 to justify their wage offer to TASS, i.e. the union figures were used against the Joint Office Committee claim. At Filton, Alan Mann, the chairman of the Industrial Committee, told me, 'the company would slaughter me if I used the salary census'. Wage bargaining was based on inflation and on comparability with Rolls-Royce and Westland Helicopters.

The ending of national agreements meant the ending of national unification of the membership around wages. The debate about bench marks and salary targets really obscured the fact that the 'figures' or 'occupational groups' were irrelevant if there was no co-ordinated campaign at a national level to realise these targets. The significance of 'national policy' to the membership at plant level ended in 1970. But why did this happen?

One side of the equation was the development of employers' and government strategies against the growth of industrial militancy. On the other, were changes in the technical division of labour, the increasing diversity within technical work and the consequent growing heterogeneity within the TASS membership. In Chapter 5 I indicated that some TASS activists interpreted the employers' sudden enthusiasm for graduate engineers as a response to militancy and rising unionisation. A less long-term response was the resort to lock-outs. There emerged in the early 1970s, what Ken Gill, the General Secretary of TASS, referred to as a 'new mood' of employer and government confidence. Before looking at occupational changes, I will examine the consequence of this new mood.

Concentration of Technical Workers and the Employers' Offensive

The membership of TASS had been increasing in concentration during the 1960s. This reflected the growing number of mergers and concentration in British engineering. The rationalisations taking place in British engineering in the late 1960s and early 1970s affected white-collar and manual workers alike. This created the impetus for an unprecedented (outside of war time), growth in white-collar unions. Between 1964 and 1975 white collar unions in all sectors showed a considerable expansion. TASS increased its membership by 90 per cent; ASTMS, 346 per cent; CPSA 46 per cent; APEX, 73 per cent; NUBE, 78 per cent; and NALGO, 60 per cent (Carter, 1985, p. 153). Between 1966 and 1978 total white-collar union membership increased by over 2 million, and density rose from 29.8 per cent to 43.1 per cent (Price, 1983, p. 151).

TASS membership started to grow by several thousand per year instead of by just two thousand. Between 1968 and 1974 the union grew by 50 000. Growth was in the large plants, and it was in the larger units that the employers began challenging TASS's guerilla campaigns with lockouts. Where TASS members were concentrated in large numbers, there was less room for the employers to buy peace through status provisions, good wages and conditions. By 1973 53 per cent of the 114 000 members were located in just 46 companies. For TASS this level of concentration had two major consequences. Firstly, it meant any industrial action in a large plant was very expensive when dispute benefit was guaranteed. Secondly, it created a greater degree of differentiation between technical staff in small and medium units and those in the larger combines. Concentration helped spread unionisation and the development of combine committees with their own in-house dispute funds independent from the official structure of the union. The union leadership encouraged growth because the membership was easier and cheaper to service if they were located in large groups with their subs checked off at source. But there are also disadvantages if the members are involved in all-out disputes and dispute benefit is set at a high percentage of nett pay. This contradiction came together when the employers began to challenge the guerilla-style tactics developed during the minimum wage campaign through lockouts, victimisations and a more organised response to TASS.

The change in the engineering employers response to TASS was part of a much wider change in the period as both State and capital attempted to come to terms with the economic crisis by attacking organised labour. The union withstood a thirteen-week lockout of 1766 members by the Shipbuilding Employers Federation in 1967. In the course of that protracted dispute, the 100 per cent dispute pay was reduced to 80 per cent and the union spent £250 000, over 50 per cent of its yearly subscription income on the dispute. Following this lockout by the Shipbuilders Employers, a second was threatened in 1969, and there were lockouts of 180 DATA members at BAC Preston in Summer 1968; at GEC Netherton, 1969; and C. A. Parsons Newcastle in 1970 and 1972. A thirteen-week lockout of TASS members at Rolls-Royce, in the summer of 1970, exposed TASS's 'weakness' in the face of the employer's offensive. It showed how the union could be brought to the edge of bankruptcy by paying high fixed dispute benefit for a large dispute, and polarised opinion within TASS about how best to go forward. It began as a wage claim in Coventry, with traditional sanctions and a tactical strike of twenty-four TASS members. It ended with 950 TASS members at Coventry being locked out, and the Company threatening to lock out all 5000 TASS members at Rolls-Royce Derby, Glasgow and Bristol. It cost TASS well over £250 000 and ended with a compromise on the full wage claim for all the Rolls-Royce plants. The membership was levied as it had been with the shipbuilding lockout, and responded by raising over £100 000 in support of those on strike. This was the last of the TASS national levies.

The Chairman of the Joint Office Committee at Rolls-Royce, Coventry, the centre of the dispute, reflected on the dispute:

It was the employers coming to terms with the classical guerilla action that had characterised TASS in the '60s.

On the other hand there were the special conditions of
Rolls-Royce's impending bankruptcy. Whether it was a
conscious attempt to take us on or whether they were forced
to do that I don't know.

The new mood of 'confidence' (or 'desperation') amongst
the employers was met with by TASS attempting to build
stronger links with manual workers in the workplace. In the
GEC Netherton lockout, for example, the *DATA* journal
carried an article about the dispute written by activists from
DATA and the AEF. The DATA leadership were projecting
closer links at factory level and through an amalgamation as
a way to retaliate against the employers. The article ended
by saying:

> Solidarity won the day. Undoubtedly the prospect of
> DATA amalgamated with the AEF, the largest union in
> the factory (500 members), contributed towards the spon-
> taneous supporting action of the shop floor.
>
> (*DATA Journal*, October 1969)

However after the Rolls-Royce struggle the Executive
Committee was more cautious about backing disputes. Within
the broad left there was a regrouping of forces with the
Communist Party pushing a policy of broadening out the left,
which helped to isolate what can be called a 'left opposition',
who became identified with 'adventurism' and 'militancy'
that threatened to 'bankrupt' the union. A 'left opposition'
member I interviewed summed up the points of agreement
between themselves and the Communist Party:

> in response to the employers' lockout tactic there was the
> question of developing combine activity, increased
> subscriptions, levies and giving the Divisional Council the
> authority to have levies. And of course *central to all these
> policies was attempts to get meaningful developments in the
> amalgamation.*

Both left 'factions' were adjusting to the new situation of
employers' opposition and rising redundancies where the

tactics of the 1960s on their own were inappropriate. Both
saw the need for 'politics' to answer the employers' offensive,
but the left opposition wanted politics on the shop floor, while
the official broad left emphasised formal links within trade
union and Labour Party bureaucracies, with a reduced
emphasis on industrial struggle. Another leading left oppositionist told me:

> We were advocating an emphasis on fighting disputes. This
> strategy could be summed up as more reliance on the
> membership and more confidence in their ability to under-
> stand and fight than the leadership would be prepared to
> give them.

To the broad left the Rolls-Royce dispute epitomised the
expense and danger of mass strikes, to the left opposition it
represented the membership rallying to support other
members in struggle. To both the weakness of TASS as a
small-craft union was emphasised by the lockouts in the early
1970s and this focused attention on closer links with manual
workers at the plant level, through combined committees and
joint activities, and at the national level through amalgamation with the AEF. Both factions were committed to
the idea of integrating technical workers into the wider
labour movement and to a left strategy inside a new union.
The amalgamation appeared to be an answer to the new climate in the technical areas. It offered a way of consolidating
objective tendencies towards unity established by DATA
militancy inside engineering during the 1960s. In addition the new confidence of employers and the State 'demanded' unity between all sections of the working class.
This was, as mentioned in Chapter 1, a period of rising
labour militancy across Europe (Crouch and Pizzorno,
1978).

The Amalgamation

DATA had flirted with amalgamating with the Association
of Supervisory Staffs, Executives and Technicians (ASSET)

in the 1950s and the Association of Scientific Workers (AScW) in the 1960s, but industrially the Amalgamated Engineering Union (AEU) was the closest to DATA. The decision to amalgamate with the AEU was supported by three-quarters of the DATA membership in a national ballot that took place in April 1970. This overwhelming support for industrial unionism was against these earlier failures of DATA to attach itself to other technical and scientific unions. Although Roberts *et al.* (1972, p. 110) identify some demand for closer ties with other technical unions within DATA, I would suggest that both politically and industrially an amalgamation with the AEU answered many of the problems facing DATA in the late 1960s. Internally, there was no organised opposition to the amalgamation. The two left factions supported industrial unionism, but as I will show, had different visions of what the amalgamated union could achieve.

Up until 1972, 70 per cent of the membership were still in the typical technical occupations that possessed this craft association. Related to this, there was the linking in certain areas, North London for example, between DATA and AEU struggles. Joint action, representation on stewards' committees, and CSEU district committees, existed in some TASS Divisions, although this 'organic unity' should not be exaggerated. It is part of TASS mythology that the need for amalgamation with the AEU can be traced back to disputes in the 1950s that exposed the industrial weakness of DATA. There were certainly informal discussions between the officials of AEU and DATA in the 1960s, but to assume a linear development from 1950 to 1970 is inaccurate. The political changes in the AEU – the slight left face on the National Committee – had very significant implications for the Communist Party thinking on the amalgamation. To assume, because of the unity in certain areas, that there was a strong degree of cohesion in the majority of factories would also be wrong. Even in factories with very strong and militant left wing DATA office committees, relations between DATA and the manual unions were often bitter. One of the strongest areas of the left opposition in DATA, Newcastle, was classically right wing in terms of the AEU. Attempts to establish relations in combined committees and joint committees in Rolls-Royce Coventry and C.A.V., London, two factories with strong left traditions on the technical side, were without any real success.

The divisions between staff and works were still strong, and as Chapter 6 revealed the craft association is contradictory, embodying both co-operative and divisive elements. Terry Rogers, who helped form a joint manual/staff corporate committee at C. A. Parsons Newcastle Upon Tyne, considered the major problem of the amalgamation residing with manual worker's attitudes to staff:

> I think the main difficulty has been the real historical attitude towards staff on the shop floor. You know, to regard them [i.e. staff] as natural allies, industrially, requires a bit of a leap of the imagination . . . Also the quite tight relationship between the various manual unions on the shop floor is far more cohesive than the projected AUEW-TASS relationship.

The 'natural' bonds between shop floor unions meant to some extent that the unity with staff was not an organic outgrowth but an organisational imposition. On the shop floor stewards represent workers who are often not in their own union and it does not need a 'formal' amalgamation for common interests, conditions and grievances to be jointly settled. The Confederation of Shipbuilding and Engineering Unions had joint manual agreements that excluded white-collar unions. Ron Whitely, an ex-Treasurer of TASS and active in the amalgamation talks throughout the 1960s told me:

> Shop stewards' committees in factories are not AUEW shop steward's committees. They're all CSEU shop stewards' committees, and this is where the umbrella cover meant that they could very easily exclude staff who were not party to any agreements with the CSEU jointly together with manual unions.

Issues affecting the whole plant – redundancies, closures, productivity deals – did create joint committees, but these were frequently short-lived, as at Filton, where the joint committees in the 1970s only lasted for the duration of the redundancies. At N.E.I. Parsons a joint manual–staff committee, lasted for almost ten years before manual unions withdrew and negotiated a separate redundancy deal with management. While rationalisation and redundancies in the early 1970s increased the number of joint white-collar/manual committees, developments from the late 1970s were moving sharply away from such examples of cooperation, towards division and self-interest. Batstone (1984), for example, in a survey of large companies representing 2 million employees in manufacturing, discovered a marked decline in inter-union committees and combines.

In many ways the objective situation (rationalisations, redundancies, State pay freezes, and industrial relations legislation) supported the amalgamation, and industrially there was a common craft tradition and respect. Nevertheless, for the amalgamation to have been made 'meaningful' would have required a very active political campaign for the equalisation in hours, holidays and other conditions traditionally reserved for staff workers. Terry Rogers thought that:

> If you wanted the amalgamation to be meaningful, I think the staff side would have had to accept that there's got to be a catching up to be done in terms of holidays and should be prepared to throw their weight behind a campaign that wasn't going to bring them any great material benefit. But would have built some understanding with manual workers.

Before the successful amalgamation in January 1971 TASS leadership had been constantly preparing the membership by emphasising the industrial advantages a unity with the three manual engineering unions would bring. This was done through leaflets and reports in *The TASS Journal* and *TASS News* of successful joint action between the AEU and TASS. There were also some reflective articles on the increased power offered by an amalgamation, one by an AEU activist said:

An amalgamation of our two unions will ensure that we
can never be broken into pieces . . . It means the forging
of a new and greater power . . ., the power that can flow
from a linking of the resources of DATA and the AEU. A
power that has never hitherto existed in the British trade
union world.

(*DATA Journal*, December 1969)

The emphasis on joint industrial action that figured in
TASS propaganda before the amalgamation was not maintained into the 1970s. There were efforts towards establishing
joint machinery at local levels, but these moves took place
in an industrial vacuum. For example, at the 1971 TASS
Conference a motion was passed which instructed the Executive Committee to press other sections in the amalgamation
to set up AUEW shop stewards' committees at factory level;
and in multi-factory companies AUEW combined shop stewards' committees. This motion was then taken to the AUEW
National Conference, where it was passed, but not acted on.
This is an example of the TASS leadership acknowledging
the 'need' for unity at the base, and Conference backing this
need, but not really campaigning to achieve it. The motion
did not call for joint committees to fight for specific goals,
e.g. 35-hour week, longer holidays, equalisation of conditions
etc., but just for the formation of committees. It lacked the
type of campaign orientation TASS developed in the 1960s.
During the 1978 national engineering strike on the 35-hour
week, TASS did not physically support the Engineering
Section. Yet joint action in 1978 could have formed durable
bonds at the base of the union.

The amalgamation between DATA and the AEF on paper
should have improved relations between technical and
manual workers. I asked all those I interviewed if this had
been the case and few thought it had. In fact several
considered that it had weakened relations by raising expectations of unity without forcefully integrating the structures
of the union at all levels. It was interesting that the absence
of united action, the failure to integrate strategy at the base,
was most strongly criticised by those I interviewed at BAe:

It's one thing to join a bigger organisation, you get more strength behind you, but I don't think we've been on very good terms since. Because everytime we've had some upheaval like we're having now, we've split off again and we argue on our own. . . . It's created more aggro between the shop floor and us.

It was considered a meaningless arrangement because it had not brought the two groups together on the ground. The technical workers I interviewed did not see the amalgamation in terms of the politics within the TUC or AEU, but whether or not relationships with the manual workers at Filton had been improved. And by this criterion the amalgamation was a failure. Worse, it had created the expectation of stronger bonds, a clear majority had supported amalgamation, and the promise of 'a new and greater power . . . that has never hitherto existed in the British trade union world'. Such expectations did not materialise, partly because there were no nationally orchestrated campaigns to integrate the two unions. This reflected the perspective on the amalgamation accepted by the dominant faction inside TASS. The problems of a common rule book, election of full-time officials and the elimination of the slight left majority on the Engineering Section National Committee, are subordinate to, or a reflection of, this fundamental problem.

The Communist Party viewed the amalgamation in terms of the political capital they could gain inside the AUEW, the TUC, the Labour Party Conference and other areas of the official labour movement. Mike Cooley, one of the TASS signatories to the amalgamation, said this about their perspective:

The Communist Party regarded the growing success of the left in the AEU as being of prime importance. The *political* affinity was regarded of more importance by Communist Party members than the *occupational* one, which is what the rest of us had been emphasising all along . . . There were also discussions inside the Communist Party on the National Committee [of the AEF]. That National Committee was continuously tied 26–26 . . . Now when

Carron went, it was still broadly 26–26 and there was a
notion going around that if TASS could get in, with whatever number of people, that this would mean that the whole
of the amalgamated union could get committed to left wing,
i.e. Communist Party policies, which would then go to the
TUC.

The 'left opposition' wanted to integrate the structure of
the union at the base, retaining the participative democracy
of TASS, together with an emphasis on industrial militancy
and joint activity. But the climate of general militancy began
to change after 1974, and this did not favour a strategy
fashioned in the conditions of the 1960s (Hyman, 1984). As
I argued in Chapter 1, theories of the new middle class and
alliance politics emerged after 1974 in the wake of a general
downturn in working class industrial militancy. The dynamic
areas of technical occupational growth were also outside the
craft tradition. Therefore closer associations with manual
workers through an amalgamation would not make the
recruitment of engineers an easy matter. For these reasons a
left opposition strategy of trying to secure stronger links with
manual workers through industrial militancy was easy to
resist because of its potential costs and risks.
    The amalgamation in 1971 created a federal structure, the
AUEW, with four sections, each retaining its own officials,
rule books and policy-making machinery. Attempts to integrate the structure quickly degenerated into, on the one hand,
accusations that the dominant section, the former AEF,
simply wanted to impose its own rule book on all sections;
and on the other, that TASS wanted to retain its undemo-
cratic system of appointing officials. By 1975 the amalgamation was organisationally moribund, with the TASS leadership refusing to submit its existing full-time officials to
election, and the right wing of the Engineering Section – now
back in the driving seat – distancing themselves from the
progressive policies of TASS. The transfer of members
between the two sections ended in 1974, and there were no
National Conferences of the full union after 1979. From early
in 1979, TASS was seeking to merge with a small manual
union to acquire procedural agreements to directly compete

with the Engineering Section. This occurred in 1981 when they joined with the National Union of Gold, Silver and Allied Trades (NUGSAT), a 3000-strong craft union. This has been followed by further mergers, TASS joining with the sheet metal workers union (NUSMWCH) in 1985. This pattern of growth through association is a new strategy for the union, and reflects the failure of the amalgamation and TASS's movement from a craft/white-collar base into a multi-level, white-collar/manual membership. Although these mergers have been with skilled manual unions, there was talk of absorbing the Tobacco Workers Union at the time of writing, thus indicating that the leadership are not necessarily committed to craft-based industrial unionism. The AUEW collapsed completely in 1986. Having limped along since the mid-1970s, the main sections finally split away, and the Engineering Section returned to its former status as the AEU.

If this experiment in industrial unionism failed, it did not leave TASS unchanged. It was behind the banner of securing the amalgamation that the union was transformed in the 1970s.

Internal Changes

TASS entered the amalgamation as a craft-union with membership concentrated within middle-range technical occupations, such as draughtsmen and planning engineers. The union had a small number of full-time officials, a high degree of lay member participation and commitment to the linking of recruitment and politics to industrial action. All this changed in the 1970s. The emphasis on industrial activity changed towards political representation; the direct support for industrial action declined; and the lay member partici-pation and control over the union gradually diminished as the number of national and divisional full-time officials was expanded. Recruitment too, was dis-associated from self-activity, as the union was 'sold' to new members on its 'professional' provision of services. The changes which I describe below reflect a movement away from the working class militancy of the 1960s, to a 'political' strategy divorced from the activity of the membership. Carter (1985, p. 198) argues that it is precisely this split which characterises the new middle class practice of ASTMS: 'the political orientation reflect[ing] and reinforc[ing] a lack of self-activity amongst large sections of the membership'. TASS, from having an integrated policy and practice, has moved closer to the ASTMS position where 'political' ideology is separated from the industrial activity of the membership.

Significant changes in the union's structure were (i) the ending of a branch-based National Conference in favour of a two-tier structure. This reduced the connection between the branch and the national policy-making structures of the union; and (ii) the reduction in the size of the Executive Committee and its re-structuring from a divisional to a regional basis, which also weakened the direct control lay members could exercise over Executive Committee members. Both changes increased the influence of full-time officials within the union by reducing branch member control. Given the continuation of an appointment, not election, system for full-time posts, these changes represented a weakening of the participative features of the old DATA.

Full-time officials also increased within the union. Between 1957 and 1971 the membership almost doubled – from 56 000 to just over 100 000 – and the number of full-time officials increased proportionately from 9 in 1957 to 18 in 1971. Mike Cooley, the President of the union in 1972, claimed that the union had a 'superstructure to cater for 150 000 members' without any increase in the number of full-time officials. However, the broad left leadership were committed to expanding the size of the bureaucracy. Between 1971 and 1980 the membership increased by 78 500, but the number of divisional organisers expanded from 18 to 38. National officials increased by one in the 1957–71 period (2 to 3) but from 3 to 8 in the second period. These structural changes reduced the association between the membership and union characteristic of craft unionism.

Cooley articulated the concern of the left opposition to the drift towards bureaucracy, in particular the fear of the Executive Committee becoming a full-time, not lay body, when, as President in 1972, he said:

It is clear that within our union political differences are emerging as to the way forward. One thing, however is vital. Our union must continue to be controlled by the lay membership which gives it the great drive and energy for which it is famous. Our rank and file control is a unique and precious thing and we should guard it well. Increasing emphasis is being placed in the TU movement on professionalism and the use of legal and economic experts . . . As far as I am concerned there are no greater experts than those who work at the point of production. Improvements in our conditions are not won by brilliant moral and statistical arguments but by organisational strength and the will to use it. That strength resides at the point of production in those steeled in actual struggle themselves. It is vital that they continue to control and guide the destiny of our union.

(DATA Journal, January 1972)

Subscription income, instead of returning to the membership directly through dispute benefit, went to pay for the administrative costs of a larger bureaucracy carrying out indirect servicing functions to the membership. Between 1960 and 1970 dispute benefit averaged 42.4 per cent of subscription income, a massive direct return to the membership. In contrast, between 1971 and 1980, dispute benefit only averaged 13.9 per cent. From being set at 100 per cent of net income, dispute benefit declined to 80 per cent in 1968, 60 per cent in 1972 and a non-guaranteed, so called flexible policy, from 1975 to date. From the advent of the latter system the average return to the membership in the 1975–1980 period was 6.2 per cent. The stress on industrial activity was dropped in the 1970s. Militancy was jettisoned for ideological reasons – it would not encourage engineers and managers to join TASS, when competitors like the EMA and ASTMS were projecting professional unionism based on a more coherent new middle class strategy. In addition the union was economically more stretched by the rising claims of administration due to the enlargement of the bureaucracy.

The ending of national agreements severed the material link between the National Conference and divisional structures of

TASS and the branch or workplace. If all the action on wages and conditions depended upon activity within the factory, then National Conference was much less important. The ending of fixed benefit loosened the tie even further, and the organisational restructuring broke the direct relationship between a branch and National Conference.

It was not only on the question of wages that a separation had occurred. Other policy, such as new technology or the 35 hour week, was passed at Conference but not acted upon in a co-ordinated regional or national manner. The responsibility for policy implementation was at plant level, and there was no encouragement to develop wider campaigns. An example from C.A. Parsons indicates this effective divorce between 'policy' and 'practice' which I am suggesting is indicative of a different class orientation of the union. Parsons' management wanted to introduce Computer Aided Design–Computer Aided Manufacture and TASS wanted shorter hours in return. In an attempt to isolate TASS, Parsons' management referred to the companies locally and nationally who had accepted CAD–CAM without substantial reductions in hours. Baldry and Connolly (1984) in their study of TASS and CAD in the West of Scotland, noted the lack of awareness amongst TASS representatives of new technology agreements and activities in their local area. They compared this with the co-ordination and knowledge of management, who were frequently members of equipment suppliers 'users clubs' which were major networks for new technology in their area. The TASS leadership at Parsons wanted to give the union the same knowledge and co-ordination as management; as this steward explains:

> All we were saying was that firms shouldn't accept new technology without getting some significant change in the working week. They should use the attempt by the employers to bring in CAD to get hours down. Now we always thought that this was union policy. We were attempting to get the Executive to give some sort of commitment to this, and to wage some sort of campaign, to put some propaganda out. Because we realised that the employers were dealing with individual office committees,

individual companies and . . . they isolate you that way. We were arguing that there should be some general policy, and we couldn't even get it through the Divisional Council. Because the people at Divisional Council were recognising the Executive Committee would be implicated in this and the union as a whole would be implicated. And while they pass motions at Annual Conference in line with this, it's just window dressing, to try and implement these motions is really ultra-leftism [laughter] . . . This is just the generally accepted hypocrisy.

Continuing within the dominant industrial practice of the union up until the mid-1970s, Terry Rogers, can only interpret the new separation between policy and practice as 'hypocrisy'. Behind this however, is the politics of the new middle class.

Leaving aside the crucial question of the implementation of policy, analysis of the motions passed at Annual Conference, reveals a massive decline in motions connected to industrial issues. Table 8.1 presents motions in three categories. Industrial, covers motions relating to industrial activity, wages, and conditions. Internal refers to all motions to do with the organisational structure of TASS. And general political/economic covers statements of policy which carried no implication for activity, i.e. abstract pronouncement on issues that did not link into a campaign. There was an increase in the number of motions from the Executive Committee after 1974, primarily to do with internal organisational issues.

There was an approximate balance of motions in the earlier

Table 8.1 *TASS Conference motions 1968–80*

	No. of motions	Industrial wages, conditions		Internal organisation		General political & economic issues		Others	
		%	No.	%	No.	%	No.	%	No.
1968–73	313	29.0	(89)	34.0	(107)	34.0	(107)	3.0	(10)
1974–80	376	16.0	(50)	60.0	(224)	22.0	(84)	2.0	(9)

Source: TASS Conference Reports 1968–80.

period: 29, 34, 34 per cent, while in the later period a gross
imbalance occurs as the union was gripped by introspection:
16, 60, 22 per cent. The distribution of motions reflects the
distribution of TASS priorities. An analysis of the percentage
of the annual Executive Committee Report to Conference
devoted to the unions' industrial activity indicates a similar
decline. Between 1968 and 1973, an average of 37 per cent
was devoted to industrial issues. The average for 1974–1980
was 21 per cent, and closer to 16 per cent if a long report on
the 1974 C. A. Parsons dispute is excluded. This reporting
partially reflects membership activity, but is also representative of an attempt to play down industrial militancy to facilitate the recruitment of engineers and managers.

TASS Policy and the Class Composition of TASS Membership

The old AESD had been built on draughtsmen. The title of
the organisation changed in 1960 to DATA (Draughtsmen
and Allied Technicians' Association). The emphasis was still
on draughtsmen, although 'other technicians' were a growing
group in engineering. The amalgamation with the AEF in
1970 saw DATA change to TASS – the Technical and Supervisory Section of the AUEW (1971). This changed again in
1973 to Technical, Administrative and Supervisory Section
of the AUEW. In all these changes the base in technical
staff was maintained, although the pond the union fished in
embraced all staff within engineering. The appointment of a
women's organiser in 1974 following the failure of efforts to
get APEX into the amalgamated union, meant TASS actively
recruited in clerical areas, although not with much success.
Figures on the composition of the TASS membership in 1978
reveal a concentration within middle-range technical occupations, i.e. the traditional base of the union. Of the 183 000
members, 65.6 per cent (120 000) were technical staff, 16.8
per cent (30 000) were engaged in original work in design
and production areas, i.e. qualified engineers; and 18.1 per
cent were in management, administrative and clerical grades,

(TASS, 1979). I pointed out in Chapter 2 that draughtsmen have been declining as a group for several decades. The technical occupations that have increased are within computer-based activities and among the growing number of graduate engineers. As a percentage of the total white-collar workforce in engineering and allied industries, professional engineers have increased from 7 per cent in 1965 to 11.9 per cent in 1979. An equally dramatic increase has been in the field of management, which as Chapter 7 revealed, has become more fragmented in the post-war period. In the same period and the same industrial sectors, all management grades increased from 22.9 per cent to 30.6 per cent of total white-collar employment. The losses have been amongst general administrative and clerical grades and draughtsmen. The decision to begin an aggressive recruitment drive amongst professional engineers, and later amongst managers, had to do with the growth of these groups in the 1960s and 1970s.

TASS conferences and publications during the late 1960s, acknowledged the relative decline of draughtsmen, and the growth in the technologist area. The recruitment leaflets during the period stressed the importance of designers, technologists and engineers joining a militant trade union, and the hopelessness of the 'middle ground' they were considered to be defending (TASS, 1971). The propaganda emphasised the technical or craft quality of the TASS membership and the common associations within engineering between designers and draughtsmen. All these recruitment efforts were towards getting the new members into joint bargaining units. A break came in the mid 1970s in terms of who was to be recruited, both engineers **and** managers and in the way they were to be organised. I characterise the policy of the period up until the mid 1970s as 'recruitment through militancy' and the policy of the post-1976 period as 'recruitment through autonomy' (Smith, 1986). In the latter period, TASS no longer used the practice of recruiting senior technical staff by drawing them into militant wage struggles. Neither did their policy statement stress the militant nature of the union, but rather its servicing facilities and importantly, the autonomy of professional engineers, their separateness, and lack of obligation to become associated with wage militancy of other technical workers. The recruitment of professional engineers in the first period had little to do with the recruitment of managers. The decision in 1976 to recruit among managers was really separate from the long-standing commitment inside the union to organise professional engineers. The machinery established to separate the higher sections of membership initially involved different agreements and bargaining units at factory level, and from 1978, separate branches. The argument was largely that of how best to recruit these new groups, of adapting the organisation to suit the level of consciousness of the new layers. A national spokesman I interviewed in 1981 both explained and supported the policy in these words:

> If you look at the development of this union and look back at the application forms over the years, you will see that there has been a long-term trend, in the union, to remove questions from the application form about the background, the status, the age, the sex and the training of the applicants. There has been a long-term trend to make the union more open. It's that simple. And if you remove progressively the restrictions on entry, as you become an all-staff union, the process accelerates. And just as you don't submit applicants to a blood and urine test, neither do you submit them to an ideology test . . . You must ask the question, did TASS successfully recruit professional engineers and managers under the policies that were in force in the first part of the 1970s? And the answer is no! So, you just have to learn from experience . . .

This movement away from 'craft exclusiveness' toward a more open union was actually *halted* in the mid-1970s by the decision to institutionalise hierarchical features of the work situation of technical workers within the union. The establishment of management or professional engineers-only branches, introduced a new exclusiveness through multi-level unionism, as it split TASS membership into what was referred to at Filton as 'super TASS' and 'TASS ordinaire.'

The two TASS branches at Filton represented the *class* divide that emerged in the union in the 1970s. Changes in the union's structure and policies were, at one level, an accommodation to the emergence of *new middle class* interests of managers and qualified engineers. The stresses on bureaucratic service, autonomy from other workers' industrial action, and distance from the labour movement were emphasised by the TASS managers I interviewed. The militancy and emphasis on lay-member activity of the earlier period reflected the solid working class base of the union amongst draughtsmen. The run-up to the amalgamation was seen very much as a way of ideologically integrating the white-collar and manual sections of the working class. Recruitment of higher technical workers in this period was aimed at securing their commitment to the working class, using the activity of draughtsmen to force through unionisation. From the mid-1970s, in the interests of expanding the membership to support the extension of the bureaucracy, recruitment of engineers and significantly, managers, was used as a justification for abandoning militancy and active unity with manual workers. By using class analysis the political struggles inside TASS over policy changes begin to make more sense. In the early 1970s the TASS leadership used a working-class practice to pursue the integration of engineers. In the mid-1970s it used the new middle class to restructure the union away from a craft form and working class politics.

Chapters 5 and 7 demonstrated that qualified engineers and managers occupy significantly different class places in the social relations of production, places that ideologically predispose them towards professionalism and elitism. Trade unionism can challenge, accommodate or support these ideas through policy and institutional practice. It cannot *overcome* them through activity or ideological questioning. TASS at BAe refused or were unable to challenge UKAPE in the early 1970s, and consequently latent ideas of elitism and separatism were allowed an organisational expression. TASS nationally backed an aggressive challenge to UKAPE in the early 1970s. The routing of UKAPE at C.A. Parsons, under the glare of national publicity, weakened its overall influence and blocked the development, evident at BAe and other plants, of the organisational fractionalism within TASS at Parsons. The success at C.A. Parsons cannot be explained solely through the quality of trade union leadership, although this was important as I have discussed elsewhere (Smith 1986). It also reflected the greater homogeneity amongst technical workers and the confidence they accumulated during successful wage campaigns in the 1960s. This militancy created its own contradictions, in terms of employer and State reaction as I have indicated, and culminated in the amalgamation with industrial unionism in the early 1970s. Recruitment amongst the new grades of technical workers in this context initially represented a continuity with working class practice. The union remained committed to the principle that 'industrial activity gave rise to recruitment' (*TASS Journal*, June 1972).

This changed in the course of the 1970s when the union, operating within a more conservative political and industrial environment and a failed amalgamation with manual trade unionism, faced increasing competition for members. The decision of the EMA to recruit outside the power engineering industry was used as a pretext for making an accommodation to the ideas and values supported by explicit new middle-class unions (the EMA). The allocation of separate arrangements for managers and engineers has created a form of class and organisational federalism in TASS, which is in marked contrast to the ideology of class unity and integration around at the time of the amalgamation. The shift from industrial to political campaigning, discussed earlier, is a reflection of the way the leadership have used the new membership, which lacks the craft traditions, to abandon militancy. The entry of managers into TASS has altered the practice of the union and weakened ties with manual workers. For instance a TASS convenor I interviewed at Rolls-Royce, Coventry, said that management unionisation had made TASS's relations with shop-floor unions much more difficult.

Along any one-dimensional measure of union character or unionateness, the official structure and policies of TASS in both the 1960s and currently, would indicate a working class orientation. The formal features of the union's commitment to the labour movement – affiliation to the TUC and Labour Party, involvement in industrial action, etc. – are present in both periods. By using this analysis, the changes described within this chapter are hard to explain. Some coherence is obtained by using what I have described as the 'new Marxism of trade unionism'. Within this analysis, the 'union' as an institutional totality is not the focus, but rather the specific class position of the membership and the interaction between union policy and practice in relation to class composition. However, this perspective requires careful application, in particular, it has to be sensitive to conjunctural conditions within the rest of the class structure. It also has to take on board the union traditions within particular plants, the differences between C.A. Parsons and Filton being a case in point. An abstract analysis of the growing class fractionalism within TASS and amongst technical labour does not, of itself, reveal the dominance or dynamic of class practices between different groups or within different periods. Nor can we read off the broad traditions within which these different class fractions operate, for instance the centrality of craftism as a major ideological and institutional practice within British engineering. However, with these qualifications or cautions, I think such a class analysis of TASS offers a systematic interpretation of developments inside the union over the last three decades.

Conclusion

This book has explored the class situation of British technical workers through a Marxist perspective. Weberian approaches to class were rejected because of their tendency to fragment class relations into an infinite variety of market properties, without capturing the contradictory movement of class consciousness and conflict within capitalist societies. My review of Marxist literature on intermediate workers focused upon two oppositional models, those of the new working class and new middle class. New working class writing drew attention to the growing internal differentiation *within* the working class, while new middle class models argued that there was a new class divide *between* the working class and the bourgeoisie. In a critique of aspects of both approaches I have argued that a more dynamic approach to class should retain functional location of class defined through the relations of production, while integrating this into historical variations in the conditions of class relations within particular social formations. New working class writing retained some of this historical movement, but falsely allocated technology the central role in determining the pattern of relations between wage labour. In practice, relations within the working class are influenced by organisation, politics and ideology which different groups bring into their work and working relations. These are influenced by particular conditions and types of production, but there is no linear determination. A central component of the affinity between class and activity is trade union organisation. My analysis of TASS examined how collective organisation interacts with and shapes class relations.

Focusing attention upon social relationships in the production of surplus value places the division between capital and waged labour at the centre, and internal divisions within the latter at a secondary level of analysis. By this method the main determination of non-supervisory technical workers' class position is given by their condition as productive wage labourers and the relationships of exploitation accompanying this location. It is *capital* which exploits technical workers, rationalises and intensifies their work and generally shapes their experience of wage labour. It is therefore their relationship to the capitalist class which stands in a dominant relationship to them, and defines their position in the class structure. Unlike foremen or managers, who act for capital in the labour process, the majority of the technical workers studied here lacked supervisory authority or control over manual workers. However, their position of indirectly productive workers within 'mental' labour, made their relationship with manual labour and capital more complex than that revealed through a narrow focus on their productive role. The 'political' and 'ideological' social relations at the practical level of the workplace have therefore been an essential part of my investigation of differentiation within wage labour.

Labour process analysis, especially that developed from Braverman (1974) has tackled the internal divisions within waged labour. Poulantzas (1975) and Carchedi (1977) built their analyses on a labour theory of value and the political role of supervision. Braverman focused on the mental-manual split, the symbolic and material division between the conceptualisation of work and its actual performance. Technical labour, as part of this conceptualisation process, therefore appeared on the side of management against manual workers. My analysis of the British craft tradition has indicated the continuity between manual and technical modes of conceptualisation. This continuity existed because technical occupational roles were defined alongside, and not against manual skills, and the conditions of recruitment supported, rather than blocked manual workers' transferring into the technical office. The occupational socialisation of technical workers maintained the connection with the workplace rather than the college, and confirmed the value of practical experience, which prevented technical education becoming an autonomous, alternative source of authority over manual labour. This meant technical workers' occupational identity continued to be informed by manual workers' perceptions of their competence, rather than through an independent knowledge base which excluded this evaluation.

Within the practical relations between technical and manual workers, I explained how the 'form of association' between the two groups has a major influence on their evaluation of their common or opposed interests. I outlined two basic relations which supported 'qualitative' and 'quantitative' forms of association. Those groups in marginalised, quasi-technical positions, (production controllers, rate-fixers) had a quantitative form of association with manual workers that entailed timing, evaluating and progressing their work and adopting a strong belief in the 'logic of production', an ideology dominant within management's evaluation of labour. By contrast draughtsmen, planners and NC programmers possessed a qualitative form of association that linked them to manual workers via an assessment of the product, and not the pace of production and manual labour power. This produced a concern for the nature of craftsmanship and training that, on the one hand elevated the value of their own contribution, and on the other, linked them to a common concern for 'skill' that capitalist production or Taylorism sought to degrade.

One of the groups behind deskilling practices and technological change were other, higher engineers and designers who increasingly related to the shop floor via computerised systems and sought to enhance their autonomy by a strategy of computerising the links between design and production. These groups enter technical areas without socialisation through the shops, although still within an engineering culture that places a premium on practical skills. Nevertheless they remain divorced from manual workers and disdainful of the physical skills of middle range technical staff. Moreover, given the absence of manual skills in their occupational roles and elevation of mental over physical labour, they are closer to management and within a different class position from working class technicians.

If technical workers' relationship to manual labour is complex, so too is their connection and evaluation of management. What stands out in my analysis is that most technical staff did not perceive their interests as workers to be complementary to those of management *against* the interests of manual workers. Such an alliance of forces only surfaced amongst those with a quantitative association with labour who needed to shore up their weak authority via links with the foremen. Most other technical groups related to manual labour via a reservoir of craft values, technical competence and know-how. In relation to their own labour, technical staff saw the function of management as marginal to them. Although all the managers had a technical background, and the natural avenue into management was through the department, nevertheless managers were considered irrelevant to the technical worker's job. The section leader was more involved, although it was emphasised by all those I interviewed that nobody knew the job at hand as well as the individual technical worker. This autonomy on the job, an ability to obtain technical advice within the section or office relegated the functions of the technical manager to what one programmer called 'paperwork queries'. Far from their proximity to management generating a 'management outlook' on the back of borrowed authority, technical workers maintained a strong sense of autonomy, self-management and control. It was middle management that was torn between their position as wage labour and function as coordinators for capital. They most closely conform to the definition of the new middle class proposed by Carchedi (1977).

This study has chiefly dealt with work relations, the formal and informal divisions of labour. However ideological relations and trade union practice which are central to practical class consciousness and combined trade union organisation, have also been examined against the structuring of technical work over the last two decades. My analysis of TASS explored the changing 'character' of the union against

the industrial struggles of the 1960s and 1970s. The transformations in the policy, structure and politics of the union
are not reducible to the growing heterogeneity of the membership in the 1970s, but neither are the three developments
explicable without a discussion of these class changes. The
emergence of distinct class fractions within the membership
created the basis for competing approaches towards union
development, recruitment and association with manual
unions. Differentiation within technical work between
graduate, managerial and non-supervisory technical workers
has become institutionalised within union organisation. This
contrasts with the relative homogeneity within technical work
and unionism in the 1960s. The divergent strategies to the
recruitment of qualified engineers reflected the utilisation of
working class and new middle class political practices. Similarly the lack of practical action to develop the amalgamation
with the manual Engineering Section indicated the growing
divergence between the working class political practice of the
union leadership in the 1960s and new middle class politics
of the 1970s.

Finally, this book offers evidence that technical and manual
workers in Britain are less fragmented into fractions sealed
in from each other via educational qualifications than is
suggested by models of the new middle class. Inside the
densely unionised areas of engineering there has been a tendency for the 'privileges' of staff status to disappear. This was
happening at BAe, Rolls-Royce and Westland Helicopters.
The continued access to technical occupations for shop floor
workers, a feature of the absence of strong educational credentialism, also maintained a co-operative relationship between
'office' and 'works'. Against these positive practices and tendencies, the educational barriers were strongly established at
the level of the design engineer, and computer technology is
creating what can be called a 'bifurcation' of the labour
process and 'knowledge barriers' to unity between specialised
technical workers and manual workers. I argued in Chapter
5 that the longer-term implications of computer aided design
appeared to threaten the craft tradition that has supported
the strong association between technical and manual workers.
However without more evidence of the current impact of such

technologies, scenarios of upskilling, proletarianisation and major fragmentation remain a matter of conjecture.

More research is needed into the relationship between technical and manual workers within the new industrial sectors, such as computer design and manufacturing, where technical workers are frequently in a dominant numerical position and unionisation is within a single union. In addition, closer attention to national variation in the formation of technical occupations would highlight the diversity of relationships between technical workers, manual workers and management and place the British experience in a wider context. Finally, there has been little research into the experiences of relations between technical and manual unionists within joint combine committees. The development (and perhaps decline) of such organisational attempts to bridge white-collar/manual union divisions have been seriously neglected by the literature on class and white-collar unionism. Any further research should, in the light of the conclusions of this study, and the sterility of structuralist disregard for empirical analysis, examine from the inside, rather than by external declaration, some of the contradictory forces operating within technical labour in the 1980s.

Bibliography

Abercrombie, N. and J. Urry, (1983) *Capital, Labour and the Middle Classes*, London, Allen & Unwin.

Adams, R. J. (1975) 'The Recognition of White Collar Worker Unions', *British Journal of Industrial Relations*, vol. 13, no. 1.

AESD (1963) *Report of the Proceedings of the Association of Engineering and Shipbuilding Draughtsmenu*, Richmond, Surrey AESD.

Ahlstrom, G. (1982) *Engineers and Industrial Growth*, London, Croom Helm.

Albu, A. (1980) 'British Attitudes to Engineering Education: a Historical Perspective' in K. Pavitt (ed.), *Technical Education and British Economic Performance*, London, Macmillan.

Allen, V. L. (1971) *The Sociology of Industrial Relations*, London, Longman.

Amin, A. (1983) 'Restructuring in Fiat and the Decentralisation of Production in Southern Italy', mimeo, University of Newcastle, CURDS.

Anderson, G. (1976) *Victorian Clerks*, Manchester, Manchester University Press.

Anderson, P. and R. Blackburn (eds) (1965) *Towards Socialism* London, Fontana.

Armstrong, P. (1984) 'Competition between the Organisational Professions and the Evolution of Managerial Control Strategies'. Paper presented to the Aston/UMIST Conference, *Organisation and Control of the Labour Process*, Aston University, March.

Armstrong, P. (1986) 'Work Supervisors and Trade Unionism' in P. Armstrong, B. Carter, C. Smith and T. Nichols, *White Collar Workers, Trade Unions and Class*, London, Croom Helm.

Armstrong, P., Carter, B., Smith, C. and Nichols, T. (1986) *White Collar Workers, Trade Unions and Class* London, Croom Helm.

Arnold, E. (1981) 'The Manpower Implications of Computer Aided Design in the UK Engineering Industry', paper to British Computer Society Conference, July.

Arnold, E. and P. Senker, (1982) *Designing the Future – the Implication of*

CAD Interactive Graphics for Employment and Skills in the British Engineering Industry, Sussex, Science Policy Research Unit.

Arthers, A. J. (1976) 'Managerial Unionism in the Coal, Steel and Electricity Supply Industries', unpublished M.A. dissertation, University of Warwick.

AUEW-TASS (1971) *Which Way Forward for Professional Engineers?*, Richmond, Surrey, TASS.

AUEW-TASS (1973) *Report of the Proceedings of AUEW-TASS Representative Council Conference*, Richmond, Surrey, TASS.

AUEW-TASS (1974) *Report of the Proceedings of AUEW-TASS Representative Council Conference*, Richmond, Surrey, TASS.

AUEW-TASS (1976) *Report of the Proceedings of AUEW-TASS Representative Council Conference*, Richmond, Surrey, TASS.

AUEW-TASS (1978) *Qualified Engineers: The Way Forward*, Richmond, Surrey, TASS.

AUEW-TASS (1980a) *Professional and Managerial Staff in Engineering*, Richmond, Surrey, TASS.

AUEW-TASS (1980b) *Report of Proceedings of AUEW-TASS Representative Council Conference* Richmond, Surrey, TASS

Bain, G. S. (1970) *The Growth of White Collar Unionism*, Oxford, Oxford University Press.

Bain, G. S. (1983) *Industrial Relations in Britain*, Oxford, Blackwell.

Bain, G. S. and R. Price (1972) 'Who is a White Collar Employee?', *British Journal of Industrial Relations*, vol. X.

Bain, G. S. and R. Price, (1983) 'Union Growth: Dimensions, Determinants, and Density' in G. S. Bain (ed.), *Industrial Relations in Britain*, Oxford, Blackwell.

Baldry, C. and A. Connolly, (1984) 'Drawing the Line: Computer Aided Design and the Organisation of the Drawing Office', Paper presented to Aston/UMIST Conference, Organisation and Control of the Labour Process, Aston University, March.

Bamber, G. J. (1978) 'Engineers and Managers as Trade Unionists', *British Association for the Advancement of Science*, Bath University, September.

Batstone, E. (1984) *Working Order*, Oxford, Blackwell.

Batstone.,E., Boraston, I. and Frenkel, S. (1978) *The Social Organisation of Strikes*, Oxford, Blackwell.

Bernstein, E. (1961) *Evolutionary Socialism*, New York, Schocken Books.

Birchall, I. (1980) 'The Autonomy of Theory: A Short History of New Left Review', *International Socialism*, no. 10.

Blackburn, R. M. and Prandy, K. (1965) 'White Collar Unionism: A Conceptual Framework', *British Journal of Sociology*, vol. XVI, no. 2.

Blackburn, R. M. (1967) *Union Character and Social Class*, London, Batsford.

Blauner, R. (1964) *Alienation and Freedom*, Chicago, University of Chicago Press.

Booker, P. J. (1963) *A History of Engineering Drawing*, London, Chatto & Windus.

Bowley, M. (1966) *The British Building Industry*, Cambridge, Cambridge University Press.

306 *Bibliography*

Braverman, H. (1974) *Labor and Monopoly Capital*, New York, Monthly Review.

Bristol Aircraft Workers (1975) *A New Approach to Public Ownership*, Nottingham, Spokesman.

Bristol Siddeley Engines Shop Stewards Combined Committee (1969) *The Aircraft Industry and Workers' Control*, Nottingham, Spokesman.

Brockway, F. and F. Mullally, (1944) *Death Pays a Dividend*, London, Gollanz.

Brown, K. (ed.) (1972) 'Technicians and the Capitalist Division of Labour', *Socialist Revolution*, vol. 2, no. 3.

Bulmer, M. (ed.) (1975) *Working Class Images of Society*, London, Routledge.

Burawoy, M. (1985) *The Politics of Production*, London, Verso.

Burnham, J. (1961) *The Managerial Revolution*, Harmondsworth, Penguin.

Callaghan, J. (1987) 'Marxism, Fabianism and the State' in G. Duncan (ed.) *Capitalism and the State* Cambridge, Cambridge University Press.

Carchedi, G. (1977) *On the Economic Identification of Social Classes* London, Routledge & Kegan Paul.

Carter, R. (1979) 'Class, Militancy and Union Character: a Study of the Association of Scientific, Technical and Managerial Staffs', *Sociological Review*, vol. 27, May.

Carter, R. (1980) 'Managerial and Supervisory Workers: Class, Unionism and Union Character', Ph.D. thesis, University of Bristol.

Carter, R. (1985) *Capitalism, Class Conflict and the New Middle Class*, London, Routledge & Kegan Paul.

Carter, R. (1986) 'Trade Unionism and the New Middle Class – The Case of ASTMS' in P. Armstrong, B. Carter, C. Smith and T. Nichols *White Collar Workers, Trade Unions and Class*, London, Croom Helm.

Chamot, D. (1976) 'Professional Employees turn to Unions', *Harvard Business Review*, vol. 54, no. 3.

Child J. (1985) New Technology and the Service Class', *Work Organisation Research Centre Working Paper Series* no. 6, Aston University.

Child, J. and B. Partridge (1982) *Lost Managers: Supervisors in Industry and Society*, Cambridge, Cambridge University Press.

Clarke, S. (1977) 'Marxism, Sociology and Poulantzas's Theory of the State', *Capital and Class*, 2.

Clegg, H. (1976) *The System of Industrial Relations in Britain*, Oxford, Blackwell.

Coates, K. (ed.) (1979) *The Right to Useful Work*, Nottingham, Spokesman.

Cole, G. D. H. (1934) *What Marx Really Meant*, London, Gollanz.

Commission on Industrial Relations (1972) Report No. 32 *C. A. Parsons and Co. Limited and Associated Companies*, London, HMSO.

Cooley, M. (1972) *Computer Aided Design: its Nature and Implications*, Richmond, Surrey, TASS.

Cooley, M. (1976) 'Contradictions of Science and Technology in the Productive Process' in H. Rose and S. Rose (eds) *The Political Economy of Science*, London, Macmillan.

Cooley, M. (1978) 'Design Technology and Production for Social Needs' in *New Universities Quarterly*, no. 32.

Cooley, M. (1980) *Architect or Bee: The Human/Technology Relationship*, Slough, Hand & Brain.

Cooley, M. (1981) 'Some Social Implications of C.A.D. in J. Mermet (ed.) *CAD in Medium Sized and Small Industries*, North-Holland Publishing Company.

Counter Information Services (1982) *War Lords: The UK Arms Industry*, Anti Report no. 31, London.

Crompton, R. (1976) 'Approaches to the Study of White Collar Unionism', *Sociology*, vol. 10, no. 3, September.

Crompton, R. and J. Gubbay (1977) *Economy and Class Structure*, London, Macmillan.

Crompton, R. and G. Jones (1984) *White Collar Proletariat: Deskilling and Gender in Clerical Work*, London, Macmillan.

Crossick, G. (ed.) (1977) *Lower Middle Class in Britain 1870–1914*, London, Croom Helm.

Crouch, C. and A. Pizzorno (eds) (1978) *The Resurgence of Class Conflict in Western Europe since 1968* vol. 2, London, Macmillan.

Department of Employment (1980) *Employment Gazette* June.

DATA (1964) *Report of Proceedings of Draughtsmen and Allied Technicians Representative Council Conference*, Richmond, Surrey, Draughtsmen and Allied Technicians Association.

DATA Journal (1968) 'Tracing a Dying Profession', January.

DATA Journal (1969).

DATA Journal (1972) 'President's New Year Message: Organise', January.

Davis, R. L. and J. Cousins, (1975) 'The New Working Class and the Old' in M. Bulmer (ed.) *Working Class Images of Society*, London, Routledge.

Dey, I. F. (1979) 'A Study of the Formulation and Implementation of Policies Relating to Redundancies and Unemployment', unpublished Ph.D. thesis, University of Bristol.

Dickens, L. (1972) 'UKAPE: a Study of a Professional Union', *Industrial Relations Journal*, vol. 3, no. 3.

Dunn, S. and J. Gennard, (1984) *The Closed Shop in British Industry*, London, Macmillan.

Edwards, R. (1980) *Contested Terrain*, London, Heinemann.

Eldridge, J. E. T. (1973) *The Sociology of Industrial Life*, Sunbury-on-Thames, Nelson.

Elliott, D. A. and R. H. Elliott (1976) *The Control of Technology*.

EAPM (1979) *Management Unionisation in Western Europe*, London, European Association for Personnel Management.

Engineering Industry Training Board (1970), *The Technician in Engineering*, Watford, EITB.

Fairbrother, P. (1978) 'Consciousness and Collective Action: A Study of the Social Organisation of Unionised White Collar Factory Workers', unpublished Ph.D. thesis, Nuffield College, University of Oxford.

Fearon, P. (1978) 'The Vicissitudes of a British Aircraft Company: Handley Page Ltd Between the Wars', *Business History*, vol XX, no. 1.

Finniston Report (1980) *Engineering our Future* London: HMSO.

Flanders, A. D. (1970) *Management and Unions: The Theory and Reform of Industrial Relations*, London, Faber.

Flicker, M. (1977) The Effects of Nationalisation of the Aircraft Industry on the British Aircraft Corporation Limited 1976–77, unpublished paper, Bristol Polytechnic Library.

Friedman, A. (1977) *Industry and Labour*, London, Macmillan.

Fryer, R. H. (1977) 'Unemployment, myths and science', *New Scientist*, 16 December.

Gallie, D. (1978) *In Search of the New Working Class*, Cambridge, Cambridge University Press.

Giddens, A. (1973) *The Class Structure of Advanced Societies*, London, Hutchinson.

Gorz, A. (1967) *Strategy for Labour: A Radical Proposal*, Boston, Beacon Press.

Gorz, A. (1971) 'Technical Intelligence and the Capitalist Division of Labour', *Les Temps Modernes*, August–September, Translation, Bristol University.

Gorz, A. (1976) 'Technology, Technicians and Class Struggle' in A. Gorz (ed.) *The Division of Labour*, Hassocks, Harvester.

Gorz, A. (1976) ed. *The Division of Labour* Hassocks, Harvester.

Gorz, A. (1982) *Farewell to the Working Class* London, Pluto Press.

Greenbaum, J. (1979) *In the Name of Efficiency: Management Theory and Shop Floor Practice*, Philadelphia, Temple University Press.

Halle, D. (1984) *America's Working Man*, Chicago, University of Chicago Press.

Hannah, L. (1976) *The Rise of the Corporate Economy*, London, Methuen.

Harris, N. (1983) *Of Bread and Guns*, Harmondsworth, Penguin.

Hartman, H. (1974) 'Managerial Employees: New Participants in Industrial Democracy', *British Journal of Industrial Relations*, no. 14.

Hinton, J. (1972) *The First Shop Stewards Movement*, London, Allen & Unwin.

HMSO (1965) *Report of the Committee of Inquiry into the Aircraft Industry, Appointed by the Ministry of Aviation under the Chairmanship of Lord Plowden 1964–1965*, Cmnd 2853.

Hoggart, R. (1957) *The Uses of Literacy*, Harmondsworth, Penguin.

Howard, D. (1974) 'In Memory of Serge Mallet', *Telos*, no. 7.

Hunt, A. (1977) 'Class Structure and Political Strategy', *Marxism Today*, July.

Hutber, P. (1977) *The Decline and Fall of the Middle Class: and how it can fight back*, Harmondsworth, Penguin.

Huws, U. (1984) *The New Homeworkers. New Technology and the Changing Location of White Collar Work*, London, Low Pay Unit.

Hyman, R. (1971) *Marxism and the Sociology of Trade Unionism*, London, Pluto Press.

Hyman, R. (1975) *Industrial Relations – A Marxist Introduction*, London, Macmillan.

Hyman, R. (1983) 'White-Collar Workers and Theories of Class' in R. Hyman and R. Price (eds), *The New Working Class? White-Collar Workers and Their Organisations*, London, Macmillan.

Hyman, R. (1984) *Strikes*, London, Fontana.

Hyman, R. and R. Price, (1983) *The New Working Class? White Collar Workers and Their Organisations*, London, Macmillan.

Incomes Data Services (1982a), *Harmonisation of Conditions* IDS Study 273, Sept, London, Incomes Data Services.

Incomes Data Services (1982b) *CAD Agreements and Pay*, IDS Study 276, October, London: Incomes Data Services.

Jefferys, J. B. (1945) *The Story of the Engineers 1800–1945*, London, Lawrence & Wishart.

Johnson, D. (1982) (ed.) *Class and Social Development: A New Theory of the Middle Class*, London, Sage Publications.

Jones, B. (1982) 'Destruction of Redistribution of Engineering Skills? The Case of Numerical Control' in S. Wood (ed.) *The Degradation of Work*, London, Hutchinson.

Kidron, M. (1968) *Western Capitalism since the War*, Harmondsworth, Penguin.

King, R. and N. Nugent (eds) (1979) *Respectable Rebels*, London, Hodder & Stoughton.

Kocka, J. (1980) *White Collar Workers in America, 1890–1940*, London, Sage.

Kraft, P. (1979) 'The Industrialisation of Computer Programming: From Programming to Software Production' in A. Zimbalist (ed.) *Case Studies in the Labour Process*, New York, Monthly Review.

Labour Research (1984) 'Homeworking', vol. 73, no. 7. July.

Labour Research (1986) 'The Military Takeover in Manufacturing', vol. 75, no. 7 July.

Labour Party Defence Study Group (1977) *Sense about Defence*, London.

Lazonick, W. (1985) 'Strategy, Structure and Management Development in the US and Britain' mimeo, University of Harvard.

Lee, G. (1986) 'The Adoption of Computer Based Systems in Engineering: Management Strategies and the Role of the Professional Engineer', *Work Organisation Research Centre Working Paper Series* no. 16.

Lee, G. and J. Wrench (1981) *In Search of Skill: Ethnic Minority Youth and Apprenticeships*, London, Commission for Racial Equality.

Lee, G. and J. Wrench (1983) *Skill Seekers: Black Youth, Apprenticeship and Disadvantage*, London, National Youth Bureau.

Littler, C. R. (1982) *The Development of the Labour Process in Capitalist Societies. A Comparative Study of the Transformation of Work Organisation in Britain, Japan and the USA*, London, Heinemann.

Lockwood, D. (1958) *The Blackcoated Worker*, London, Allen & Unwin.

Low-Beer, J. R. (1978) *Protest and Participation*, Cambridge, Cambridge University Press.

Lucas Aerospace Combine Shop Stewards Committee (1976) 'The Corporate Plan', unpublished report.

Lucas Aerospace Combine Shop Stewards' Committee (1978) 'The Lucas Plan' in K. Coates (ed.) *The Right to Useful Work*, Nottingham, Spokesman.

McCormick, B. (1960) 'Managerial Unionism in the Coal Industry', *British Journal of Sociology*, vol. 11, no. 4.

MacDonald, W. (1923) *The Intellectual Worker and His Work*, London.

Maclean, J. (1978) *In the Rapids of Revolution*, London, Allison & Busby.
McLoughlin, I. (1982) 'Misunderstanding the New Middle Class', *Sociology*, vol. 16, no. 4.
McLoughlin, I. (1983) 'Industrial Engineers and Theories of the New Middle Class', unpublished Ph.D. thesis, University of Bath.
Mallet, S. (1975s) *The New Working Class*, Nottingham, Spokesman.
Mallet, S. (1975t) *Essays on the New Working Class*, St Louis, Telos Press.
Mandel, E. (1978) *Late Capitalism*, London, Verso.
Marchington, M. and R. Loveridge (1983) 'Management decision-making and shop floor participation' in K. Thurley and S. Wood (eds) *Industrial Relations and Management Strategy*, Cambridge, Cambridge University Press.
Marcuse, H. (1964) *One Dimensional Man* London, Routledge & Kegan Paul.
Marwick, A. (1978) *The Deluge: British Society and the First World War*, London, Macmillan.
Marx, K. (1969) *Theories of Surplus Value*, London, Lawrence & Wishart.
Marx, K. (1976) *Capital Volume 1*, Harmondsworth, Pelican.
Melling, J. (1983) 'Supervisors and Innovation in British Industry with Reference to Engineering Production 1870–1914', mimeo., Kings College, University of Cambridge.
Melman, S. (1978) *Pentagon Capitalism*, New York.
Melman, S. (1981) 'Alternative Criteria for the Design of Means of Production' in *Theory and Society*, vol. 10, no. 3.
Mermet, J. (ed) (1981) *CAD in Medium Sized and Small Industries*, North-Holland Publishing Company.
Metcalf, D. (1977) 'Unions, incomes policy and relative wages in Britain', *British Journal of Industrial Relations*, vol. 15, no. 2.
Mills, C. W. (1953) *White Collar*, New York, Oxford University Press.
More, C. (1980) *Skill and the English Working Class 1870–1914*, London, Croom Helm.
Mortimer, J. (1960) *A History of the Association of Shipbuilding and Engineering Draughtsmen*, Richmond, Surrey, Association of Engineering and Shipbuilding Draughtsmen.
National Aerospace Shop Stewards Liaison Committee (1974) *Report on the Aerospace Industry*, unpublished report.
NEI Parsons TASS (1979) (ACAS Submission' unpublished report) Newcastle-upon-Tyne, TASS, NEI Parsons.
New Fabian Research Pamphlet (1935) *Aircraft Manufacture: A Description of the Industry and Proposals for its Socialisation*, London, Fabian Society.
Nichols, T. (1979) 'Social Class: Official, Sociological and Marxist' in J. Irvine, I. Miles, and J. Evans (eds) *Demystifying Social Statistics*, London, Pluto Press.
Nichols, T. (1986) 'Introduction' in P. Armstrong, B. Carter, C. Smith and T. Nichols, *White Collar Workers, Trade Unions and Clan*, London, Croom Helm.
Nichols, T. and H. Beynon, (1977) *Living with Capitalism: Class Relations and the Modern Factory*, London, Routledge & Kegan Paul.

Noble, D. (1977) *America by Design*, New York, Knopf.
Noble, D. (1979) 'Social Choice in Machine Design: The Case of Automatically Controlled Machine Tools', in A. Zimbalist (ed.) *Case Studies on the Labour Process*, New York, Monthly Review.
Noble, D. (1984) *Forces of Production: A Social History of Industrial Automation*, New York, Knopf.
Panitch, L. (1976) *Social Democracy and Industrial Militancy*, Cambridge, Cambridge University Press.
Parkin, B. (1974) 'The Broad Left in TASS' in *International Socialism*, no. 74.
Parkin, F. (1974a) 'Strategies of Social Closure in Class Formation' in F. Parkin (ed.) *The Social Analysis of Class Structure*, London, Tavistock.
Parkin, F. (ed.) (1974b) *The Social Analysis of Class Structure*, London, Tavistock.
Pavitt, K. (ed.) (1980) *Technical Innovation and British Economic Performance*, London, Macmillan.
Pollert, A. (1981) *Girls, Wives, Factory Lives*, London, Macmillan.
Poulantzas, N. (1975) *Classes in Contemporary Capitalism*, London, Verso.
Prandy, K. (1965) *Professional Employees*, London, Faber & Faber.
Prandy, K., A. Stewart, and R. M. Blackburn (1974) 'Concepts and Measures: The Example of Unionateness', *Sociology*, vol. 8, no. 3.
Prandy, K., A. Stewart, and R. M. Blackburn (1982) *White Collar Work*, London, Macmillan.
Price, R. (1983) 'White-Collar Unions: Growth, Character and Attitudes in the 1970s' in R. Hyman and R. Price (eds), *The New Working Class? White Collar Workers and their Organisations*, London, Macmillan.
Purcell, J. (1976) 'Managers and union membership', *R. & D. Management*, vol. 6 no. 3, June.
Rader, M. (1982) 'The Social Effects of Computer Aided Design: Current Trends and Forecasts for the Future' in L. Bannan, U. Barry and O. Holst (eds), *Information Technology: Impact on the Way of Life*, Dublin, Tycooly International Publishing.
Rader, M. and B. Wingert (1981) *Computer Aided Design in Great Britain and the Federal Republic of Germany*, Karlsruhe, Abteilung fur Angewandte Systemanalyse, Kernforschungszentrum.
Rattansi, A. (1985) 'End of an orthodoxy? The critique of sociology's view of Marx on class', *Sociological Review*, vol. 36, no. 1.
Reid, A. J. (1980) 'The Division of Labour in the British Shipbuilding Industry, 1880–1920 with Special Reference to Clydeside', unpublished Ph.D. thesis, University of Cambridge.
Ridley, F. F. (1970) *Revolutionary Syndicalism in France*, Cambridge, Cambridge University Press.
Roberts, B. C., R. Loveridge and J. Gennard (1972) *Reluctant Militants*, London, Allen & Unwin.
Roemer, J. (1982) *A General Theory of Exploitation and Class*, Cambridge, Mass., Harvard University Press.
Rose, M. (1979) *Servants of Post-Industrial Power*, London, Macmillan.
Rosenbrock, H. (1977) 'The Future of Control' in *Automatica*, vol. 13.

Rosenbrock, H. (1981) 'Engineers and the Work that People Do', *Work Research Unit Occasional Paper* no. 21.

Roslender, R. (1983) 'Trade Unionism amongst Scientific Workers in Great Britain', unpublished Ph.D. thesis, University of Leeds.

Ross, G. (1978) 'Marxism and the New Middle Classes: French Critique' in *Theory and Society*, vol. 5, No. 2.

Routh, G. (1980) *Occupation and Pay in Great Britain, 1906–79*, London, Macmillan.

Rustin, M. (1980) 'The Politics of Workers' Plans' paper given to *Conference of Socialist Economist*, Conference, July.

Sabel, C. (1982) *Work and Politics*, Cambridge, Cambridge University Press.

Salaman, G. (1981) *Class and the Corporation*, London, Fontana.

Shaiken, H. (1984) *Work Transformed: Automation and Labor in the Computer Age*, New York, Holt, Rinehart & Winston.

Singh, D. (1977) 'Becoming a Craftsman', unpublished Ph.D. thesis, University of Bristol.

Smith, C. D. (1979) 'Workers' Plans and Technical Workers', mimeo, University of Bristol.

Smith, C. D. (1982) 'Technical Workers: Class, Work and Trade Unionism' Ph.D. thesis, University of Bristol.

Smith, C. D. (1984) 'Managerial Strategies: Capital and Labour: A reply to John Child', *Work Organisation Research Centre Working Paper Series*, no. 2, Aston Univeristy.

Smith, C. D. (1985) 'Design Engineers and the Capitalist Firm', *Work Organisation Research Centre Working Paper Series*, no. 6, Aston University.

Smith, C. (1986) 'Engineers, Trade Unionism and TASS' in P. Armstrong, B. Carter, C. Smith and T. Nichols, *White Collar Workers, Trade Unions and Class*, London, Croom Helm.

Smith, C. D., J. Child, and M. Rowlinson, (1987) *Innovations in Work Organisation: The Cadbury Experience*, Cambridge, Cambridge University Press, forthcoming.

Smith, R. and D. Sawbridge (1974) 'Professional Associations, Trade Unions and Industrial Conflict', mimeo., University of Durham.

Storey, J. (1983) *Managerial Prerogative and the Question of Control*, London, Routledge.

Strauss, G. (1954) 'White Collar Unions are Different' in R. Hyman and R. Price (eds) (1983) *The New Working Class? White-Collar Workers and Their Organisations*, London, Macmillan.

Thompson, E. P. (1978) *The Poverty of Theory and other essays*, London, Merlin Press.

Thompson, P. (1983) *The Nature of Work*, London, Macmillan.

Turner, H. A. (1962) *Trade Union Growth, Structure and Policy: a Comparative Study of the Cotton Unions*, London, Allen & Unwin.

Undy, R., V. Ellis, W. E. J. McCarthy and A. M. Halmos (1981) *Change in Trade Unions: The Development of UK Unions since the 1960s*, London, Hutchinson.

Veblen, T. (1923) *Engineers and the Price System*, New York.

Wainwright, H. and D. Elliott, (1982) *The Lucas Plan: A New Trade Unionism in the Making*, London: Allison and Busby.

Watson, H. B. (1975) 'Organisational Bases of Professional Status: A Comparative Study of the Engineering Professions' unpublished Ph.D. thesis, University of London.

Whalley, P. (1982) 'The Social Production of Technical Work: the case of British Engineers', Ph.D. thesis, University of Columbia, USA.

Whalley, P. (1984) 'Engineers? The Labour Process, Labour Markets and Labour Segmentation' *Social Problems* vol. 32, no. 2, December.

Whitfield, R. (1979) 'The Labour Movement in Bristol 1910–1939', unpublished M. Lit thesis, University of Bristol.

Woodley, M. (1973) 'TASS: A Trade Union During a Period of Change', unpublished M.A. thesis, University of Durham.

Woodward, J. (1965) *Industrial Organisation: Theory and Practice*, London, Oxford University Press.

Wooton, G. (1961) 'Parties in a Union Government: the AESD', *Political Studies*, no. 9.

Wrench, J. and N. Stanley, (1984) 'Old Problems for New Workers: A Study of the Changing Patterns of Shiftworking in the West Midlands', *British Sociological Association Annual Conference*, 2–5 April.

Wright, E. O. (1977) 'Class Boundaries in Advanced Capitalism', *New Left Review*, no. 98.

Wright, E. O. (1985) *Classes*, London, Verso.

Zimbalist, A. (ed.) (1979) *Case Studies on the Labor Process*, New York, Monthly Review.

Index

Key references appear in **bold** type.

Abercrombie, N., 61
Adams, R. J., 258
Adley, Robert, 113
Ahlström, G., 71
AEF (Amalgamated Engineering
    and Foundry Workers Union),
    279, 281–7, 292
    see also AUEW
Aerospatiale, 118, 180
AESD (Association of Engineering
    and Shipbuilding
    Draughtsmen), 85, 86, 258,
    271
    becomes DATA, 292
    draughtsmen in, 7, 77
    rate-fixers in, 130
    tracers in, 147
AEU (Amalgamated Engineering
    Union), 281
    see also AUEW
age structure of workforce at Filton,
    125, 229
America, *see* United States
aircraft industry, 106–7
    in Britain, 112–16; growth of
    white collar workers, 16, 76,
    85–9, 107; management in,
    229–34, 248–50
    funding of, 107–10, 169–70

technological innovation in,
    111–12
Airbus programme, 115–16
Aircraft and Shipbuilding
    Industries Act (1977), 116,
    117
Aircraft Group, BAe, 5, 117
Allen, V. L., 60, 257
Anderson, P., 15, 101
APEX (Association of Professional,
    Executive, Clerical and
    Computer Staff), 138, 140,
    277, 292
Armstrong, P., 124, 163, 185, 190,
    231
    on white-collar unions, 256, 258,
    263–4
Arnold, E., 177
ASSET (Association of Supervisory
    Staffs, Executives and
    Technicians), 270, 280
Association of Programmes, 154
ASTMS (Association of Scientific,
    Technical and Managerial
    Staffs), 78, 249, 262, 277, 288
ASW (Association of Scientific
    Workers), 281
AUEW (Amalgamated Union of
    Engineering Workers), 122,
    282, 284–6

Engineering Section, 122–3, 287, 301
  formation and break-up, 287, 292
  see also TASS
automobile industry, 16, 76, 85, 107, 177
autonomy of technical work, 68, 97, 127–8, 227–8, 300
  manual workers' view of, 222–3

BAC (British Aircraft Corporation), 115
  formation of, 230
  introduction of NC machines, 149
  nationalisation (1977), 117–19
  Preston, 278
  see also Filton
BAe (British Aerospace), **114–19**, 232–4
  funding, 110, 116
  Guided Weapons, 117, 146, 190
  lockouts at, 103, 124
  Management Staff Association, 246, 247
  trade unions at, 122–5, 177, 190, 301
  see also BAC; Filton
Bain, G. S., 227, 247, 257–8
Baker Perkins, 269
Baldry, C., 172, 177–8, 179, 183, 186–7, 290
Bamber, G. J., 246, 247, 248
Batstone, E., 104, 283
Benn, Tony, 113, 114, 121
Bernstein, E., 73
Beswick, Lord, 116
Beynon, H., 27, 120
Birchall, I., 15
BL (British Leyland), 113, 177
black workers, 80
Blackburn, R. M., 248, 259–60, 261, 262
Blauner, R., 17–18
Boeing, 108, 115, 180, 204
Booker, P. J., 82
Boraston, I., 104

Braverman, H., **36–41**
  on deskilling, 12, 36–7, 41, 46, 85, 196
  on technical workers: class position, 37–40, 74, 185, 194; power relations, 84, 298–9
  on white-collar labour markets, 39, 257
Bristol, economic and political climate, 119–23, 125
Britain
  class structure, 66, 69–73
  technical workers in, 75–80, 97
  see also aircraft industry; craft tradition
Brockway, F., 116
Burawoy, M., 37
Burnham, J., 16

CAD (computer-aided design)
  deskilling effects of, 43, 44, 45–7
  at Filton, 157, 159, 178–83
  rationales for introduction, 171–2, 177–8
  social effects of, 164, 166–8, 290–1, 302
Cadbury, Bournville, effects of automation at, 27
calculators (occupation), 80
Callaghan, J., 71
Carchedi, G., **57–60**
  on divisions within technical labour, 194, 224
  on job descriptions, 59
  new middle class theory, 4, 58, 74, 235, 301
  on relations between manual and technical labour, 195, 298
Carter, R., 66, 69–70, 73
  on ASTMS, 270, 288
  on management, 230–1, 237, 248
  on TASS, 124, 288
  on white-collar workers: class position, 14, 58; militancy, 16, 245; unionism, 256, 258, 259, 261, 262, 264–6, 273, 277
C.A.V., London, 282
Chamot, D., 234, 247

chemical industry, 16, 27, 76, 85
Child, J., 15, 27, 164, 245, 258
Churchill, T. I. (company), 269
Clarke, S., 56
class
  position of white-collar workers,
    3–5, **13–74**, 185, 192–4, 235,
    297–302
  and unionism, 262–7, 266, 267
Clegg, H., 247
clothing of technical workers, 129
Cocks, Michael, 113
Cole, G. D. H., 15–16, 71–2
computer staff, 103–5
computerisation, 183, 302
  effects on work organisation:
    electrical planning, 128,
    207–8; rate-fixers, 157;
    production control, 139
Concorde programme, 94, 115,
    170–1
  ending of, 112, 118, 189–90
  funding, 110, 116
  and specialisation in design
    work, 90
conditions of work at Filton, 96–7
Connolly, A.,
  on introduction of CAD, 172,
    178, 179, 186–7, 291
  on specialisation in design work,
    183
consumer goods industries, 67
Cooley, M., **41–9**, 112, 164, 185,
    267
  on class position of white-collar
    workers, 29, 45
  on decline of craft tradition, 43,
    177, 194
  on design work, 86, 89–90, 160–1
  on deskilling effects of new
    technology, 43–7, 103, 111,
    168, 182, 186
  on TASS policy (as President,
    1972–73), 273, 274–5, 285–6,
    288–9
cost control engineers, *see* rate-
    fixers
Cousins, J., 14, 70, 73

CPSA (Civil and Public Services
    Association), 277
craft tradition in Britain, 27, 43,
    194
  aided trade unionism, 70–1
  effect on class structure, 68–9,
    192
  structures relations between
    technical and manual
    workers, 175–7, 195–6,
    216–18, 224–6, 299
  under threat: decline in
    differentials, 157; growth of
    graduate engineers, 77–8, 157,
    176, 185; result of
    computerisation, 211
Crompton, R., 11, 256, 261, 263,
    264
Crossick, G., 70, 71
Crouch, C., 280
CSEU (Confederation of
    Shipbuilding and Engineering
    Unions), 281, 282

DATA (Draughtsmen and Allied
    Technicians Association),
    forerunner of TASS, 278, 279,
    280–1, 292
Davis, R. L., 14, 70, 73
denationalisation of BAe (1981),
    116
Denny, Archibald, 82–3
Denny, William (company), 82–3
design draughtsmen, 86, 88–90
  see also design engineers
design engineers (designers)
  craft experience dying out, 197
  and new technology, 155, 162–3,
    166–74, 177–87, 300
  numbers at Filton, 158–9
  relations with managers, 173–4
  view of hierarchy of work,
    159–62, 164–6
design of work, 164–8
deskilling effects of new technology,
    43–7, 103, 111, 145, 150–1,
    167–8, 182, 186, 300
Dey, I. F., 107, 112–13

Dickens, L., 258
differentials between manual and
    technical workers, 96–9, 157,
    206, 214, 268, 271–2
differentiation of technical
    occupations, 85–91
distribution of technical workers in
    British industry, 76
division of labour between manual
    and technical work, 126–9,
    155–7, 193–7
draughtsmen, **199–206, 212–16**
    decline in numbers, 76–7
    impact of new technology on,
        128–9, 146, 184
    origins of occupation, 82–3
    relations with manual workers,
        199–201, 205–6, 212–16
    respect for practical skills, 159,
        200–2
    separation from designers, 86,
        88–90, 145
    wage differential from skilled
        manual work, 97
    women, 78
Dunn, S., 258
Dynamics Group, BAe, 117

economic and political climate,
    effect on class structure,
    15–17
education of British technical
    workers, 78, 79t
Edwards, R., 133
electical goods industry, 16, 76
electrical planners, 128, 199,
    207–11
electricity industry, 25, 85
electronics industry, 23, 85, 107
Elliot, D. A., 44, 137, 168, 216
EMA (Engineers and Managers
    Association), 249, 296
embourgeoisement theory, 3, 18, 70
employers
    Engineering Employers
        Federation, 258, 275
    influence on unionisation of
        management, 247

response to TASS militancy, 276
employment in Bristol, 119–21, 125
Engineering Design Organisation,
    Filton, 89, 100, 123, 129,
    158–91, 202, 203, 232
Engineering Employers
    Federation, 258, 275
engineering industry, 76–7, 81
Engineering Industry Training
    Board, 76
established technical occupations,
    155–7
estimators, 80, 124, 128–9, 197, 229

Fairbrother, P., 59
Fearon, P., 88
Federation of Professional
    Workers, 72
Filton site, **117–19**
    commercial department, 137
    customer liaison, 197
    division of labour at, 126–9
    industrial disputes at, 101–3,
        214–15
    job titles at, 91–3
    management at, 230–46
    redundancies at, 107
    unionisation of middle
        managers, 246, 248–54
    wage bargaining at, 276
    workforce at, 80, 117–19
Fine Tubes strike, 123
Finniston Report (1980), 45, 94
First World War, effects of, 85, 87,
    99, 107, 147
Flanders, A. D., 247
France, 17–18, 27, 94–5, 110
Frenkel, S., 104
Fryer, R. H., 234, 247

Gallie, D., 19, 26
GEC, 17, 110, 278, 279
Gennard, J., 16, 76, 126, 257, 258
Giddens, A., 227
Gill, Ken, 104, 275, 276
Gorz, A., 3, 16, **28–36**, 74, 84, 194
government influence on aircraft
    industry, 107–16

grading schemes, 99–100, 187
graduate engineers, *see* professional
  engineers
Greenbaum, J., 25
Grunwicks dispute, 123
Gubbay, J., 11

Halle, D., 27
Handley Page, 87–8
Hannah, L., 231
Harris, N., 108
Hawker Siddeley, 115, 117
Heseltine, Michael, 117
hierarchy in technical work, 145,
  158–68, 164–6
higher technical occupations, 192,
  195
Hinton, J., 212
Howard, D., 18, 50
Hunt, A., 56
Hutber, P., 73
Hyman, R., 11, 13, 56, 58–9, 261,
  286

industrial disputes, 100–5
  impact of new technology on,
    103–5
  manual unions in, 152, 214–15,
    216
  strikes: engineering strike (1978),
    284; at Filton, 124–5; at Fine
    Tubes, 123; at Rolls-Royce,
    278
  TASS involved in, 16–17, 101–2,
    103, 152, 232, 244–5, 268–70,
    277–80
industrial relations orthodoxy
  (theory of white-collar
  unionism), 256, 257–8
inspection (occupation), 80
Institute of Electrical Engineers,
  189
Institute of Production Engineers,
  154

James, Tom, 122
Jeffreys, J. B., 80, 81

jig and tool design
  assembly, 124, 199–206, 229
  machine shop, 143–57, 246
job identity, 91–100, 156
Johnson, D., 6, 12–13, 14
Jones, B., 149, 220

Kidron, M., 109
King, R., 73
Kocka, J., 71
Kraft, P., 111

Labour Party Aerospace Group,
  113
labour tradition in Bristol, 119–23
Lazonick, W., 163
Lee, G., 80, 183, 189
Littler, C. R., 15, 71, 82
Lockheed, 108, 115, 180
lockouts, 103, 124, 278–80
Lockwood, D., 37, 60, 227, 257
lofting department, 203
Loveridge, R., 16, 76, 126, 257, 263
Low-Beer, J. R., 4, 14, 25
Lucas Aerospace, 42, 102, 137, 190,
  193
Lucas Plan, 44–5, 185

McCormick, B., 247
MacDonald, W., 72
McDonnell Douglas, 108, 115, 180
machine tool industry, 47
Maclean, J., 81–2
McLoughlin, I., 259, 267
Mallet, S., 3, 16, **18–28**, 103,
  197–9
managers, **227–55**
  features of work, 68, 230–2,
    234–6, 240–1
  relations with technical workers,
    170–4, 188–9, 227–46, 300–1
  unionisation of, 246–55, 294–5
Mandel, E., 26
Mann, Alan, 102, 103, 122, 123
manual trade unions, 107
manual workers
  hours and conditions, 96–7
  relations with technical workers,

68–9, 84, 192–7, 224–6, 245;
designers, 174–6, 188, 190,
198–9; draughtsmen, 94,
199–206, 212–16; electrical
planners, 207–11; NC part
programmers, 154–5, 211,
216–24; rate-fixers, 211
Marchington, M., 263
Marcuse, H., 18, 19
marginalised technical jobs, *see*
quasi-technical jobs
Marwick, A., 85
Marx, K., 57, 64,
on definition of productive
labour, 52
on growth of white-collar
workers, 11–12, 17
on managers as agents of capital,
68, 237
Melling, J., 71, 81, 82, 83
Melman, S., 109–10, 112, 169
merit payments, 240
metal goods industry, 76
metallurgists, 76, 78
metals industry, 76
Metcalf, D., 247
Mills, C. Wright, 195–6
militancy among white-collar
workers, 16–17, 123, 177
see also industrial disputes
mining industry, 247
More, C., 70–1, 81, 83, 84–5
Mortimer, J., 71, 77, 82, 258, 268,
271
motor vehicle industry, 16, 76, 85,
107, 177
Mullally, F., 116

NALGO (National and Local
Government Officers
Association), 262, 277
National Aerospace Shop Stewards
Liaison Committee, 122
nationalisation of British aircraft
industry (1977), 115–16,
229–34, 248–50
NC (numerically controlled)
machines

impact of, 134–5, 149–51, 165
operators, 217–20, 226
NC part programmers, 149–55,
215
managers, 228, 229
and new technology, 149–51,
155, 157
relations with manual workers,
154–5, 211, 216–24
relations with production
control, 137
NEI Parsons (Northern
Engineering Industries), *see*
Parsons
new middle class theory, 4, 49–66,
297
new technical occupations, 84–5
new technology
effects on class structure, 14–15
effects on work design, 43, 46,
186–7; designers, 155, 162–3,
166–74, 177–87, 300;
draughtsmen, 128–9, 146,
184; electrical planners, 128,
207–8; rate-fixers, 157;
production control, 139
and industrial action, 103–4
new working class theory, 3,
17–36, 297–8
Nichols, T., 27, 51, 61, 120
Noble, D.
on effects of new technology, 46,
47, 149–50, 172, 184–5, 220
on engineer as force of
capitalism, 41–2
on innovation in aircraft
industry, 111
on social aspects of work design,
162, 164–5
NUBE (National Union of Bank
Employees), 277
Nugent, R., 73
NUGSAT (National Union of
Gold, Silver and Allied
Trades), 287
numbers of technical workers in
British industry, 76–7

numerically controlled machine
  tools, *see* NC machines
NUSMWCH (National Union of
  Sheet Metal Workers,
  Coppersmiths, and Heating
  and Domestic Engineers), 287

office environment, 129
oil industry, 25, 26
one-dimensional man thesis, 17–18
origins of technical jobs, 80–5

Palmer, Arthur, 113
Panitch, L., 258
Parkin, B., 101, 271
Parkin, F., 60
Parsons, C. A. (company), 100,
  190, 193
  management at, 177, 240, 242
  qualifications of technical
    workers at, 79t
  trade unions at, 44–5, 282, 283;
    disputes, 268–70, 278, 290;
    industrial action, 16–17, 102;
    TASS recruitment, 295–6;
    wage bargaining, 276
Partridge, B., 258
pattern bargaining, 272–3
Pizzorno, A., 280
planning engineers
  conflict with rate-fixers, 135–6
  development of occupation, 80,
    81–2
  force in TASS, 188
  relations with manual workers,
    211
  relations with production
    control, 137, 139
  respect for practical skill, 159
Plessey, 110, 269
Plowden Report (1965), 109,
  111–12, 115, 117
pointsmen, 211
political influences on aircraft
  industry, 112–14
Pollert, A., 120
Poulantzas, N.,

on characteristics of technical
    workers, 6, 26
  on class position of white-collar
    workers, 4, 74, **49–57**, 298–9
  on Mallet, 25
  on managers as agents of capital,
    235
  on relationship of manual and
    technical workers, 84, 195,
    224
Prandy, K., 246, 248, 259, 260, 267
premium bonus scheme at Filton,
  131, 132–4
Price, R., 56, 227, 277
production controllers, 156, 197,
  211, **136–42**
production cycle at Filton, 92
Production Engineering
  Organisation, Filton, 207
productive labour, technical work
  as, 68, 141, 156, 222, 268, 269
productivity deals, 134
professional and graduate
  engineers, 157
  at Filton, 186
  growth of, 76–7, 293
  identified with management, 69
  recruitment in TASS, 185, 293,
    301
  women, 78
progress chasing, 80
Purcell, J., 247

qualitative and quantitative
    relationships, 6–7, 197,
    299–300
quasi-technical occupations, 155–7
  production controllers, 136–42,
    192, 197, 299
  rate-fixers, 130–6

Rader, M., 177, 178, 183
radio and electronics industry, 23,
  85, 107
rate-fixers, 80, **130–6**, 157, 211
Rattansi, A., 12, 64

redundancies
  at Filton: 112–13, 119, 234, 247,
    283; effect on age structure of
    workforce, 125, 229
Reid, A. J., 7, 71, 81, 82–3, 147,
  268
Ridley, F. F., 27–8
Roberts, B. C.
  on DATA, 281
  on technical workers in Britain,
    76, 126
  on white-collar unionism, 16,
    257, 258, 262; TASS, 268, 272
Rogers, Terry, 273, 282, 283, 291
Roemer, J., 63
Rolls-Royce, 114–15, 177, 276, 280,
  301
  Bristol: designers at, 190;
    disputes at, 152, 224, 278;
    TASS at, 102, 123, 179, 193
  Coventry: DATA at, 282;
    disputes at, 278–9; TASS at,
    102, 193, 296
Rose, M., 18, 19, 26
Rose Foregrove, 269
Rosenbrock, H., 43, 47, 164, 184
Ross, G., 18, 50
Routh, G., 97
Rowlinson, M., 27, 164, 245
Rustin, M., 45

SAIMA (Shipbuilding and Allied
  Industries Management
  Association), 249
Salaman, G., 26–7
scientists, numbers in British
  industry, 76, 78
Scottish Aviation, 117
Second World War, effects of,
  86–7, 99, 271
self-employment among engineers,
  189
Senker, P., 177
Shaiken, H., 151, 155, 164, 172, 220
shipbuilding, 5, 71, 81, 82–3
Shipbuilding Employers
  Federation, 278

shop floor workers, *see* manual
  workers
Shorts Brothers, 114, 117
SIMA (Steel Industry
  Management Association), 248
singh, D., 225
Snilma, 180
social identity and status of
  technical workers, 75, 93–6,
    146–7, 256–7
  draughtsmen, 93–4
  NC part programmers, 154, 155
social stratification theory (of
  white-collar unionism), 256–7
Stanley, N., 177
steel industry, 248
Stevenage-Bristol Division, BAe,
  117
Stewart, A., 248, 260
Storey, J., 231
Strauss, G., 262
strikes, *see* industrial disputes
subcontract work, 114–15, 118,
  204, 232

TASS (Technical, Administrative
  and Supervisory Section),
  AUEW
  at Filton, 122–4, 158, 188, 228;
    consultations on CAD, 178–9;
    industrial disputes, 101–3,
    113, 124–5, 232; success in
    securing work, 233;
    unionisation of management,
    123, 174–5, 228, **244–55**, 263,
    296
  formation of (previously DATA),
    9, 287–7, 292
  industrial disputes, 101, 113,
    232, 245: at C. A. Parsons,
    268–70, 272; at Rolls-Royce,
    152, 179, 224; at Westland,
    105
  membership and recruitment,
    91, 130, 185, 190, 258, 262, 270,
    292–7
  occupational base, 267–8, 270,
    277

TASS *cont.*
  policies, 78, 115, 166, 183, 245,
    268, 271–8, 287–92, 301
  surveys, 78, 229
technical–clerical divide, *see* quasi-
    technical occupations
technical education, 77, 84–5
technical publications, Filton, 197
technical workers
  in Britain, 75–80, 97–9
  defined, 1–2, 66–8
technological change, *see* new
    technology
TGWU (Transport and General
    Workers Union), 122
Thompson, E. P., 59
Thompson, P., 37
Thomson-Houston (company), 20,
    23, 24
time control clerks, 81
timing of technical work, 127–8,
    143–4
Tobacco Workers Union, 287
tool design
  assembly, 124, 199–206, 229
  machine shop, 143–57, 246
tracers, 79–80, 129, 147–9, 197
Trade Union Redundancy
    Committee, 133
trade unions
  in Bristol, 121–3
  at Filton, 113–14, 123–5, 246–55
  white-collar, 16–17, 256–67, 277
  see also under individual trade unions
training of technical workers, *see*
    craft tradition; education

UKAPE (United Kingdom
    Association of Professional
    Engineers), 123–4, 158, 188,
    246
  competition with TASS, 176,
    190, 295
unemployment in Bristol, 119
unionateness, 260–2
unionisation of middle
    management, 123, 174–5, 228,
    244–55, 263, 296

unions, *see* trade unions
United States
  aircraft industry in, 107–8, 150
  status of engineers in, 94, 95
Urry, J., 61

Vickers, 269

wages
  disputes, 214, 244–5, 268–70
  at Filton, 96–9
  TASS minimum wage campaign,
    272–6
Wainwright, H., 44, 137, 216
war, effects on technical jobs, 85,
    87, 99, 107, 111, 147, 271
Watson, H. B., 72, 163, 189
Weber, M., 11, 13, 60
Weirs, Glasgow, 82
West Germany, 110
Westland Helicopters, 105, 114,
    117, 177, 276, 301
Weybridge-Bristol Division, BAe,
    117, 118
Whalley, P., 71, 185
White, Sir George, 230
white-collar unions, 16–17
  character, 259–62
  growth, 256–9, 277
  new Marxist theory, 262–7
  see also under individual trade unions
white-collar workers
  in Britain, 69–74
  theories for growth of, 10–13
Whitely, Ron, 282
Whitfield, R., 120–1
Wingert, M., 177, 178
women
  in technical work, 78–80, 147–8
  in wartime manual work, 85
Woodley, M., 271
Woodward, J., 17
Wooton, G., 271
works productivity scheme at C. A.
    Parsons, 268–9
Wrench, J., 80, 177
Wright, E. O., 4–5, 6, **61–6**, 195,
    264